CW00540056

LAWRIE BOND

MICROCAR MAN

LAWRIE BOND

MICROCAR MAN

An Illustrated History of Bond Cars

Nick Wotherspoon

PEN & SWORD TRANSPORT

First published in Great Britain in 2017 by
Pen & Sword Transport
an imprint of
Pen & Sword Books Ltd,
47 Church Street,
Barnsley,
South Yorkshire
S70 2AS

Copyright © Pen & Sword Books Limited, 2017

A CIP record for this book is available from the British Library.

ISBN 978 1 47385 868 8

The right of Nick Wotherspoon to be identified as the Author of this Work has been asserted by him in accordance with the Copyright, Designs and Patents Act 1988.

All rights reserved. No part of this book may be reproduced or transmitted in any form or by any means, electronic or mechanical including photocopying, recording or by any information storage and retrieval system, without permission from the Publisher in writing.

Printed and bound by Replika Pres Pvt. Ltd

Pen & Sword Books Ltd incorporates the Imprints of Pen & Sword Aviation,
Pen & Sword Maritime, Pen & Sword Military, Wharncliffe Local History,
Pen & Sword Select, Pen & Sword Military Classics and Leo Cooper.
For a complete list of Pen & Sword titles please contact:
Pen & Sword Books Limited

47 Church Street, Barnsley, South Yorkshire S70 2AS, England

E-mail: enquiries@pen-and-sword.co.uk

Website: www.pen-and-sword.co.uk

Dedication

This book is dedicated to my late dear friend Martin D. Whittaker, a truly gifted hands-on engineer who could turn his skills to almost anything and with whom I spent many happy hours developing my obsession for old cars.

A6814
WL9599
19

Lawrence 'Lawrie' Bond in a rare pose for the camera at Shelsley in 1951 in his Type C 500cc Racing Car.

Contents

Acknowledgements

Over the years I have been extremely fortunate to have had the support of many individuals without whom I would not have been able to complete either my initial 1993 work on 'Lawrie' Bond and the machines connected with him, or this new book. I would like to thank everyone who has helped me with my research by providing me with advice, information, photographs or other documentary material. Special thanks go to those who have given me a personal insight into the life and work of the enigmatic Lawrie Bond, though sadly a number have passed away in the intervening years and from them I now only have the detailed notes I kept at the time. I am especially grateful to: Mrs Pauline Stephenson, Miss Viki Bond and Mr Raymond Bristo. Also to Mr R. Robinson, Mr P. Patterson, Mr Jon Goddard-Watts, Mr Jon Derisley, Mr B. Parkins, Mr Chris Featherstone, Mr Rowland Eastham and Ms Islene Walsh.

I would like to thank the following former employees of Sharp's Commercials/Bond Cars Limited for their contributions and patience, again some have now passed away: Mr Alan Pounder, Mr John Woods, Mr Jim Kenyon, Mr Roy Atkinson, Mr Tom Gratrix and especially to the late Colonel C.R. Gray, whose excellent commentary on his part in the story of Bond Cars formed the foreword to my previous work and is included in this book for its historical merit.

I would also continue my thanks to the following for all their help, photographs, loan of material, access to vehicles, etc: Jean Hammond, Guy Singleton (Bond Equipe Register secretary, TSSC), Bruce Pilbrough (former Bond Equipe Register secretary, TSSC), Peter Jacklin (TSSC), Chris Gardner, Robert Buckby (BOC), Martin Boddy (Bug Club), Mike Costigan (TSSC), Nigel Halliday (Berkeley Enthusiasts' Club), Stan Cornock (BOC), Nick Manders (BOC), Nick Kelly (VMCC), Duncan Rabagliati (Five Hundred Owners' Association), Bernard Cowdrey, Don Pither, Gordon Hill, Cliff Ray, Peter G. Reed, David Crawford, Jim Bassett, Ian Gibson, T. Rowe, Peter Williams and the National Motor Museum Archives. Alan Currans (The Acceleration Archive), Mike Shepherd, Tom Karen, David Ratner, Robin Spalding, Andrew Argyle, Eric Antony Watkiss, Harry Kraemer, Roger Phillips, Roy Jaggar, Christian Künnecke, Bob Purton, Sascha Fillies (PS.SPEICHER, Einbeck), Dermot Elworthy, Andrew Tart, Rhona Bell, Tim Monck-Mason, Marty Richardson, Charlie Banyard Smith, Alan Waring, Geoff Toyer (BEC), Dave Perrin (BEC), Ian Harrop (VMSC), Clive Stanley, Thomas Touw, Ron Biggin, Lesley Cook, Justin Scratch Platts, Mike and Paula Cooper, Adam Turpin, and Clive and Andrea Steggel.

Finally, I give my thanks to all the writers responsible for the various books and journal articles that I have consulted during my research. I have tried to include details of more substantial works within the text where possible. My apologies to anyone I may have omitted.

Nick Wotherspoon, 2017

Foreword

My father Lawrence Bond's car designs were way ahead of their time. He was always thinking of his next design and if he wasn't at his drawing board working, he had paper and pencil at hand. As a child, some of my happiest memories of my father are when we were at the races and motor shows.

Though how I came to love motor racing so much is an enigma, as my first experience was very frightening. I was with my father and step-mother Paula in the pits. I can't remember if it was Goodwood or Brands Hatch (?) Anyway, a car came in and promptly burst into flames, only a few feet away. I was so scared I was shaking like a leaf. My father gave me a drink from his hip flask to help with the shock, saying to only take a tiny sip. Obviously I knocked it back. I have hated the smell of whisky ever since!

Then there were the Motor Shows at the Olympia Exhibition Hall, Earls Court Exhibition Centre, and the Racing Car Show at the Royal Horticultural Hall, Westminster. I just loved being on the stands, meeting all the famous racing drivers and celebrities of the day, as my father was always in demand and very much admired by them. Mind you, he was also a very quiet and shy man, and at the end of the day, to me, he was 'just my dad'.

Viki Bond 2016

Prologue

Written in 1993 by the late Colonel C.R. Gray MBE TD CBIM

The year 1948, following closely upon the ending of the war in Europe and the Far East, brought with it many problems for industry throughout Great Britain. During this transitional period from wartime production to the requirements of everyday life there were shortages of just about everything needed by the manufacturing industry, and much of what was required was rationed. Steel could only be obtained on licence and to obtain a licence it was necessary to show that it was required for the manufacture of goods for export, in order to help the appalling state of the economy which prevailed after six years of war. Petrol was severely rationed, as were many other basic materials and those which were not officially rationed were rigidly controlled by their suppliers in an endeavour to share out what was available. Most of these supplies, naturally enough, went to their established customers.

This was the situation in which we at Sharp's Commercials Limited found ourselves when we were notified by the Ministry of Supply, for whom we had been rebuilding military vehicles, that our contract would come to an end later in the year as by then what was left of the Armed Forces were fully equipped with new or rebuilt vehicles and no more would be required. It was at this point in time that I was approached by Lawrie Bond, a meeting which led to the introduction of the Bond Minicar and to the pioneering of ultra-lightweight motoring, subsequently to be followed by manufacturers with such familiar names as Heinkel and Messerschmitt, and a host of others who were not so successful. In retrospect, and with the hindsight of business knowledge acquired over the years since 1948, our decision to proceed with the introduction and manufacture of the Bond Minicar was indeed an optimistic and perhaps a bold one for all the odds were against us, but we were a young team filled with enthusiasm and prepared to work hard for long hours in order to achieve our objective.

We had a factory and above all we had a loyal and skilled workforce of some sixty or seventy men and a handful of ladies. Their skills were not necessarily in manufacturing, but the workforce in those days were more prepared to adapt themselves, and their loyalty and dedication were a major factor in our success in producing cars from scratch in such a short time. Progress, of course, is not only dependent upon enthusiasm, but also upon the ability of a number of people in responsible positions within a company. Initially the team consisted of: Roy Atkinson, General Manager responsible for manufacture and production, who remained in that position throughout the life of the Bond Car Company; John Woods, who was Production Manager; the late Fred Atkinson, Manager of Body Production; and the late Charlie Hollins, Service Manager. Regrettably Charlie Hollins died at the Oulton Park race circuit in Cheshire where some of the early Equipes were being tested. As the Company grew, others joined us and each played a valuable part in assisting the progression. The late Lawrie Austin joined us as Buyer, the late Ken Wallace as Sales Manager and Douglas Ferreira as Assistant Sales Manager. Tom Gratrix joined as Company Secretary and later became Managing Director, and last, but by no means least, Alan Pounder, designer and draughtsman, who was responsible for much of the design work in the later models and for the Bond Scooter, Trailer Tent and so on. When I look back now, I realise more than ever what sterling work was done by these fellows.

The commencement of production was followed by years of happiness brought about by a sense of achievement, interspersed with periods of crisis and worry. There is great satisfaction in producing something as novel as the Minicar then was and receiving the plaudits of the press, especially when one had to fight to obtain the materials with which to do so. There were crises when design faults appeared in cars already in the hands of owners. There were worries and many sleepless nights when our sales were hit by legislation beyond our control and stocks of cars piled up - for stocks had to be financed and bank managers in those days were not quite so benign as they appear to be today. Nevertheless, I look back on those years with satisfaction and with so many happy memories that the worries fade into oblivion. And nothing brings me more joy than to go along to Morecambe each year for the annual Bond Minicar Owners' Club Rally and see so many of those cars which we produced thirty and forty years ago, and to talk to their owners among whom such a pride of ownership exists today.

Unfortunately with advancing years, one's memory is not so good as it used to be, and I am unable to recall exact dates and details of the various modifications we made or indeed many other points made in the narrative of this book, but I am sure that Nick Wotherspoon has carried out a great deal of research and has got the facts right. I congratulate him on his efforts, for I know that this publication will be of great interest to the many students of the history of the motor car, for this indeed was a new era in motoring. Colonel C.R. Gray MBE TD CBIM

Introduction

My first close encounter with a Bond car occurred many years ago when I was invited to inspect a somewhat dilapidated Equipe GT that was languishing in a back garden near Preston in Lancashire. As the last of several old fencing panels that had formed a protective covering over the vehicle were pulled away, I was confronted by a surprisingly striking little fast-back-style coupé, albeit painted a rather garish bright orange colour. My invitation stemmed from the fact I had earlier turned up for a meeting in my Triumph Herald and the owner of the Bond had immediately thought his abandoned project would be of interest to me. I had to confess that although I had often seen the spartan little three-wheeler Bonds at various classic and vintage car events, I knew little about the more glamorous Equipe sports cars that the Preston Factory also produced, other than they were indeed based on Herald components. Following consultation with Chris Gardner, who was the Triumph Sports Six Club (TSSC) Bond Register Secretary at the time, I realised that this was the earliest model of the Equipe and indeed a rare vehicle, with only some twenty-five believed to have survived, so a few days later a deal was struck and I became its owner.

After a few essential repairs, an MOT and a quick re-spray, I began to use the Equipe on a regular basis, including commuting into Preston and attending a number of local classic car shows, and soon found I would regularly be approached by people eager to tell me all about the car and the Preston Firm that built it: Sharp's Commercials. Having a keen interest in local history, I was soon hooked and began to record what were often conflicting accounts, as well as seeking out documentary material related to these vehicles and arranging to meet people who had worked for the Company. Unfortunately, it soon became apparent that comparatively little in the way of archival material, such as production records from the Bond Factory, has survived. It would seem that when the Factory was cleared out following its closure by Reliant in 1970, any material which held no commercial value was simply consigned to the skip. This, it is understood, included the contents of both the publicity department and the drawing office. Fortunately, however, some material was saved by one or two employees, including hand-written production records, photographs, press cutting scrapbooks and even service-training films. At that time much of this surviving material was still in the hands of former employees who were most generous in allowing me free access.

The reminiscences of former employees and other individuals connected with Bond cars have formed important primary source material for my research and wherever possible all such information was verified using the documentary sources available and by cross-referencing with other oral accounts. It is possible, however, that over the years recollections may have been obscured, although every effort has been made to avoid any errors. One area which has been a source of much confusion over the years has been the various company names under which the different vehicles that have carried the Bond name have been built. Briefly, the story began with the forming of the Bond Aircraft and Engineering Company towards the end of the Second World War, which then produced a handful of racing cars and then the prototype 1/8th Litre Shopping Car in early 1948, following the Company's move from Blackpool to Longridge. The design was sold to Sharp's Commercials Limited in nearby Preston, who then developed it and turned it into a more viable commercial proposition, but retained the Bond name for their vehicle.

Lawrie Bond pursued his interest in two-wheel vehicles through his company at Longridge with the Bond Minibyke. This design was also sold, this time to Ellis Limited, of Armley, Leeds, who also continued to market the machine using the Bond name. For his next project Lawrie Bond shortened his company name to BAC, presumably to try to overcome the confusion that had been created! This situation continued until BAC was closed down in 1953, coinciding with the decision by Ellis Limited to abandon production of the Minibyke. The respite was short lived, however, as Lawrie set up Lawrence Bond Cars Limited at Loxwood, in Sussex. In the meantime Sharp's Commercials Limited (the apostrophe was dropped in the mid-1950s) continued to market subsequent models of the Minicar under the Bond name. Finally, in 1964 the problem was largely eliminated when, following the success of the new Equipe sportscars, the Company changed its name to Bond Cars Limited. This was followed the next year by the closure of Lawrence Bond Cars Limited in Loxwood and at last sanity prevailed - until Reliant came up with the Bond Bug!

The one common thread running through the story is Lawrence 'Lawrie' Bond himself, a largely forgotten and often misunderstood genius - certainly a talented and accomplished engineer, if somewhat eccentric. His obsession with saving weight proved the Achilles heel of a number of his designs, as it was sometimes taken to the point of weakness, which could lead to premature structural failure. However, Lawrie was at least persistent and never afraid to try out new ideas, although his apparent lack of business sense or the patience to develop his ideas into commercially-viable propositions may have been a factor that led to a number of his designs falling by the wayside. Today, he is, however, probably best known for being the designer and originator of Britain's first, and later most successful, three-wheeled microcar - The Bond Minicar. A tiny and incredibly economical vehicle that provided many people with an accessible form of personal motor transport in the harsh post-war austerity period. Readers of this book will soon realise that there is much more to the story of Bond Cars than just 'those funny little three-wheelers' and hopefully this often mistakenly held image will be dispelled. But Lawrie Bond's legacy is far more than that, as in addition to being a prolific automotive designer, he is unique in being responsible for such a diverse range of vehicles, especially his microcar designs. Without him, the Bond Minicar would of course have never happened, though purists may only credit him with the basic design of the first four models, and we would not have the stylish Berkeley, which still turns heads today. He was also responsible for the Opperman Unicar, a sound concept that never quite found its niche and the pretty Stirling from the same Company, which showed so much promise, but faded into obscurity just as it seemed to have such a bright future. Finally the Bond 875, hampered by strict weight legislation that saw its design compromised and which became the eventual victim of company politics after Reliant's takeover. It then remained unloved by enthusiasts for years, but is now being recognised for its innovative design and becoming sought after in its own right. Surely with such a range of microcars to his credit, Lawrie Bond deserves the title of the 'Microcar Man'!

Chapter One

Lawrence 'Lawrie' Bond

Note: Lawrence Bond regularly used the shortened version of his first name 'Lawrie' amongst friends and family, who recall he preferred the form 'Lawrie', as associated with the spelling of his full first name, although perhaps inevitably the press usually insisted on using the form 'Laurie'!

Lawrence 'Lawrie' Bond (1907-1974) was an accomplished engineer, draughtsman and vehicle designer, who has been described in many ways in the past, from 'a weight-saving genius' to a 'maverick designer' and even 'fanatic'. Today, he is, however, probably best known for being the designer and originator of Britain's first and later most successful, three-wheeled microcar - The Bond Minicar. This diminutive, lightweight and incredibly economical vehicle provided many people with an accessible form of personal motor transport in the harsh post-war austerity period. But few people realise just how prolific a designer Lawrie Bond actually was or how diverse was the range of projects that he was involved in. His work ranged from the well-known, such as the Bond Minicar or the Berkeley, to the obscure Opperman Unicar and the BAC Gazelle scooter. There was also a whole range of vehicles for which he had no input, other than the use of his name, culminating in the futuristic Bond Bug.

Lawrence Bond was born on 2 August 1907 in Preston, Lancashire, the son of Frederick Charles Bond (1873-1963), a clothing maker born in Liverpool who became a well-known local historian and artist, and his wife Margaret Ellen Morphy (c1876-1957), born in Ballinamallard, Fermanagh, Ireland. He had one sibling, a younger brother, Frederick Bond (1910-1997). The family lived in the Broadgate area of Preston, close to the centre of the town, and Lawrie was educated at Preston Grammar School. Details of his early career are vague, but he is believed to have served an apprenticeship with a local firm, Atkinson and Company Ltd, engineers and wagon builders. This was probably at their Kendal Street Works in Preston, where up until 1929 the Company was still building steam-powered wagons.

By the early 1930s he worked in the drawing offices of engine and gearbox manufacturers Henry Meadows Limited in Wolverhampton, then from there went on to work as a draughtsman with the Blackburn Aircraft Company at Brough, where he married Mary Marjorie Lambert in 1934. The exact nature of his work at Blackburn Aircraft is not clear, although it is believed he did some design work on the Blackburn B.26 Botha, a three-seat twin-engined reconnaissance/torpedo bomber that entered RAF service in 1939. He is also believed to have worked on the development of the Cirrus series of aero engines, which had been bought by Blackburn Aircraft in 1934 and which were used in a number of training aircraft, including the Blackburn B.2 trainer, which was initially used by the Company's own flying school at Brough. His time here was to be an important influence on his later design work, which frequently featured weightsaving aircraft construction techniques and materials.By 1944 he had set up his own small engineering workshop just outside Blackpool, Lancashire, employing some 20-30 workers, the Bond Aircraft & Engineering Company (Blackpool) Limited, which manufactured aircraft and vehicle components under Ministry of Supply contract, and had its office on Queen Street in the centre of the town. The end of the war saw the closure of his Blackpool premises, however, and in 1947 he married for the second time to Pauline Freeman and moved to a small workshop with attached living accommodation, located on Towneley Road, off Berry Lane, Longridge, Lancashire, immediately behind and adjoining the former fire station. It was here, with now only a handful of staff, and with paid work varied and often unreliable, that Lawrie began to turn his own designs into reality, initially concentrating on his passion for motor racing.

500cc Racing

Following the Second World War, the initial post-war austerity period of the late 1940s gave rise to a situation which did little to encourage the return of motor racing. Strict rationing was still prevalent on many goods, including petrol, and many raw materials for industry were in short supply. In addition, most of the pre-war motor racing circuits were either in a poor state of repair, or, like Brooklands, had been taken over completely for war work. This left few venues for motorsport, and the shortage of materials and financial resources meant that few, if any, new racing cars were likely to be built. However, before long, a number of the well-known sprint and hill-climb courses were holding organised events, attracting large crowds looking for hard-to-find and much needed entertainment, as the mainly pre-war machines battled it out. Soon a new class of smaller, lightweight, racing cars began to appear at these events, as ever-resourceful motor racing enthusiasts sought to overcome the prevailing difficulties by using what was available.

By 1946 a new post-war 500cc class had evolved, based on low-cost, motorcycle-engined specials that had begun to appear just before the war. The new 500cc formula (later becoming Formula Three and adopted by the FIA in 1950) soon inspired a variety of new specially-built racing cars, usually powered by Norton and JAP (J.A. Prestwich) engines. As Lawrie Bond set about designing and building his own new racing car, the residents of Longridge became used to seeing

Lawrie Bond in his amazing tiny 500cc Type B Doodlebug Special at its début at Shelsley in 1947.

him testing his tiny 500cc vehicle up and down the road outside the workshop on Towneley Road. Testing was also carried out at nearby Jeffrey Hill, where he arranged for a friendly local policeman to 'close' the narrow road that runs up and along the crest of Longridge Fell, and the immaculately-dressed Lawrie Bond would frequently end up covered from head to toe in oil by the end of the day. Lawrie later referred to this car retrospectively as his 'Type B' racing car, though there seems to be no evidence at all that this was not his first foray into racing car design and building, but the car may have undergone a change of engine during development which could account for this. The bright yellow 500cc Bond Special made its debut on 21 June 1947 at the famous Shelsley Walsh hill climb in Worcestershire. This tiny, but extraordinary machine caused quite a stir at this event and was nick-named the 'Doodlebug' Bond Special by the motoring press.

The 500cc Bond Special was built using aircraft construction techniques and materials, with a monocoque-style shell using sheet aluminium to achieve its ultra-light weight. Power was provided by a 499cc Rudge Whitworth Ulster motorcycle engine driving the reinforced front wheels. Suspension was non-existent, other than the slight cushioning effect provided by the tyres, and the whole thing was so light that packets of wetted sand had to be used as ballast to keep the car on the course! This, together with the tiny wheels which gave the car almost zero ground clearance, caused the car to leap about on bumps in a quite alarming manner. In spite of the extra reinforcement pieces welded to the front driving wheels, the engine still proved too powerful for this ultra-lightweight little vehicle and Lawrie Bond had to resort to gluing the front tyres to the rims to prevent the wheels spinning uselessly within them when setting off. Despite its odd

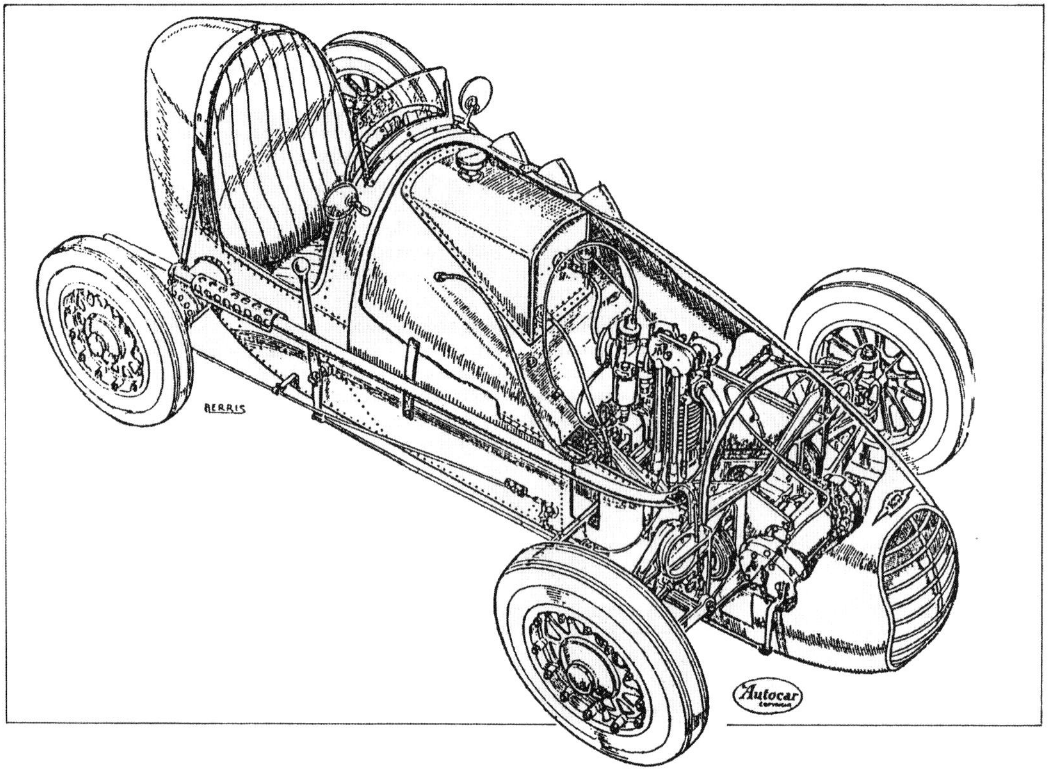
BERRIS
Autocar

Cutaway of the Bond Type C 500cc Racing Car for the new National Formula. Weighing less than 400lb and sold for £585 + £163.5s purchase tax, it made a highly promising recruit to the ranks of 'manufactured' 500cc Racing Cars.

appearance, the 500cc Bond Special was by no means the slowest at Shelsley, coming fifth in its class out of eight starters with a respectable time of 54 seconds, and being likened to a 'jet-propelled yellow slug' by *The Autocar*'s racing correspondent.

Lawrie Bond, in fact, went on to win the 500cc class at Jersey's Bouley Bay hill climb on 24 July of that year, with a time of 69.7 seconds in front of the reportedly larger-than-expected crowds, especially considering the number of other events scheduled for that date. The other events may have helped, though, by keeping some of the competition away.

Unfortunately, on his return to Shelsley Walsh on 27 September, disaster struck when Lawrie lost control of the car after mounting a bank on coming out of the 'esses' and rolled it quite spectacularly! Fortunately he was wearing a crash helmet (unlike a number of other drivers of the time at such events). However, he still came off the worse for wear due to being thrown out of his car - from which he suffered a broken jaw and damaged front teeth, but he was able to walk to the waiting ambulance and was driven to the bottom of the hill, whilst his somewhat rather dented 500cc Special was bodily carried off the course by a couple of marshals.

National 500cc Formula

With the rapid growth in the numbers of 500cc competitors at such events, the need for a National 500cc Formula was recognised, and this was to be introduced in 1948. Because the 500cc Bond Special did not conform to the new National 500cc Formula, Lawrie Bond set about designing and building a new racing car for the 1948 season. The new Type C Bond (as the car became known) was a far more ambitious project than his previous machine and the resulting vehicle was certainly very professional in its appearance. The Type C was constructed using an extremely lightweight stressed aluminium-skinned semi-monocoque shell, built around an Elektron alloy casting that acted as a frame for the 497cc Speedway JAP engine as well as supporting the wishbone-type independent front suspension. This suspension comprised an alloy lower true wishbone with the upper member being a two-part single arm incorporating a segmented rubber disc forming a simple, but effective damper. A similar system was used for the rear suspension, with the wheels carried on trailing links. Transmission was via a primary chain to the four-speed motorcycle-type Burman gearbox and then a secondary chain to a short central driveshaft on which the differential was mounted. Power was then transmitted to the front driving wheels by universally-jointed half shafts. The wheels were also specially designed and manufactured by Lawrie Bond, again being made of Elektron alloy, with detachable split rims to avoid damage when tyres were changed. Finally, steering was achieved by a system of steel cables and bobbins reminiscent of early cycle cars, and the brakes were also cable operated, with the front brakes being mounted inboard in order to reduce unsprung weight.

The Type C Bond was widely regarded as an extremely advanced design, and, with its incredibly low dry weight of just 398lb, much was expected of it. In fact, provision had to be made for extra ballast in the form of detachable weights to be carried to bring the car up to the 500lb minimum weight under the new 500cc Formula. Running on special alcohol fuel with Castrol 'R' lubricating oil, the engine was said to produce 38/40bhp and gave the racing car a power-to-weight-ratio of 230bhp per ton with a claimed top speed in excess of 100mph. The car was due to make its first competition appearance at Silverstone in September 1948 at the first joint JCC (Junior Car Club) and BARC (British Automobile Racing Club) meeting, but unfortunately it was not ready in time for it to qualify. It is reputed, however, that a youthful Stirling Moss was persuaded to try the car out there, possibly with a view to racing the Type C. His impressions of the car are not recorded, but as he was already building up quite a reputation in his Speedway JAP-engined Mk II Cooper, it seems unlikely to have been taken as a serious suggestion. Moss, in fact, took first place at the meeting on 18

Early photo of the Bond Type C 500cc Racing Car, circa 1948, with Charles Fothergill 'driving'.

49

Two Bond 500cc Type C Racing cars at Altcar in 1951. No. 49 was driven by Lawrie Bond – behind it is No. 48 driven by Rowland Eastham. Apparently No. 48 was slightly faster at this event, although unfortunately final placings and times are not known.

September and, significantly, all the top three placed drivers were in Coopers.

Despite expectations, the Type C Bond appears to have achieved little success either in competition or as a commercial venture, as it was also promoted as being available to order. Apparently just three cars

were built and of these only one is believed to have been sold, at a cost of £585 plus £163 purchase tax - a lot of money in 1948! However, the Type C Bond became the subject of considerable interest among those involved in motor racing at the time, and it certainly helped establish Lawrie Bond's reputation in the design field. During the late 1940s and early 1950s, he was a frequent competitor at many of the well-known motor-racing venues - including Silverstone, Brough, Shelsley Walsh, and Prescott - with his former 'apprentice' Raymond Bristo as his mechanic and often using an old Chevrolet truck borrowed from Sharp's Commercials for transport. Although he was not conspicuously successful in competition, he did become a prominent figure at such events and was acquainted with many celebrated motor-racing personalities of the period.

It was also during the late 1940s that Lawrie Bond began work on a number of new projects, this time unconnected with his motor racing interests and probably motivated by the realities of the need to generate income! He began to concentrate on more practical applications of his ideas in his somewhat cramped workshop and yard, rather grandly titled 'Towneley Works' at Longridge, despite its very modest accommodation. This was also home to Lawrie Bond and his

Another early photo of the Bond Type C 500cc Racing Car, circa 1948 with unknown driver, taken on Towneley Road, Longridge.

Centre spread from the original Bond Type C 500cc brochure. The text in the brochure describes the Type C single-seater racing car as an entirely new design developed from the successful Type B Midget Bond racing car:

'The new Type C is a much larger car than its predecessor, incorporating many improvements as a result of extensive research and experience gained racing the very small Type B car. The new Type C complies fully with the Class 1 formula laid down by the British 500 Club, except for the total dry weight, which is only just over 3½cwt, and in order to make the car eligible for any events which may be governed by these rules, detachable ballast weights are provided, which, when fitted, raise the total dry weight to just over 500lb. For the more important Open and International events these ballast weights may be removed, giving the obvious advantage of a lighter car.

'The front suspension is independent with wishbones and special rubber suspension unit; the rear uses a trailing link and rubber unit. Built-in shock absorbers front and rear. Both front and rear wheels have a high roll centre, giving entire absence of roll, resulting in exceptional cornering stability.

'Body and frame are single stressed skin unit of aluminium. The full mass weight of engine, gearbox/transmission is over the front-wheel drive axle,

ENGINE	Speedway J.A.P. single cylinder racing engine. O.H.V. Push rod operated. Bore 80mm. Stroke 99mm. Capacity 497c.c. Compression ratio 14 : 1. Max. B.H.P. 38/40 at 6,000 r.p.m. Fuel, special alcohol. Lubricating oil, Castrol " R."
GEARBOX	Racing close ratio 4-speed. Positive change. Ratios, 1 : 1.26 : 1.57 : 2.67.
TRANSMISSION	Front wheel drive by roller chain throughout, allowing easily changed final gear ratio. Primary $\frac{5}{16}$in. x $\frac{1}{2}$in. Roller chain. Secondary $\frac{3}{8}$in. x $\frac{5}{8}$in. Roller chain.

STEERIN

BRAKES

FRAME

justable cable and drum, giving absolutely
d sensitive steering without backlash.

ernal expanding mounted inboard, allowing
unsprung weight. Rear, internal expanding
s and wheels cast integral in light alloy. Cable
:hroughout.

Frame combined into an extremely light and
sed skin aluminium alloy structure.

SUSPENSION

Front: Independent with wishbones and special rubber suspension unit. Rear: Trailing link with special rubber suspension unit. Special built-in friction-type shock absorbers, front and rear.

DIMENSIONS

Wheelbase 5ft. 10in. Track 3ft. 9in. Overall length 9ft. 6in. Tyres 4.25 x 15. Petrol tank capacity 1 gallon. Weight approx. $3\frac{1}{2}$ cwts.

PERFORMANCE

Power weight ratio = 0.75 lb. per B.H.P. = 230 B.H.P. per ton. Maximum speed over 100 m.p.h.

resulting in over 80 per cent of the total weight of the car is concentrated over the front driving wheels, reducing wheelspin to an absolute minimum and giving superb directional stability.

'The Type C Bond is full of ingenious and unusual features which contribute to its amazing performance. The extreme ease of handling and remarkable feeling of safety, coupled with a terrific acceleration and high maximum speed over 100mph (*power weight ratio is given as 230bhp per ton*) make driving a really thrilling experience.'

This recently-restored Type C Bond 500cc Racing Car, belonging to Charlie Banyard-Smith, made its debut at the Goodwood Revival in 2015. It is one of two surviving Type C Bonds, the other, having been heavily modified, is now stripped and awaiting restoration. (*Photo: A.E. Watkiss.*)

wife Pauline, where they lived in a small flat above, along with his several large dogs which were allowed to roam the premises freely. Here Bond worked with only a handful of employees and occasionally with his father, Frederick Charles Bond, who did some pattern work, and fashioned out of sheet aluminium the handmade badges that adorned the various racing cars, motorcycles and scooters which were produced. Working conditions and hours were somewhat unusual, to say the least; Lawrie Bond often did not appear until midday and then - if he wanted to try out a new idea - he would carry on for 36 hours or more without a break. Money was always short and pay was often irregular with a bonus always being promised 'when things got better'. Later on Bond also employed two further 'assistants' or 'apprentices' at the works - one of these was Mr Roy Robinson who recalls that Lawrie Bond modified his bicycle by adding some experimental sprung front forks, which he was working on - they were not a success!

As Bond preferred to manufacture as many components as possible himself, rather than buy items in from other companies, the small workshop was fairly well-equipped with three lathes, a guillotine, a pillar drill, welding and brazing equipment, and so on. The only work that had to be contracted out was the casting of the alloy components

JAP

During the restoration, the Type C Bond was returned to its original Speedway JAP engine specification, having spent many years fitted with a Pre-Unit alloy Triumph 500 twin engine, installed by previous owner Dermot Elworthy. (*Photo: A.E. Watkiss.*)

Cockpit view of Charlie Banyard-Smith's beautifully restored Type C Bond 500cc Racing Car. (*Photo: A.E. Watkiss.*)

that were frequently incorporated in his designs. This work was usually done by a firm in nearby Preston, although most of the pattern work and final machining of such components was still done in the Longridge workshop. During quiet periods, other, sometimes unusual, projects were taken on - these ranged from manufacturing wrought-iron garden furniture and gates to building a complete shooting gallery for Blackpool Pleasure Beach that incorporated a specially-designed ball-bearing-firing machine gun!

The First Bond Minicar

It was in November 1948 when what was to become perhaps the best-known of Lawrie Bond's vehicle designs was formally announced to the motoring press. This was the first production model of the Bond Minicar, which was to be manufactured by Sharp's Commercials, a long-established commercial vehicle concern in Preston, Lancashire, following an agreement between Lawrie Bond and the Company's Managing Director, Lieutenant-Colonel C.R. Gray. The prototype for this amazing little three-wheeled vehicle had been built at Lawrie's Longridge workshop earlier that year and had already received considerable attention from the motoring press. Originally intended as a local runabout/shopping car for Bond and his wife, the prototype had become a regular sight around the small town of Longridge and began to arouse interest, leading to a realisation that there might, in fact, be considerable commercial potential for such a vehicle under the economic conditions prevalent at the time. It was decided to see if a market did indeed exist for such a machine, and Lawrie's wife Pauline, who had previously worked in London's Fleet Street and had many press contacts there, now put these to good use. This resulted in articles on the new '1/8th Litre Bond Shopping Car', as it was initially called, appearing in many of the major motoring and motorcycling journals in May 1948. Although it was made clear that the vehicle was still at the prototype stage and production was still some time off, this coverage did indeed bring in a considerable number of serious enquiries, but left Bond with a major problem of where to build his new microcar. Owing to the lack of space at Towneley Works, the prototype had apparently been built on the first floor of the premises and lowered through a trap door to the workshop below, although at only 195lb this would not have presented any great problem.

Lawrie and wife Pauline demonstrating the prototype 1/8th Litre Bond Shopping Car on Towneley Road, Longridge.

As with the Type C Bond racing car, the new Bond Shopping Car was also built using aircraft-style construction techniques and materials. The bodyshell was a semi-monocoque structure made almost entirely of sheet aluminium. It was described in *The Motor* as a 'Short Radius Runabout' powered by a 125cc Villiers motorcycle engine (probably a Mk 9D) fitted with a side-mounted carburettor and three-speed gearbox, with its normally handlebar mounted gear change lever now mounted on the

(Right). Austere layout of the instrument panel on the Bond three-wheeler. Note steering-column gear change mounting.

The ⅛-Litre Bond Shopping Car

(Above and right). Modern treatment of the bodywork is evident in these two views of the Bond shopping-car.

(Left). Close-up of the 125 c.c. Villiers engine-cum-gearbox unit which is mounted directly over the single driving wheel. The "radiator" louvres are arranged to concentrate cooling air direct on to the cylinder.

Early Press coverage of the announcement of the prototype 1/8th-Litre Bond Shopping Car in May 1948.

steering column. The engine was rated at 3.25bhp at 3,800rpm giving the new vehicle a claimed practical cruising speed of 30mph whilst carrying two adults and, sensationally for the time, an anticipated 100mpg fuel economy. This would indeed be a big selling point as despite its diminutive size and the fact it was a three-wheeler, it would still be eligible for the same petrol ration as received by cars up to 9hp (engine size approx 1,100cc), the difference being that the Bond would be able to cover some 1,800 miles over a six-month period compared to only 540 miles for the conventional small car. The engine/gearbox unit was mounted on a centrally-positioned single-front steering fork which was attached to a front bulkhead. Transmission to the single

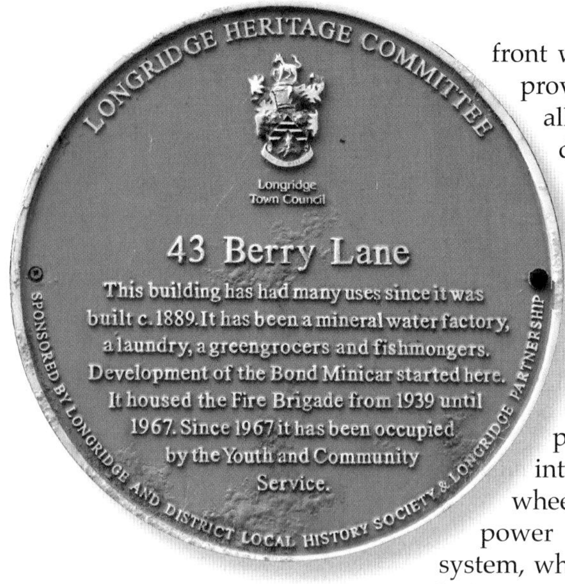
LONGRIDGE HERITAGE COMMITTEE
Longridge Town Council
43 Berry Lane
This building has had many uses since it was built c.1889. It has been a mineral water factory, a laundry, a greengrocers and fishmongers. Development of the Bond Minicar started here. It housed the Fire Brigade from 1939 until 1967. Since 1967 it has been occupied by the Youth and Community Service.
SPONSORED BY LONGRIDGE AND DISTRICT LOCAL HISTORY SOCIETY & LONGRIDGE PARTNERSHIP

Blue plaque on the front of the Old Fire Station, 43 Berry Lane, Longridge, commemorating the rear of the building's role in the Bond Minicar story.

front wheel was via chain and suspension was to be provided by a sprung trailing link, which would also allow for front wheel removal without the need to disturb the chain drive. Steering was achieved by a steel cable and bobbin (or drum) arrangement as used on the Type C Bond, and reminiscent of early pre-war cyclecars, but today only really likely to be used to steer boats fitted with outboard motors. Rear suspension was basically non-existent, apart from rubber mountings incorporated into the light alloy castings that held the stub-axles. Braking was provided by a cable and rod system operating internal expanding shoe-type brakes on the rear wheels only. The Villiers flywheel generator provided power for the ignition and the basic 6-volt lighting system, which incorporated side-mounted headlamps and a small offset single tail lamp. There was no electric starting, but instead a hand-operated, universally-jointed, pull rod operated by the driver from inside the vehicle that was attached to the engine's 'kick-start' lever. Following testing of the prototype it was reported that it could indeed cruise at 30mph with two adults aboard and also easily climbed a short 1-in-4 gradient. In the testers' opinion it was perfectly suited to local journeys and would make an ideal shopping car, though there were reservations about reliability and the requirement for better weather protection. Lawrie had stated to the press that he hoped to commence production of several vehicles a week within only a few months and that the price would be approximately £150 plus purchase tax, which would make the selling price with tax just under £200.

Unfortunately, good business sense was never one of Lawrie Bond's strong points, and as he began to realise that his little runabout did in fact have considerable commercial potential, he also found himself with something of a dilemma, as realistically he did not have the resources or space to put the Bond Shopping Car into production. But Lawrie had heard that a local firm called Sharp's Commercials had a Government contract for refurbishing military vehicles that was coming to an end and so he approached the firm's managing director, Colonel C.R. Gray, who also lived in Longridge at that time, stating that he wished to lease their empty factory in Preston in order to manufacture his new vehicles. This arrangement was not acceptable to Colonel Gray, but after some consideration and inspection of what Gray thought to be a rather crude and not altogether reliable prototype, an agreement to build the cars was reached. The new vehicle was to be called the 'Bond Minicar' and the first twenty-five or so Minicars were produced using Lawrie's original jigs, probably in order to fulfil orders he had already taken. Their appearance is thought to have differed

Lawrie Bond's workshop was at the rear of the-then Fire Station, which fronted on to Berry Lane, Longridge, and Towneley Works was accessed from this yard on Towneley Road. The whole building currently serves as Longridge Youth and Community Centre.

from the rather streamlined prototype, being somewhat simplified and more rounded and probably closer to the eventual production model, though narrower and slightly longer at 4ft 4in width and 9ft length. But exactly what changes were made to the specification of this first batch is unclear, though an interim sales leaflet, which appears to have been drawn up by Bond, notes a modest increased overall weight of 220lb and the provision of a convertible-style hood for weather protection.

Initially Lawrie Bond apparently received a small royalty payment for each Minicar sold, but after the first batch of vehicles had been built, Colonel Gray soon realised that a certain amount of development was required before the Bond Minicar could go into full production, and work on this began almost immediately. This was carried out at Sharp's' Ribbleton Lane Works in Preston with the help of Lawrie Bond and two of his former employees from Longridge, Alan Pearson and Fred Atkinson, who both now joined Sharp's Commercials Limited. The result was a quite different vehicle, with a remodelled bodyshell and completely redesigned front suspension amongst the main features, which gave the production model of the Minicar an increased weight of 340lb. The new production version of the Minicar was announced to the motoring press in November 1948 and immediately it aroused considerable interest, being the first of the new post-war class of microcars to be put into production in the UK. A publicity trial was arranged in early 1949 in which a Bond Minicar was driven from Preston to London (a distance of 228 miles) by Lawrie and well-known

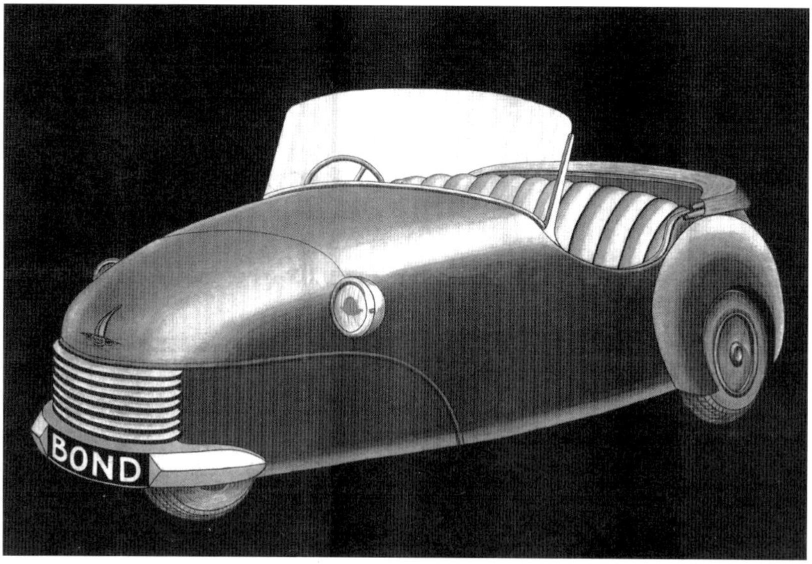
BOND

Lawrie's sketch of the proposed Bond Minicar from a very early pre-production sales leaflet he had produced. Note the angled rear wheel arches and his own Bond badge on the bonnet!

motorcycle journalist C.P. Read. This trial led to considerable press interest in the Minicar: articles appeared in a number of newspapers marvelling at the recorded fuel consumption of almost 100mpg from a 'car' which was priced at under £200. The trial even attracted the attention of Pathé News, featuring in one of their newsreels as the cheapest British car available and with fuel costs at only 'a farthing a mile'! The publicity generated, together with the numerous enquiries from would-be purchasers which started to arrive at the Preston Works of Sharp's Commercials, soon convinced Colonel Gray that he had

One of the first Minicars built by Sharp's Commercials seen outside Lawrie Bond's Towneley Works in Longridge in late 1948. From left to right: Alan Pearson, Fred Atkinson and Raymond Bristo.

backed a winner. It was not long before full-scale production of around fifteen Minicars a week began at the Ribbleton Lane Factory, after a few final modifications were required to overcome some faults that had become apparent during the trial. Although the arrangement between Gray and Lawrie Bond was soon dissolved, Bond continued to do development work on the Minicar for Sharp's Commercials, but before long he was working on new projects of his own and he began to lose interest in the vehicle. Always looking for finance for his next project, Lawrie was tempted into selling the design and manufacturing rights to the Minicar to Sharp's Commercials, who continued to build the vehicles under the Bond name that had by now become synonymous with the Minicar concept.

Bond Minibyke

During the late 1940s Lawrie Bond had turned his attention to the design and development of a range of small lightweight motorcycles and scooters. The first of these was eventually announced in February 1950. This followed the appearance of a gleaming, specially prepared, prototype machine at the Motorcycle Show in September 1949, featuring chromium-plated steel components and highly-polished aluminium bodywork. This machine attracted a great deal of attention, and became the subject of much comment. It became known as the Bond Minibyke. This unconventional machine predictably utilised mainly aluminium alloy construction in order to achieve a very light weight of 91lb and was powered by a 98cc Villiers Mk 1 F engine with a two-speed gearbox. The frame consisted of a large tapered tube, oval in section and formed from rolled sheet aluminium riveted together on its underside. This tube, with its integral fuel tank, terminated at the rear end in a large structural aluminium mudguard which enclosed most of the rear wheel, with the front end closed by the cast-aluminium headstock. The front wheel was supported by two rigid steel strips which formed the front steering forks (although from April 1950 the rigid strips were replaced with tubular telescopic dampers following persistent failure of the former) and was enclosed by a similar mudguard to that at the rear. The engine was hung on a 1-inch x $^{1}/_{4}$-inch steel-strip frame in the form of a wide loop below the main tube and protected by large leg shields at each side.

LTB 365

Lawrie Bond introduces his new Minibyke to the press in early 1950 – note the early rigid steel strip front steering forks.

98 c.c. BOND MINIBYKE
PERFORMANCE AND ECONOMY IN COMFORT
£55
plus purchase tax
LTB 365
BOND AIRCRAFT & ENG Co LTD
TOWNELEY WORKS, LONGRIDGE, LANCS.
50 MPH
200 MPG

Early advert for the Bond-built Minibyke, claiming an ambitious 50mph top speed and 200mpg fuel economy.

The rigid rear wheel was supported by a steel 'U'-shaped strengthening frame attached to the bottom edge of the aluminium mudguard which enclosed it. As with other Bond designs there was no suspension at the rear, and it was intended that any shock from bumps on the road would be absorbed by the sprung saddle and the large 4.00 x 8in low-pressure tyres. The wheels were also of Bond design and incorporated steel split rims bolted to alloy hubs containing 4-inch drum brakes.

Due to its particularly light weight and relatively inexpensive price, at £69.17s.0d, including purchase tax, the Minibyke did prove a limited commercial success, despite problems with the flexibility of the steel strip engine frame, and production reached around twelve a week from the Towneley Works at Longridge. This success led to the introduction of a Deluxe version with telescopic front forks as standard and powered by a 125cc JAP engine with a three-speed gearbox. Unfortunately, problems with the supply of this engine meant that few of this version were actually built at Longridge. In November 1950, Lawrie was again tempted by an offer for the manufacturing rights to the Minibyke and the design was sold to Ellis Limited of Armley, Leeds, who continued to build the machines (still under the Bond Minibyke name) up until 1953. Prices for the two machines they produced were £85.10s.2d for the 98cc standard version and £100.2s.1d. for the 125cc Deluxe, both inclusive of purchase tax. During Minibyke production at Leeds numerous minor changes were made to the design, including replacement of the steel strip engine cradle with a stronger, more rigid, tubular component. This modification meant that a more conventional chain adjuster was now required to replace the original method of deforming the steel strip cradle with a jacking screw. However, persistent problems with premature frame failure proved to be inherent in the design of the

OHY 736

Late 1950, 98cc model Minibyke, now with tubular telescopic dampers forming the steering fork struts.

The late John Ellis (of Ellis, Leeds, Ltd) proudly displays a 125cc JAP-engined, Leeds-built Bond Minibyke, which he kept for many years in his own collection. (*Photo: D. Crawford.*)

A 1951 Ellis-built Bond Minibyke, now in the British Scooter Collection. This machine is fitted with a 98cc Villiers engine and has the later Ellis-designed tubular engine support frame. (*Photo: R. Spalding.*)

Minibyke and undoubtedly contributed to the eventual decision to cease production. Ellis Ltd offered a slight reduction in their prices in March 1953, which was soon followed in August with the announcement that Minibyke production had been discontinued as a result of 'uneconomic circumstances'. During the somewhat troubled production run, only around 750 Minibykes were built in total, with about 150 of these being produced at Longridge and the remainder being Ellis-built machines.

BOND
...VOOR

Later, slightly more exuberant, advertising for the Minibyke, again depicting an Ellis-built machine despite the Bond badge, from a Belgian/Dutch distributor.

BAC Lilliput and Gazelle

Following the transfer of Minibyke production to Leeds, work began on the manufacture of another of Lawrie's new designs of motorcycle, which was to be sold under the new abbreviated company name of 'BAC' (Bond Aircraft and Engineering Company). Like the Minibyke it was to be a relatively small machine characterised by its light weight - both features Lawrie believed would become especially desirable as more and more people began to live in flats, and would need to be able to carry their machines up to their floor for storage. The new machine was to be named the 'Lilliput' due to its diminutive size and was introduced in February 1951, and although it was indeed very small, it was of a much more conventional appearance than the Minibyke. It was built using a single-loop tubular frame attached to the headstock with two tubular triangular extensions forming the chainstays at the rear to support the rigid rear wheel - similar in many respects to a conventional bicycle frame.

The prototype in fact used Dunlop heavy duty 20in delivery bicycle rims laced onto Sturmey-Archer hubs with internal expanding brakes. However, following pressure from Dunlop (who considered that the use of their rims on even such a small motorcycle was potentially dangerous), Bond was forced to modify his design. This he did by manufacturing his own somewhat crude rims from 18-gauge steel on a modified lathe. As with the Minibyke, two versions of the Lilliput were offered: one with the 98cc Mk 1 F Villiers engine and two-speed gearbox at £74.5s.11d, and the other with the 125cc JAP engine and three-speed

BAC
LILLIPUT

Original, rather conservative, sales leaflet cover for the BAC Lilliput.

B·A·C
Lilliput
CK 960

Beautifully restored 1951 98cc BAC Lilliput. Standard original colours were maroon for mudguards, chain guard, front forks and top of tank, with bronze for the frame and tank sides. This scheme may be unoriginal, but it still gets my vote!

gearbox at £83.3s.8d, (both inclusive of purchase tax). Overall the Lilliput was not particularly successful; approximately 200 were built and production rarely exceeded 10-12 a week. However, difficulties with the supply of 125cc JAP engines remained a problem and this led to the 125cc Deluxe version of the Lilliput being discontinued in late 1951, although the 98cc Standard model continued until October the following year. Although an innovative design, and with very light weight, the Lilliput was not considered to be particularly cheap -

Lilliput

Villiers Mk 1F engine detail on the restored 1951 98cc BAC Lilliput.

BAC
GAZELLE

Original sales leaflet cover for the BAC Gazelle. Note the early strip steel cage engine protection for the rider and the early type-specific fuel tank.

especially when compared to the better-known and more conventional machines available at the time.

Whilst the production of the Lilliput continued, Lawrie Bond had already begun work on a new design of motorcycle - this time it was a departure from his previous machines, being a scooter-type machine called the 'Gazelle', which was introduced at the Motorcycle Show at Earls Court in November 1951. This new machine was the subject of much interest at the show - as surprisingly, it was the only all-British scooter to be exhibited - and was competitively priced at £99.13s.4d. (including purchase tax). Another exhibit on Lawrie Bond's stand at this show which also attracted the attention of the motoring press was his new design for a motorcycle engine rotary-valve cylinder head.

The new Gazelle used the 122cc Villiers Mk 10 D engine and featured a fairly conventional scooter layout. The rider was seated over the engine (which was protected by a rather curious cage-like metal grille), and ahead of the fuel tank which was situated immediately behind the saddle. One very unusual feature of the Gazelle was the

Raymond Bristo and Pauline Bond outside Towneley Works, Longridge, circa 1952, in a 122cc BAC Gazelle combination, one of only two such combinations believed to have been built before production ceased in 1953.

JJU·997

This 1953 BAC Gazelle Scooter, now in the British Scooter Collection, is probably the only surviving example. It is fitted with a 98cc Villiers engine, and has the later 'improved' design of engine guard and a Lilliput fuel tank over the rear wheel. Presumably towards the end of production BAC were using whatever was to hand to keep costs down. (*Photo: R. Spalding.*)

dual role of the rear frame tubes, which not only supported the rigid rear wheel, but also acted as the exhaust pipes as well! The twin-tube mainframe also featured a hollow ribbed transverse stiffener positioned immediately below the engine which enclosed the two short transverse bracing tubes and acted as the exhaust silencer. Following the end of Lilliput production in October 1952, a 98cc version of the Gazelle was introduced together with the option of a lightweight sidecar weighing only 47lb for the 122cc model. Suspension was again somewhat basic, relying largely on the 4.00 x 8in low-pressure tyres to absorb some of the bumps, but with telescopic forks fitted at the front. The Gazelle achieved little success; relatively few were built before late 1952 when Bond sold the design and manufacturing rights, and handed the Gazelle over to a firm of manufacturing, development, and consultant engineers by the name of Projects and Developments Limited, located on Hodson Street in nearby Blackburn, Lancashire.

Oscar Scooter

Finance for the work that Projects and Developments Ltd were to undertake on the Gazelle design was provided by entrepreneur, financier and sometime-racing driver Roger Dennistoun 'Dennis' Poore, an old acquaintance of Lawrie Bond (through their mutual interest in motor racing) who was later to become known as one of the key figures behind British Manganese Bronze, and the creation of Norton-Villiers-Triumph Ltd in the late 1960s and early 1970s. Raymond Bristo was recruited by Projects and Developments Limited, and he left BAC to begin work on an intensive fourteen-month development and testing programme at Blackburn, which was to result in an almost completely new scooter.

The resulting machine was to be available with either a 122cc or 197cc Villiers engine, which was now fully enclosed along with the fuel tank in a moulded glass fibre rear bodyshell (being one of the first scooters to use this material), and provided with an electric starter and a new exceptionally quiet exhaust system. This body shell pivoted upwards from the front end, offering excellent access for maintenance, and the rear suspension utilised a swinging arm system at the rear, to give a very smooth and safe ride. Unusually, the foot platform extended alongside the rear bodywork to provide running board type footrests for a pillion passenger or to allow two suitcases to be carried, one on each side of the machine. The front bodywork was also glass fibre and in one piece, completely covering the front wheel and front steering forks, fitted with a recessed 6in headlamp, as well as providing weather protection for the rider, with an optional Perspex windscreen, and an integral facia panel for instruments and the ignition switch. The tubular steel frame of the Oscar was also much improved over the Gazelle design, and unusually featured bonded rubber 'Flexitor' suspension units front and rear, and flexible rubber engine mountings to eliminate vibration passing through to the frame. Wheels were steel disc type and interchangeable, with provision to carry a spare being provided, and both could be changed quickly, with the rear wheel detachable without disturbing the chain. Gear change was carried out using two pedals located on the front right-hand side of the foot platform - left to make an

OSCAR
THE BRITISH DESIGNED AND BUILT "OSCAR" has—
★ Accommodation for two persons on a comfortable dual seat. Space for two large suitcases and all are well protected from weather and mud
★ Silence and Smoothness which is remarkable; achieved by an exclusive design of exhaust silencer together with resilient rubber mounting of the entire engine, and exhaust system.
★ Exceptional Stability and Safety ensured by the use of specially large wheels rigidly mounted on both sides to supple rubber suspension units.
★ Outstanding Non-skid characteristics built into the design by unique suspension and correctly proportioned braking between front and rear wheels.
★ Both Road Wheels interchangeable and easily removed by a single bolt without disturbing either final drive chain or brakes. A cushion drive is provided.
★ Beauty of Line, Accessibility, and is easily cleaned.
"OSCAR" IS ON STAND 52 AT EARLS COURT.
PROJECTS & DEVELOPMENTS LTD., BLACKBURN, ENGLAND

Press announcement for the new Oscar Scooter by Projects and Developments Ltd of Blackburn, Lancs.

Remarkably, both the Oscar Scooters believed to have been completed by the time the project was abandoned in late 1953 appear to have survived. This one is preserved in remarkably original untouched condition. (*Photo: I. Harrop.*)

upward change and right for a downward change. Even more unusually, a third pedal to the left-hand side of the foot platform operated both the front and rear brakes together, using a compensator to ensure most pressure was applied to the front to prevent the possibility of skidding, though a more conventional handlebar brake lever for the front brakes was also provided for use as an emergency brake.

Described as a design prototype, the new Oscar scooter made its debut at the 1953 Motorcycle Show at Earls Court, where it aroused considerable interest, not just due to the fact it was a new all-British scooter, but also because show goers were impressed with the attractive modern design and highly professional standard of finish - one of the show stand machines even featuring a lightweight sidecar. The *Motor Cycle* magazine gave it a full two-page write up and were clearly highly impressed. International sales were obviously anticipated as the Oscar also made an appearance at the Frankfurt Show, where it was almost equally enthusiastically received. But motoring journalists wanting to test ride the machine were disappointed to find no machines were available and only a select few were granted short, supervised, rides. Firm details regarding pricing and production dates proved equally elusive, and, soon after the shows, Dennis Poore collected the handful

Rear view of the 1953 Oscar Scooter. Note the two gear change pedals to the right of the foot platform – apparently changing down a gear whilst also braking with the third pedal to the left (not visible) leaves the rider in an uncomfortably precarious position, perhaps making it just as well the Oscar did not go into production! (*Photo: I. Harrop.*)

of prototypes that had been built from Blackburn and no more was heard of the Oscar scooter.

Rotary Valve Development

In the meantime. Lawrie Bond had continued with development work on his Type C racing-car design, including plans for the installation of a BMW 496cc twin engine and further experimentation with his rotary valve design. A working test engine was built and tested, based on a 500cc JAP engine using his own rotary valve head, in one of the Type C Bond racing cars. This testing did not prove a success, however, because of problems with the oil seals resulting in both the car and the driver receiving a liberal coating of oil! The single-cylinder test engine used a chain driven valve enclosed in a finned and jacketed oil-cooled cylinder head, as had been seen on the mock-up engine exhibited at the Motorcycle Show. Though others had tried, also unsuccessfully, Lawrie's variation on the rotary valve theme caught the attention of Norton's Joe Craig who was looking for a means of extracting more power out of their works competition engines. Norton took up the design and Lawrie Bond worked with Joe Craig on the project at the Norton's Bracebridge Street Factory in Birmingham to produce a new experimental engine, this time with the valve driven by a vertical shaft and bevel gear arrangement. Two years' work apparently resulted in only a modest improvement in power from 35bhp to 47bhp, but with poor reliability and with frequent seizure of the valve, oil leaks, and fouling of the plug when power was eased off. In 1954 Norton called a halt to the project and Lawrie Bond went back to his drawing board to come up with a new rotary valve design, this time to create an air-cooled 2.5 litre V8 racing-car engine, which would be very compact, allowing the building of a very streamlined racing car. In the meantime he had sold his Longridge Workshop and most of its contents, and moved to the village of Wormley, near Godalming, in Surrey, where he hoped to concentrate on his freelance design work. The racing-car engine design was purchased (together with a rather familiar looking test engine based on a 500cc Speedway JAP unit that was intended to prove the principle for the design) by Connaught Engineering, who were considering building their own engine at this time. Connaught were apparently very impressed with the extremely well-produced design drawings (a trade mark of Lawrie Bond) for this engine which incorporated gear-driven rotary valves and had an overall height of just 14 inches. After some further testing, Bill Warham at Connaught concluded that although the basic principle was sound and did show potential, it would require much development - and therefore money - so the idea was sadly abandoned.

Shortly after Lawrie moved south in mid-1953, another of his designs caught the attention of the motoring press. This was a form of fuel-injection device that could be fitted in place of a conventional carburettor on car and motorcycle engines. The device was reported as being suitable for sports or touring purposes on motorcycles and cars with normal engine-driven fuel pumps or gravity-fed fuel systems. For racing purposes, where it was claimed the full potential of the device could be best utilised, a pressurised fuel system would be used. Among the claims made for the Bond fuel-injection system were increased power output from the engine while at the same time reduced fuel consumption. This was to be achieved through eliminating fuel wastage, by ensuring thorough atomisation of the fuel, and an unrestricted air flow through the induction system. On paper the Bond fuel injection or fuel-metering device appeared similar to a number of other contemporary designs, the main difference being the use of pressure from the engine cylinder to operate a plunger-pump which was to force the fuel into the induction system. This allowed for the quantity of fuel 'injected' to be automatically adjusted according to the throttle setting and also - it was claimed - to give the added advantage of easier starting. Despite the interest shown by the motoring press and the apparent advantages of the system, it would appear that the design never progressed beyond the initial design stage. As with many of Lawrie Bond's prolific designs, the Bond fuel-injection system appeared impressive in theory, but little is known about its actual performance in prototype form and the idea seems to have been abandoned due to lack of any serious commercial interest in the project.

Sherpa Scooter

Lawrie Bond's final foray into two-wheel designs was announced in November 1955 in the form of a newly-designed machine he named the Sherpa Scooter. This new scooter received a surprising amount of press coverage after Lawrie had turned up outside the Motorcycle Show that year at Earls Court on his prototype machine, which he displayed in the exhibitor's car park, as he did not have the funds to cover the expense of a stand at the show! The appearance of the new Sherpa was quite conventional and somewhat reminiscent of the Italian scooters becoming very popular at the time. It was powered by a 98cc Villiers engine with a two-speed gearbox and, as might be expected, featured light weight construction, this time utilising glassfibre bodywork to achieve an overall weight of 123lb. The machine featured 8in wheels with swinging arm suspension at the front and trailing arm at the rear. As far as is known, only one prototype Sherpa scooter was ever built, and it faded into obscurity when an anticipated contract to supply them for Police use failed to materialise and the project was abandoned.

YPG 225

Lawrie Bond on his Sherpa Scooter prototype in 1956.

Lawrence Bond Cars Ltd

These apparent setbacks do not seem to have worried Lawrie Bond, however, as he was busier than ever. In 1956 he bought garage premises at Loxwood in Sussex and set up a new workshop under the title 'Lawrence Bond Cars Limited'. Meanwhile his former associate Raymond Bristo had left Projects and Developments Limited in Blackburn and was now working as a motorcycle mechanic in Preston,

LAWRENCE BOND CARS LTD
ESSO

Lawrence Bond Cars Limited premises at Loxwood in Sussex.

Lancashire. Bristo was persuaded by Bond to move down to Loxwood to manage the new garage premises. Lawrie must certainly have needed the help at that time, as 1956 also saw the announcement of two new lightweight vehicles of Bond's design.

Chapter Two

The Berkeley

BERKELEY
B

The first of Lawrie's new designs appeared in late 1956 and had been designed at the request of Charles Panter, more formally known as Charles Maxwell Roscoe de Buire Panter (1911-1993), who was at that time the Managing Director of a company called Berkeley Coachwork Limited, located at Biggleswade in Bedfordshire. Like many small manufacturing companies in post-war Britain, this Company had evolved, partly out of necessity and also in order to try to capitalise on the opportunities provided by emerging new markets, as the country recovered from the years of conflict and began to rebuild its economy.

Their story began with Charles Panter's involvement with a furniture manufacture named Shrager Brothers of Bridport Road, Edmonton, London, which had become involved in war work early in the conflict, manufacturing mainly wooden parts and sub-assemblies for aircraft. As the threat of bombing in and around London intensified, they moved to Old Warden Aerodrome in Bedfordshire, where they set up a Civilian Repair Unit (CRU) as part of the Civilian Repair Organisation (CRO), a branch of the Air Ministry. Here they specialised in the repair of civilian aircraft impressed into service with the RAF for training purposes, etc., including: Desoutter, Heston Phoenix, Leopard Moth and Vega Gull. They also repaired military training aircraft, such as the Miles Magister and Master, and Percival Proctor, and later carried out modifications to American-built aircraft for RAF service, such as the Harvard advanced trainer and Mustang fighter.

At the end of the war and with the aircraft repair contract work coming to an end, the Company took stock of the skills and materials they had available, and looked to how these could be applied to the huge demand for emergency / temporary housing. The first design they came up with, in July 1946, was named the Berkeley Carapartment, a large trailer caravan with styling cues obviously taken from American 'trailers' of the period. The first of these were built, alongside the last aircraft the Company were working on, in Old Warden's No.

Sales literature for the amazing double-decked leviathan that was the Berkeley Statesman Caravan, though at 42cwt, the Humber Super Snipe Mk III illustrated, with its 4.1 litre engine, was one of the few cars able to actually tow it.

JTM 733
Move into the 'STATESMAN'
BERKELEY'S big caravan-house

1 Hangar. It was advertised as embodying aircraft design features and manufacturing principles, and featured a wedge, shaped front end that housed a large washroom, and was more of a small flat on wheels than a traditional caravan. Despite apparently having poor towing characteristics (perhaps not an issue for its main intended use as temporary housing), it did, initially at least, sell and the Company were soon looking for alternative premises to accommodate increased production. This they found nearby, as another important wartime manufacturing company, Pobjoy (Aeroengines) Ltd was by now scaling

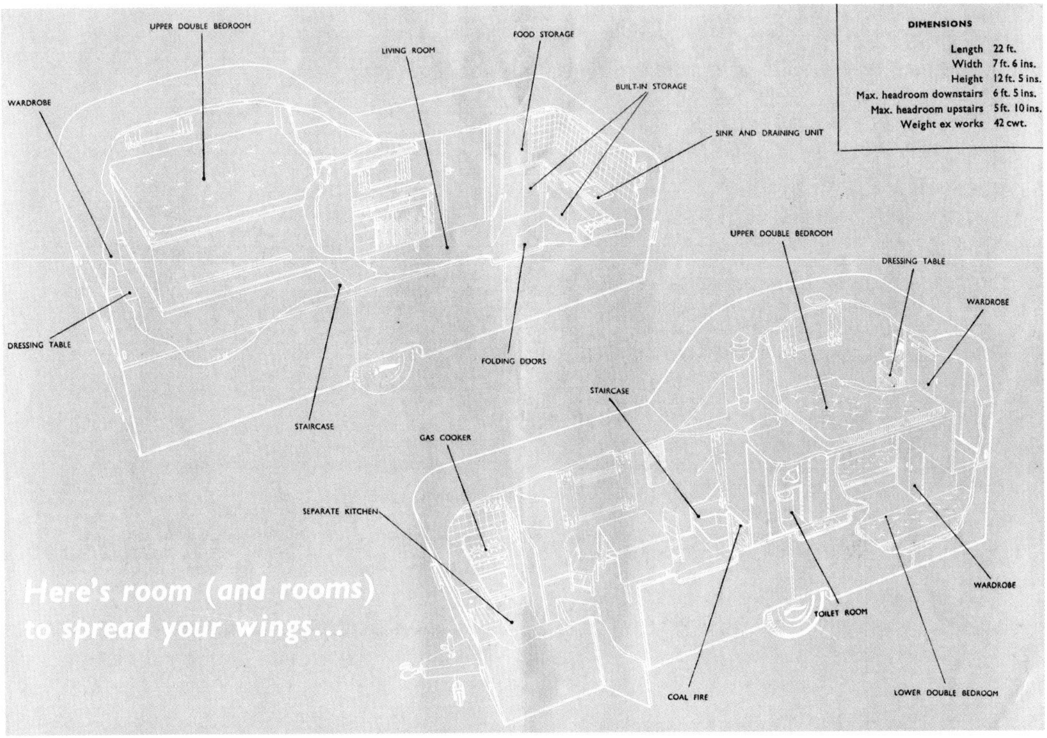
DIMENSIONS
Length 22 ft.
Width 7 ft. 6 ins.
Height 12 ft. 5 ins.
Max. headroom downstairs 6 ft. 5 ins.
Max. headroom upstairs 5 ft. 10 ins.
Weight ex works 42 cwt.
UPPER DOUBLE BEDROOM
LIVING ROOM
FOOD STORAGE
BUILT-IN STORAGE
WARDROBE
SINK AND DRAINING UNIT
DRESSING TABLE
FOLDING DOORS
STAIRCASE
GAS COOKER
SEPARATE KITCHEN
UPPER DOUBLE BEDROOM
DRESSING TABLE
WARDROBE
STAIRCASE
WARDROBE
TOILET ROOM
COAL FIRE
LOWER DOUBLE BEDROOM
Here's room (and rooms) to spread your wings...

Cutaway of the Berkeley Statesman revealing its separate rooms, coal fire, kitchen and staircase to the master bedroom.

down their operation and no longer needed their factory premises in Hitchin Street, Biggleswade. The Company bought and moved into these new premises in late 1946 and a new company was set up in 1947 - Berkeley Coachwork Limited - to manufacture the new caravans, with Charles Panter appointed as Managing Director, whilst Shrager Brothers went back to their main business of furniture manufacture in London.

The Company continued to build the Carapartment, now re-named Berkeley Baronet, and soon added new models, mainly concentrating on larger 'mobile apartment' style caravans. In 1949 they introduced the 28-foot Ambassador, the largest caravan available on the UK market at that time, with two double-bedrooms and separate toilet room! By now they had over 500 employees and were producing around 60 caravans a week. By 1950 they were described as 'the largest producer of caravans in the UK' and brought out a smaller 12ft 6in Messenger Tourer in response to the changing market, which began to look more to caravans as a leisure product. Berkeley Coachworks continued to maintain their market position by introducing a variety of specialist designs and features as well as experimenting with the use of new materials and production methods. Their designs included the Berkeley Deputy of 1951, which featured removable fittings and opening-end panel, giving it a dual role as a car-storage garage in winter! The diminutive Berkeley Caravette was introduced in 1953 and was advertised that it could

At the other end of the scale Berkeley also produced the Caravette 'pod caravan', which could be towed by a 500cc motorcycle combination or suitably powerful microcar. An ingenious feature was that the caravan shell could be lifted from the chassis and replaced with a box trailer body, making it a dual-use product. (*Photo C. & A. Steggel.*)

even be towed by a 500cc motorcycle combination - a forerunner of today's miniature 'pod' caravans. But perhaps rather unfortunately, the Company is more often remembered for the double-deck Berkeley Statesman of 1951, a true leviathan of a caravan, complete with an internal staircase to a first-floor double-bedroom, which had the option of a roof sun-deck and veranda outside! Inside it boasted a bathroom, with toilet, sink and shower, a coal fire in the sitting room for heating, and a kitchen approved by *Good Housekeeping*. At over 7ft wide and 12ft 4in high it was hardly a practical towing proposition, and at over

AJB 473A

Amazingly, one Berkeley Statesman Caravan survives to this day, albeit only saved following a major restoration. It is seen here at the Goodwood Revival, alongside a rare Berkeley Caravette, in this case towed by a Mk G Estate Bond Minicar. (*Photo: C. & A. Steggel.*)

Wooden body buck for the Berkeley nearing completion under the watchful eye of Lawrie Bond (*left*).

£1,065 + £10 purchase tax, you could buy a conventionally-built small home for considerably less at the time - though apparently the US Air Force did buy several to use as married quarters on one of their UK bases.

By the mid-1950s, despite Berkeley Coachworks' best efforts, they were losing their leading position in the UK caravan market, which was becoming decidedly over-crowded, and this, coupled with the by, now very much seasonal nature of the demand for leisure caravans, had led the Company to look for ways of cutting production costs. One tactic was to look to new production methods and materials, and at about this time the development of glass-reinforced plastic (GRP) appeared to offer an ideal solution. In theory GRP construction offered the means to build a lightweight caravan cheaply - in practice it provided neither. In 1956 Berkeley Coachworks announced an innovative 15ft tourer named the Berkeley Delight that featured a shell constructed entirely from GRP, moulded in two side halves and bolted

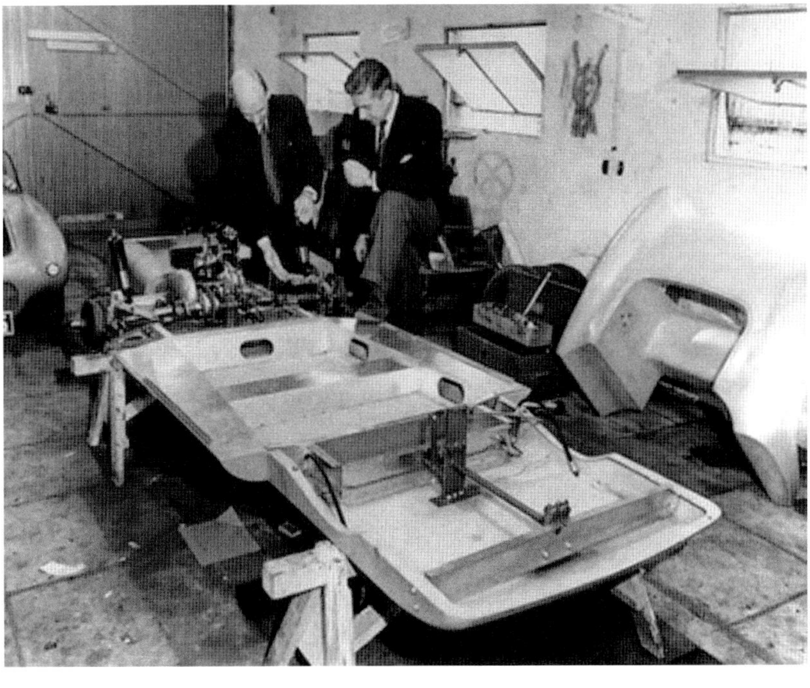

Lawrie Bond (*left*) and Berkeley MD Charles Panter discuss the finer points of the Berkeley Sports' chassis and drive train as one of the prototype cars takes shape. (Photo: A. Waring.)

together. However, the Delight proved costly and time-consuming to build, which led to an expensive finished product and limited sales, but it did give the Company valuable experience in working with GRP.

Whilst caravan production continued, Charles Panter had decided the answer was to diversify into motor vehicle production, setting up a new company - Berkeley Cars Ltd - and eliciting the assistance of Lawrie Bond to design a vehicle utilising GRP construction techniques. The brief was to produce a good-looking, lightweight, motorcycle-engined, soft-top sports car that would be competitive in both performance and price - ideal for the enthusiastic driver to maintain, race and repair. Initially two prototypes were completed and by mid-1956 were being extensively tested locally, frequently being seen around Biggleswade, often with Charles Panter or Lawrie Bond at the wheel. The Berkeley Sports car was announced in September 1956, with articles appearing in both *Motor* and *Autocar* magazines, and shortly after was revealed to the public in October of that year at the London Motor Show at Earls Court with a proposed price tag of just under £575.

First Berkeley Sports

The initial model of the Berkeley Sports was designated Type SA322 (Sports Anzani 322cc), later sometimes referred to as the B60, presumably to make it more consistent with subsequent model designations.

Pauline Bond at the wheel of a prototype Berkeley on trade plates, circa 1956. Note the car is not yet fitted with headlamps.

BERKELEY

Early sales literature for the 322cc Berkeley Sports was relatively sophisticated for the time.

It featured a bodyshell of semi-monocoque construction in glass-reinforced plastic with bonded in steel and aluminium strengthening tubes and box sections. This shell was moulded in three main sections. The central section was a rigid reinforced floor pan, likened at the time to a 'punt', to which was bonded the complete front bodywork

Now where's the fuel filler? Period shot from early Berkeley sales literature.

POWER
BP

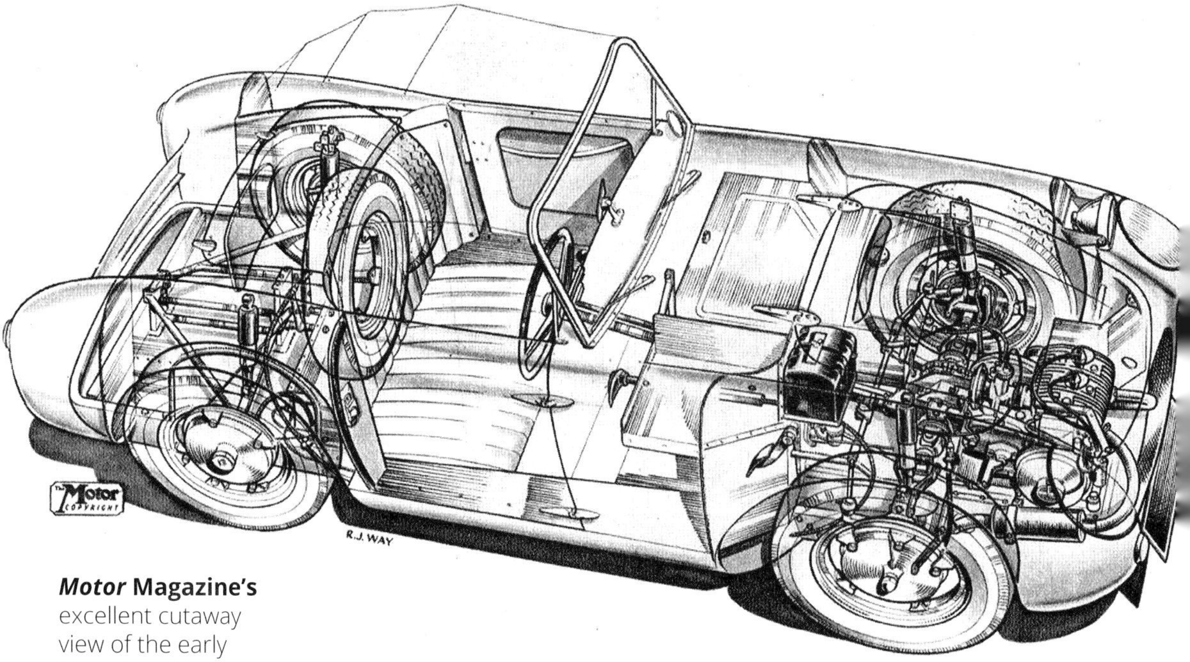
Motor
COPYRIGHT
R.J. WAY

Motor **Magazine's** excellent cutaway view of the early Anzani engined SA322 Berkeley Sports.

section, comprising front wings, scuttle, door pillars and dash. The rear bodywork section comprised rear bulkhead, wings and luggage compartment.

It was said to be the lightest and smallest four-wheel car on the market at that time and was considered to offer 'practical sports car performance with excellent economy'. This was the opinion of John Bolster who tested the car for *Autosport* with Lawrie Bond later in

40
12
11

Early 1956 Berkeley Sports, seen as found, awaiting restoration in the workshop area of the Hammond Collection (*see appendices*). This vehicle is one of only approximately 160 fitted with the 322cc British Anzani engine before the Company changed to the Excelsior engine, and one of very few that retain its original engine.

Close-up view of the engine compartment of the Hammond Collection's 322cc Anzani-engined Berkeley Sports. Note the distinctive curved twin exhaust pipes, often visible through the grill on old photos, enabling the model to be positively identified.

September 1956, recording an average fuel consumption of over 50mpg with a top speed of 70mph. The car boasted all-round independent suspension using unequal-length wishbones at the front and swing axles at the back with combined coil springs and telescopic dampers made by Girling (who also provided the very efficient hydraulic brakes). The front-mounted transverse engine was a specially tuned and modified 322cc air-cooled British Anzani two-stroke, vertical twin, which featured a rotary inlet valve located on the central journal of the crankshaft and was fitted with a Siba Dynastart motor/generator. Transmission was via the engine's integral Albion three-speed gearbox with reverse; a three-plate clutch was used with a secondary chain-drive to a spur-type differential and final drive to the front wheels via Hardy-Spicer universally-jointed half-shafts. Considering the size of the car, the cockpit was surprisingly roomy, providing reasonable and comfortable accommodation for two adults, with a somewhat cramped, very occasional, space for one person behind the seats - though to be fair, this was only advertised as suitable for two small children - but only if the spare wheel was moved to a tray under the dashboard in the front passenger footwell! The controls were relatively basic, but quite conventional, although the steering column-mounted gear change was said to take some getting used to. Finally, the car had a 12-volt electrical lighting and starting system, via the Siba Dynastart coupled direct to the crankshaft.

Production of the Berkeley Sport began in October 1956 and sales were no doubt helped by the positive reaction in the motoring press, who praised its handling and road-holding as well as regularly quoting its

NAS 705

Very nicely restored 1956 Berkeley SE328 Sports. (*Photo: Revival Automotive.*)

NAS 705

This view of the SE328 Berkeley shows the distinctive sloping door pillars that were a feature of early models. Also note the non-original rear lamps – many Berkeleys were subject to modifications by their owners over the years and whilst purists may wish to see these replaced, surely they are also part of the history of the car? (*Photo: Revival Automotive.*)

claimed top speed 'in excess of 65mph'. However, despite the Berkeley's diminutive size, at 10ft 3in in length, 4ft 2in wide and weighing only 5.5cwt, the 322cc engine was only rated at 15bhp at 4,800rpm, meaning performance could only really be rated as adequate, with a top speed of 60mph being more realistic. By January 1957, and with some 163 vehicles having been built (Berkeley Enthusiasts' Club figures), the choice of engine for the Berkeley Sport was being questioned. Originally designed as a water-cooled outboard boat engine, where its smooth running was considered a significant advantage, the Anzani 322cc Uni-Twin engine, as used in the Berkeley, had been modified to

Again-excellent attention to detail in the nicely-appointed cockpit of this restored SE328 Berkeley Sports. (*Photo: Revival Automotive.*)

Nicely-detailed engine bay of the SE328 Berkeley, showing the 328cc Excelsior Talisman twin-cylinder engine and bulkhead-mounted fuel tank with filler cap that had to be accessed by opening the bonnet. (*Photo: Revival Automotive.*)

air-cooled configuration for motorcycle use. But the air cooling proved less consistent, which could lead to engine seizure, and the unorthodox design and fine tolerances used in its construction led to it gaining a reputation for being overly complicated and difficult to repair. The solution was to switch to the 328cc Excelsior Talisman, a twin, two-stroke engine using the same Albion three-speed gearbox and column-mounted gear change (until around June 1957, when a floor-mounted gate-style gear lever was substituted). The Talisman gave an increased

TBM 215

Jon Derisley, who later went on to race with Lotus, lifts a rear wheel of the Berkeley on the Long Club Circuit during the Silverstone 6-hour Relay Race.

power output of 18bhp - only 3bhp more, but an increase of 20 per cent over the Anzani! The new Excelsior-powered Berkeley Sport was given the type designation SE328 (Sports Excelsior 328cc, also sometimes incorrectly referred to as the B65) and the change seems to have been well received, particularly as the Berkeley was already starting to gain quite a reputation in competition events.

Berkeley Cars Ltd had made their racing aspirations for their vehicle clear from the start and soon reinforced this with a well publicised test-drive around the Goodwood Circuit in a camera-equipped Berkeley Sport by none other than Sir Stirling Moss for BBC News in September 1956. Apparently he was very impressed and a photo of him driving the Berkeley enthusiastically made the front cover of *Autosport* Magazine the same month. By the following year Berkeley cars were making regular appearances across the country at motor-racing events and the Company put together their own team, with Lawrie Bond acting as manager. A local Biggleswade car and caravan dealership owner with rally driving experience, Ian Mantle, became one of the Berkeley Team drivers, as did Albert Cheney ('Bert') Westwood, a well-known pre-war rally and trials driver. Other drivers using their own Berkeley cars in competition were also sponsored by the factory, such

Lawrie Bond, (*far right*) acting as the Berkeley Team Manager, looks on during the National 6-Hour Handicap Relay Race at Silverstone on 17 August 1957.

SYL 663

as Jon A. Derisley, R.A. ('Alex') Jamieson and Jon Goddard-Watts. Events in 1957 included the BARC (British Automobile Racing Club) meeting on 10 June at Goodwood, during which Jon Goddard-Watts set a new under 350cc lap record at 58.62mph. At a speed trial at Brands Hatch, Jon Goddard-Watts came first in a class for standard sports and saloon cars up to 1,000cc, and it was noted his time was faster than thirty-three other entrants driving cars up to ten times the engine size of the 328cc Berkeley. Back at Goodwood for the BARC members meeting he won a five-lap handicap race at an average speed of 58.86mph and broke the under-350cc circuit lap record he had previously set, raising it to 60.002mph (though he later raised it again to 64.48mph!).

Berkeley cars also participated in events at Aintree, Wicklow, Silverstone and Snetterton. In August at the British Racing and Sports Car Club (BRSCC) meeting at Brands Hatch there was even a 'Berkeley Only' event, attracting thirteen participants for a ten-lap race with a 'Le Mans' style start - again Jon Goddard-Watts proved unbeatable! Also in August was the 7th National Six-Hour Relay Race held at Silverstone, in which the Berkeley Company entered a team of four cars driven by Jon Goddard-Watts, Nelson Graham, Alex Jamieson and Jon Derisley, with Lawrie Bond acting as team manager. Thirty-nine teams entered, with cars ranging from D-Type Jaguars down to Goggomobiles, of which twenty-five teams finished, many with only one car left running. Cars were assessed by the distance they were likely to be able to cover within the race-time limit, which dictated how many laps they were required to complete to finish - for the Berkeleys it was 137 (with a 45-lap credit). Although not amongst the winners, they ranked 14th overall, and remarkably three of the Berkeley cars completed the event, with an average speed of over 61mph. Not all events went quite according to plan though, as in June when only one out of six Berkeleys that entered the Eastbourne Rally managed to complete all the driving tests, with Lawrie Bond, Charles Panter and Ian Mantle being amongst the drivers. Only Panter managed to finish, although he had lost a lot of time due to an electrical fault, whilst the hill-test section proved impossible for others, as their cars were set up for racing and the gearing used proved unsuitable.

Berkeleys to the USA

All this competition success, and the associated positive publicity it generated, did not go unnoticed outside the UK either, which fitted in well with Berkeley Cars Ltd intentions for their little vehicle as a viable export proposition - particularly for the US market. From the initial design stage it had always been intended that the car could be built as either right-hand or left-hand drive, though to meet some US states' vehicle lighting regulations it initially required pod-mounted 'frogeye' style headlamps to be fitted on top of the front edge of the

STM 317
TM 733

Early export model Berkeley Sports with 'Frogeye' headlamps fitted to conform to minimum headlamp heights required by some US states' vehicle lighting regulations for road use. (*Photo: A. Waring.*)

car for road use, rather than the car's distinctive Perspex-covered headlamps mounted within the front wings. Later a slightly more streamlined export headlamp fairing was produced. Despite the apparent questionable appeal of such a small car in the American market, it transpired there was indeed a demand, and by early 1958 articles and road tests were also appearing in US motoring magazines, including *Road & Track* and *Sports Car Illustrated.*

Some 1,259 SE328 Berkeleys were built in total and the model continued to be available in the US up until the end of 1958, with some 555 having been exported there (J. Stein, *British Sports Cars in America 1946-1981*). They were available through a number of distributors, the largest being Berkeley Cars of America, in New Haven, Connecticut. Others were located in: Pensacola, Florida; Hollywood, California; Denver, Colorado and Lubbock, Texas.

However, by mid-1957, there was popular demand, especially from America, for a more powerful engine for the Berkeley, and fortunately the Company did not have to look too far for a solution. The origins

GSB 520
PVG 454

of the Excelsior Motor Co. can be traced back to 1874, with their first 'motor-bicycle' appearing in 1896, and by the 1930s Excelsior motorcycles were highly regarded in the UK with a reputation built on their competitive racing machines. Post-war they struggled to find their place in a changed market and although still designing and building motorcycles, they found that there was a demand for their versatile 328cc Talisman engine for microcars, including the Berkeley, Opperman Unicar and later models of the Frisky. Apparently looking to diversify and pinning their hopes on the continued popularity of these small vehicles, Excelsior put considerable effort into developing the Talisman engine, primarily for the Berkeley, by utilising the 328cc engine's vertically split crankcase and sectional crankshaft assembly to add an additional cylinder and centre section, creating a new three-cylinder 492cc engine. Equipped with triple Amal carburettors and a four-speed Albion gearbox, the new engine was rated at 30bhp and was still small enough to fit in the Berkeley, though, necessitated relocating the battery and moving the fuel tank to the rear of the car. The changes gave the new SE492 model an increased kerb weight of approx 6.5cwt, but it offered an estimated top speed of 80mph.

Production of the new SE492 (Sports Excelsior 492cc, also sometimes referred to as the B90) began in October 1957 and initially it was offered alongside the 328cc current Standard and Deluxe models, which continued to be produced until April 1958, though now with twin Amal carburettors. The 1957 Motor Show at Earls Court in October was used as the venue to unveil the new Berkeley 500 model (as it was initially referred to in the Company's advertising) to the public, and a new

Later Berkeley SE328 produced for the American market at the Bubblecar Museum (*see appendices*). It now features more streamlined fairings to house the raised headlights required to comply with US regulations.

Standard SE492 Coupe with fixed hardtop and external door handles appeared on the Company's stand, priced at £397.14s (+ £200.4s purchase tax), with the Standard Open model at £381.15s (+ £192.4s tax). Whilst the Deluxe version of the SE328 had been offered with an optional accessory removable glass fibre hardtop, the new Fixed Head Coupe appears to have been a much more practical proposition and may well have helped with some of the body flexing problems that were beginning to appear due to the increased power of the car, but sadly it seems it never went into production.

Berkeleys in International Motorsport

Berkeleys continued to appear regularly in motorsport, with several notable international successes, including class wins in the 1958 Monza twelve-hour race, driven by Lorenzo Bandini, and in the 1959 Mille Miglia where they came first and second (actually the Mille Miglia Rally, the original race having been stopped after 1957 due to a series of fatal accidents). Also in 1958, the Royal Motor Union of Belgium announced the Liege-Brescia-Liege Rally, a new rally created specifically for cars with engine capacities under 500cc, with a very challenging 3,336km (2,073 miles) route over all types of roads, including more than 20 mountain passes. Designed to test small cars to their limits and prove that they could provide a practical alternative to larger and more conventional vehicles, the Rally attracted entrants from all over Europe, with a wide variety of vehicles, and must have appeared a perfect publicity opportunity to the Berkeley Company.

The Berkeley contingent comprised of six cars. Three were SE492s, of which two were driven by well-known Berkeley drivers A.R. (Tony) Wheeler and Alex Jamieson, plus one driven by a Dutch Berkeley importer, H. Van Zalinge. The remaining three were SE328s, one driven by Bert Westwood accompanied by Robin Noel Richards, one by H. P. Fenton and the final one by an invited celebrity team of Pat Moss and Ann Wisdom, who had just won the ladies class in the 1958 Alpine Rally, where they had come 10th overall. Back-up for the works-sponsored cars was provided by Ian Mantle in another non-competing Berkeley, and drivers were warned about the risks of the Excelsior engines over-heating and seizing if pushed too hard in the expected high mid-July temperatures. It seems the Berkeley Company had become well aware of the new three-cylinder Excelsior's limitations owing to the restricted airflow around the more tightly-fitting engine, but conditions on the rally were to prove such that the 328cc cars suffered too. Regular seizing forced frequent cooling stops until the engines gave up altogether. Other mechanical failures and a minor accident saw all six Berkeleys fail to finish, despite a valiant effort by Ian Mantle towing the Moss Team's car through Yugoslavia and back to Italy to try and keep them in the event. But the rally proved hard on all the cars and drivers alike,

BERKELEY
foursome
VMJ 464
Here for the first time is a car which gives you sports car zip and performance plus really good carrying capacity.
A true 4-seater, the Berkeley Foursome has ample room in the back seats for two. Alternatively you will find you can fit in a surprising amount of luggage, golf clubs or other gear.
Developed from the 492 c.c. 2-seater, whose reliability has been proved in scores of rallies, the Berkeley Foursome enables you to go places fast—*and* take more with you.
BERKELEY CARS LTD., BIGGLESWADE, BEDS, ENGLAND

Period sales literature for the Berkeley Foursome extolling the virtues of its increased passenger and luggage space.

with only thirteen out of the twenty-nine starters completing an event that would have tested the mettle of even the most robust conventional vehicles of the day.

In the USA, demand for the new model remained strong, though not up to some of the Company's reported ambitious export estimates, but here too overheating issues and problems with the new three-cylinder two-stroke engine's reliability were beginning to emerge, leading to significant numbers of warranty claims. In the meantime, back in the UK, Berkeley Cars Ltd had been working on adding a new model to the range, and in light of some of the problems they were now experiencing with their two-seat Sport model, their choice of an enlarged four-seat sports model seems perhaps a little surprising. The Company had already recognised that there was a problem with the body flexing on the two-seat models and their engineers had been working on improving

Lawrie's lightweight 'chassis' and bodyshell design by using new steel strengthening members and suspension mounting points. The result was a new strengthened shell that compensated for the enlarged engine compartment and stresses from the new 492cc engine, though externally there were few changes, other than the revised filler cap location and the front-door pillars now straight at 90 degrees to the sill, rather than sloped back. It would appear Berkeley thought the problems solved and bravely went on to utilise the possibilities offered by the front-wheel drive layout to now enlarge the bodyshell and maximise the passenger accommodation. The new Berkeley Foursome was to still be powered by the same 492cc Excelsior three-cylinder engine and it was announced that it would appear on the Company's stand at the 1958 Earls Court Motor Show in October. It seems there must have been intense activity at the factory to get the prototype ready in time, with *Motorsport* magazine even reporting in their show preview that it would not be appearing. However, appear it did, fitted with a striking optional removable hardtop, and clearly caused something of a stir, with lengthy review articles appearing in both *The Motor* and *Autocar* magazines, who seemed to share the view that there was indeed a niche market for the vehicle, which no other manufacturer had yet attempted to fill. However, another car appearing at the show, which had already made its competition debut earlier in the year, was soon to have a significant influence on the future of the Berkeley, in the form of the Austin Healey Mk I 'Frogeye' Sprite. It seems that the popularity of vehicles such as the Berkeley had not gone unnoticed and now a major car manufacturer, BMC, had decided to enter the low-cost, small, open competitive sports car market.

Berkeley Foursome

The introduction of the Foursome saw the two-seat SE492 Sports renamed the Twosome with minor changes to specification and strengthening changes to the bodyshell, giving a slightly altered appearance to the door lines. The Foursome wasn't cheap, costing £699.12s in standard form, rising to £727.19s with the hardtop, compared to £573.19s for the Twosome, and the motoring press was already questioning the Berkeley Company's claims regarding its 'true four-seater' capacity. It seems the perceived market for the car was either not ready for the Foursome or potential customers were not prepared to put up with the car's shortcomings. With continued body-flexing problems, a cramped interior and the 492cc engine struggling to maintain performance when fully loaded, orders were sparse and only twenty-two Foursomes were built before production was discontinued.

With the Foursome having failed to open a new market for Berkeley Cars Ltd, it also appears that matters were coming to a head in the US, when a shipment to a Berkeley dealership was stopped from entering

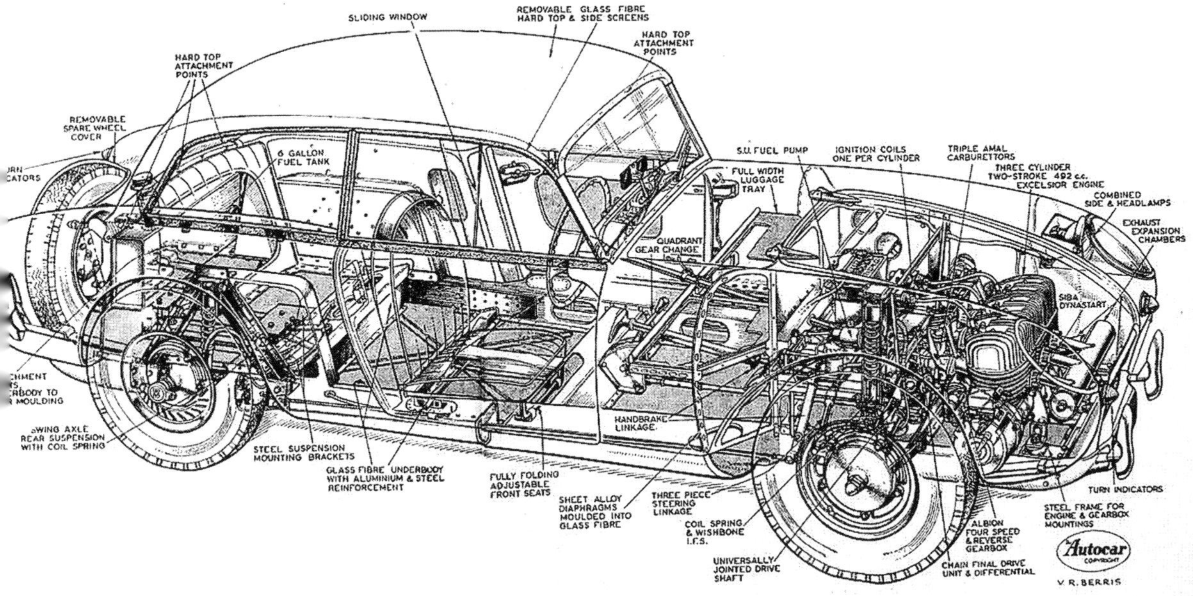
SLIDING WINDOW
REMOVABLE GLASS FIBRE HARD TOP & SIDE SCREENS
HARD TOP ATTACHMENT POINTS
HARD TOP ATTACHMENT POINTS
REMOVABLE SPARE WHEEL COVER
6 GALLON FUEL TANK
S.U. FUEL PUMP
IGNITION COILS ONE PER CYLINDER
TRIPLE AMAL CARBURETTORS
THREE CYLINDER TWO-STROKE 492 c.c. EXCELSIOR ENGINE
COMBINED SIDE & HEADLAMPS
EXHAUST EXPANSION CHAMBERS
FULL WIDTH LUGGAGE TRAY
QUADRANT GEAR CHANGE
SIBA DYNASTART
SWING AXLE REAR SUSPENSION WITH COIL SPRING
STEEL SUSPENSION MOUNTING BRACKETS
GLASS FIBRE UNDERBODY WITH ALUMINIUM & STEEL REINFORCEMENT
FULLY FOLDING ADJUSTABLE FRONT SEATS
SHEET ALLOY DIAPHRAGMS MOULDED INTO GLASS FIBRE
HANDBRAKE LINKAGE
THREE PIECE STEERING LINKAGE
COIL SPRING & WISHBONE I.F.S.
UNIVERSALLY JOINTED DRIVE SHAFT
ALBION FOUR SPEED & REVERSE GEARBOX
CHAIN FINAL DRIVE UNIT & DIFFERENTIAL
TURN INDICATORS
STEEL FRAME FOR ENGINE & GEARBOX MOUNTINGS
Autocar
V. R. BERRIS

***Autocar* magazine's** excellent cutaway drawing of the Berkeley Foursome showed that, on paper at least, the new design looked impressive.

the country by the authorities and the cars had to be returned to the factory. The Company urgently needed to respond to the situation, as there was still a demand for the cars in America, with some 490 of the 666 SE492s produced being sold in the US. But it was by now clear that the Excelsior two-stroke engines were unsuitable for the different driving conditions and warmer climates encountered there. Both at home and in the US, there had always been a demand for more power and this factor was also taken into account as the Company considered a new engine for the Berkeley.

This time they turned to the well-known British motorcycle manufacture, Royal Enfield, who had built their first motorcycle in 1901 and more recently had adapted well to the post-war market,

Factory photo of the prototype Berkeley Foursome. (*Photo: A. Waring.*)

Factory photo of the prototype saloon version of the Berkeley Foursome, with the added strength of the hard top probably going some way to improving the body rigidity and flexing problems that plagued the model. (*Photo: A. Waring.*)

Rare surviving 1960 Berkeley 492cc Foursome, note the straight-door pillars denoting the strengthened bulkhead developed for the SE492. (*Photo: D. Perrin.*)

leaving them in a good position to develop new and highly regarded motorcycles and engines. The engines chosen for the Berkeley were both 692cc vertical twin-cylinder four-stroke units: the Super Meteor, rated at 40bhp, and the similar, but more highly tuned and slightly higher compression Constellation, rated at 50bhp. The engines were

Engine compartment of the 1960 Berkeley 492cc Foursome, with the three-cylinder Excelsior Talisman engine. Note the widened engine bay and absence of fuel tank (*now moved the rear of the car*), which would be the same layout on the SE492. (Photo: D. Perrin.)

fitted with specially-designed chain case to enable a conventional Bendix-type starter to be used, and came with a separate Lucas dynamo to power the car's electrics. Transmission was via an Albion gearbox with four speeds plus reverse with duplex chain drive to the differential. Externally the cars were very much different in appearance from the preceding Berkeleys, with a totally redesigned front end to accommodate the taller engines, prominent unfaired headlights and a large grille to increase airflow. The two new models were named using a new simplified style of nomenclature to indicate their claimed top speed - the B95 and B105 respectively. A smart hard-top equipped example of the former was unveiled to the public at the Geneva Motor Show in March 1959. Prior to the launch, testing of the new model had been very thorough and well reported, including significant trials conducted at the Royal Enfield Factory - no doubt a prudent move by Royal Enfield as they would have wanted to

In any event
You can have fun with your Berkeley B.95. In sports car racing or rallies you will find that the B.95 is difficult to beat. For just driving about town, or long journeys, you have power and performance you can use because of superb road-holding and braking. Brilliant design and first-class workmanship combine in a fast, safe sports car of outstanding performance.
Read the specification overleaf and you'll see why——
BERKELEY
B.95
VNM 414

Period sales literature for the Berkeley B95 promoting the competition potential of the new model.

WJN 896
5

1960 Berkeley B105 on display at the Bubblecar Museum (*see appendices*).

ensure their engines did not lose any reputation by association, should problems have arisen with the new Berkeleys.

Three-Wheel Berkeley

Though many of the identified problems with the Berkeley Sports models were now effectively resolved, it must have been clear to the Company that they could not rest on their laurels, as sales figures, especially for exported vehicles, were still woefully short of anticipated levels. Price was also becoming an important factor, with their new B95 now offered at £659 including purchase tax in the UK - uncomfortably close to the new Austin-Healey Sprite at £699. To this end Berkeley Cars Ltd had also been working on a new 'back to basics' approach, which could take advantage of the UK's purchase and road tax (Vehicle Excise Duty) rates and driver licensing laws, already exploited by manufacturers of small three-wheel vehicles, such as the Bond Minicar. There was a significant demand for this class of vehicle in the UK at the time - they could be driven by motorcycle licence holders, especially attractive to those now needing to transport their families, and they attracted around half the rate of purchase tax when new and a similar

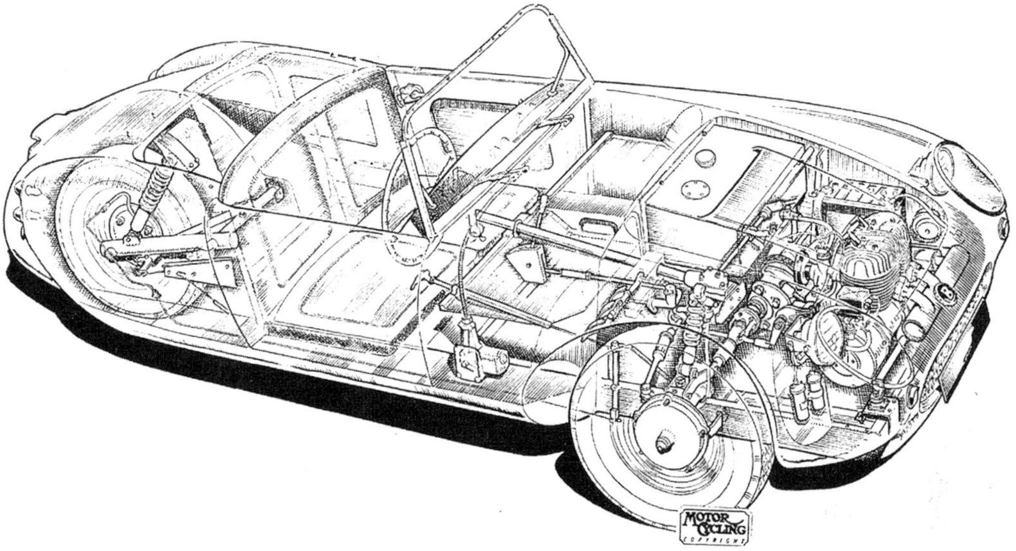
MOTOR CYCLING
COPYRIGHT

Motor Cycling magazine's cutaway drawing of the Berkeley T60, showing how the car was simply, but effectively, converted to a three-wheeler.

reduction in Road Tax payable annually. Naturally, most of these vehicles' designs were driven by economy, and it could be said that their performance and appearance usually reflected this! In light of the Berkeley's sporting character, it is perhaps understandable why the Company seem to have been reluctant to go down this route, but the new Berkeley T60 they came up with couldn't have been more different from Lawrie Bond's previous three-wheelers.

In the UK there had been a tradition of sports three-wheelers from Morgan, whose first three-wheeler Runabout had appeared in 1909. The Company began production of two-seat three-wheelers in 1911, and, just before the First World War, began to achieve a reputation in competition events. Morgan sports three-wheelers continued to gain popularity and competition success through the 1920s and 30s, but post-Second World War restrictions in allocation of steel designed to favour vehicles built for export led the Company to scale down three-wheeler production, as there was little demand abroad for such cars. By mid-1952 Morgan ended three-wheeler production altogether, leaving a potential gap in the market that it now appeared the Berkeley T60 might fill. In fact, the Berkeley T60 had one big advantage over the old Morgans - its front-wheel drive layout, which meant that the power was transmitted through two wheels as opposed to the Morgan's single rear-wheel drive layout, and this helped give the Berkeley cars their renowned handling and road holding.

Whilst the T60 retained the front-wheel drive layout of the four-wheel Berkeleys, the rear bodyshell was redesigned to accommodate a single rear wheel mounted on a trailing arm with an Armstrong coil spring and damper unit. The frontal appearance was unchanged from the

YSL 701

Front view of a nicely-restored 1960 Berkeley T60 Convertible. (*Photo: D. Perrin.*)

YSL
701

Rear view of the 1960 Berkeley T60 Coupe Convertible, showing the neat conversion of the four-wheel shell to a smart three-wheeler. (*Photo: D. Perrin.*)

earlier cars, with characteristic faired in headlamps, and the new rear appearance was considered sympathetic to the lines of the vehicle and allowed for the inclusion of an occasional seat, only really suitable for small children and additional luggage space. The T60 was announced in August 1959 via a feature article in *Motor Cycling* magazine and it was subsequently road tested in *The Motor Cycle* magazine in October, where it was noted that, 'No matter what antics were performed there was never any indication that they were driving a three-wheeler.' The mechanical specification of the T60 also followed the 'back to basics' approach, as it was powered by the 328cc Excelsior Talisman twin-cylinder two-stroke engine with the Albion four-speed gearbox, with a reverse gear and electrics via a Siba Dynastart unit. But the road test noted favourably on the car's 'lively' performance, with impressive acceleration and excellent, 'almost startling', fuel consumption figures. With the car offered at £399.19s including purchase tax, or with hardtop at £412.10s, Berkeley Cars Ltd had certainly achieved their aims, and the three-wheeler became one of their best selling models.

Later in 1959 two further four-wheel models were announced and featured on the Company's stand at the Earls Court Motor Show in October, in the form of the QB95 and QB105, both of which utilised the larger bodyshell previously developed for the Foursome combined with the technical specification and features of the B95 and B105 models. The new vehicles were now more conservatively described as 'occasional four seaters' or 'roomy two seaters with additional luggage space' in the style of the grand tourer. Apart from the two vehicles appearing at the show, the 'Q' models do not appear to have gone into production and it is not certain whether the cars were a serious proposition or a simple means to provide new models for the show stand, and which at least demonstrated the potential of the Berkeley as a more versatile car. But by this time the B95 was being offered at £628 in open form and the similar B105 at £652, whereas the more conventional Austin Healey Sprite was now offered at only £632, all inclusive of purchase tax. Quite how the QB95 at £680 and the QB105 at £703 (with hard-top versions at £713 and £727 respectively) could have been expected to attract buyers is difficult to envisage.

The Bandit

Though by 1960 Berkeley Cars Ltd's days were numbered, there was no obvious sign of this in the Firm's activities, with production of the new three-wheeler now well underway in response to a healthy order book, and the new B95 and B105 models now becoming available in the US, where initial press response was very positive. The Company also seemed to recognise that Lawrie Bond's Berkeley design had probably now reached the limit of its evolution and began to plan for a new more ambitious sports car to take them forward. By now Lawrie Bond

Motor
CRESSWELL

Motor Magazine's cutaway drawing of the Berkeley Bandit showing a much more mechanically conventional car, albeit with some very advanced features for its time, though it doesn't really do justice to Tojeiro's lightweight chassis/frame that formed the basis of the vehicle.

was fully occupied with his own Formula Junior racing-car project and in any case the Company were looking for a much more orthodox design to compete with the more conventional small sporting cars that they were now up against. Early in 1960 they commissioned John 'Toj' Tojeiro to design them a lightweight sports car chassis/frame to accommodate Ford Anglia 105E 997cc running gear, and which would be fitted with a glass fibre body. Tojeiro had built up quite a reputation for lightweight racing and sports car chassis frames, including perhaps his best known creation, the lightweight spaceframe that formed the basis for the AC Ace in 1953. Styling was not his forte, however, so this was done by prominent British landscape artist Cavendish Morton, who had already styled several racing and sports-car designs in conjunction with Tojeiro. The result was the stylish Berkeley Bandit, launched at the 1960 Motor Show in London's Earls Court in October, and which featured an impressive technical specification, including Ford's Macpherson strut front suspension with disc brakes, and rear -wheel drive with specially designed independent rear suspension utilising as many standard Ford components as possible. Press reports and company sales literature also spoke of tuning parts being available such as a Weber carburettor, and other engine options including the lightweight all-aluminium FWA Coventry Climax engine, again hinting at competition possibilities. The new Bandit seems to have made quite an impression, but as with Tojeiro's previous designs, all this did not come cheap, and no doubt the costly development of this completely new and relatively sophisticated vehicle was reflected in the asking price of £798.18s including purchase tax, making the new car a lot less competitive on price than the Company must have hoped.

700 CNM

One of the only two prototype Berkeley Bandit vehicles actually built, used as the original press review car at the model's announcement. (*Photo: D. Perrin.*)

Although Berkeley Cars Ltd obviously pinned a lot of their hopes on the Bandit, it was intended, at least initially, to complement their existing models, and to this end two other new vehicles were announced towards the end of 1960, both complementing the popular T60. The first appeared in September in the form of the B65, which essentially

Rear view of the Berkeley Bandit, showing the clean lines of the new vehicle. (*Photo: D. Perrin.*)

featured the improvements made to the late SE492 Sports models, but fitted with the twin-cylinder 328cc Excelsior engine. This was possibly another attempt at a back to basics approach, with the new designation fitting nicely into the existing range of model names based on the vehicles' top speeds. Whilst the potential market for the B65 might seem hard to understand, the other new model, the T60/4, launched in October in the form of an improved three-wheeler, made far more sense. It seems that Berkeley's three-wheeler had indeed appealed to motorcycle licence holders, now needing to transport their families, but the small rear child seating featured on the T60 had proved too limited and the rear suspension not really up to the task of supporting even small rear passengers! The new T60/4 featured a revised rear bodyshell, allowing room for more realistic seating accommodation for two children, with revised soft and hard top options to suit and uprated rear suspension that could cope with the load.

Berkeley's Demise

Despite having all the indications of an active company with a bright future ahead of it, by December 1960 it was all over for Berkeley Cars Ltd. Dealing with the numerous warranty claims for their Excelsior-powered models in the US had no doubt hit profits hard, and although the Company had taken positive steps to rectify the situation, developing new models was always going to be expensive, leaving the Company with substantial debts. Added to this the caravan market was undergoing drastic changes, and Berkeley Coachworks, like a number of established makers, was getting left behind, as the trend for more modern, lightweight, competitively priced caravans gathered pace. The caravan market began to take-off, with a growing demand for models that could easily be towed by the smaller, more fuel efficient, cars that were being introduced. Those firms that could produce exactly what the public wanted, in sufficient quantity to keep the price as low as possible, began to dominate the market, whilst most of the stragglers quietly disappeared.

With Berkeley's traditional income from caravan sales falling, the banks got nervous at the level of credit required and withdrew their support for the Company, meaning that all car production ceased and the factory was forced to close by the end of December. Of the models that were in production at the end, some 200 B95/105 vehicles had been built, with around 10 having been exported to the US. Fewer than 20 B65s are thought to have been made, but the three-wheelers fared better, with 1,800 T60s and 40-50 T60/4s having been built, giving an overall total of a little over 4,000 vehicles completed during the duration of the Company. The Bandit never made it into production and only two were built, the prototype and the show car, one of which survives to this day.

Lawrie Bond certainly still believed that the Berkeley cars had a future, but he lacked the capital to back his convictions. He did, however, make an approach to Colonel Gray to suggest a merger between Berkeley Cars Limited and Sharp's Commercials Limited, but sadly this was not considered a viable proposition and Berkeley Cars Ltd was wound up in February 1961. Charles Panter did attempt to revive the caravan side of his business in 1962, re-launching Berkeley Coachworks' innovative all-glass fibre Delight model, as the rather appropriately-named Berkeley Encore, but the anticipated sales failed to materialise and Berkeley Coachworks Ltd was finally wound up in January 1967.

Berkeley Tributes

Since the demise of Berkeley Cars Ltd, it is perhaps hardly surprising that such an innovative little vehicle has attracted a number of attempts to revive the character of these cars. In 1970 Dave Ratner set up a company called Berkeley Developments in Chaddesden, Derby, initially supplying parts and restoration services to keep existing Berkeleys on the road, but soon moved into modifying the cars and offering conversions to different power plants. The Company offered a number of more modern motorcycle engine options, and later more radical modification of the cars to allow various BMC/BL Mini engines and running gear to be fitted.

In around 1991 a second company appeared, the Berkeley Motor

118 KTN
6
5
WJN 896
GSB 520
4
PVG 464
3
GB

An impressive line-up of late-model Berkeleys at the Bubblecar Museum. Left to right: 1960 T60 Convertible; 1960 B105; SE328 LHD and 1960 T60 Coupé.

Berkeley Developments' final model, the prototype Bandit. (*Photo: D. Ratner.*)

Company, formed as a sideline to his existing garage business by Berkeley enthusiast Andrew Argyle and based in Sileby, Leicestershire, again offering parts and restoration services. A chance meeting with Dave Ratner, who came to Andrew's assistance after his T60 developed engine problems whilst attending a Berkeley club event, resulted in a discussion during which Andrew mentioned his experience with

Engine bay of Berkeley Developments' prototype Bandit showing Mini-derived powerplant and suspension. (*Photo: D. Ratner.*)

glass fibre work. This in turn led to the two joining forces with more ambitious plans to produce new-build replica and kit cars based on the Berkeley designs, and Andrew Argyle set about producing new moulds whilst Dave Ratner supplied some original ones.

The first of these 'new Berkeleys' appeared in 1992, in the form of a replica T60 three-wheeler, offered with either Mini or Citroen 2CV engine and running gear, though none are believed to have been built with the latter option. The car was built on a newly-designed steel-ladder frame chassis and named the Bandini (after the famous Italian racing driver, Lorenzo Bandini, who at one time raced Berkeleys). However, most, if not all, of these 'new' vehicles did seem to still use parts from original Berkeleys, presumably for registration purposes, and being hand-built they were time consuming to produce, with only around seven having been completed before Berkeley Developments moved to a new base at Langley Mill, Nottinghamshire, in around 1996. Though Berkeley spares and restoration did remain the Company's main business, an additional four-wheel Cammarota model (after another Italian racing driver, Raffaele Cammarota, who at one time raced Berkeleys alongside Bandini) was now offered, again with various Mini engines. Production was still limited, with around five cars being built before production

Late model Ibis Berkeley from New Zealand. (*Photo: T. Monck-Mason.*)

JAPAN MINI DA
MO
TUL
MOTOR OIL

ceased around the time Andrew Argyle sold his garage business circa 2000, though he continued glass fibre work for film props, including Daleks, K-9 and the Tardis for the BBC!

Dave Ratner's Berkeley Developments continued, however, and in 2001 he announced a new quite different model named the Bandit - a larger, much more modern looking four-wheel open-top vehicle, but still with obvious Berkeley styling cues. Only a single prototype was completed and this was later sold as a complete project with hopes that the new owner would take up production, but it appears this was not the new owner's intention and the car has not been seen for some time.

Meanwhile, during the 1980s, over in New Zealand Ian Byrd and Tim Monck-Mason began developing their own homage to the Berkeley, starting off with an already much modified original Berkeley shell (believed to be a B95). The idea was to further modify the car to take front and rear Mini subframes, but disaster struck early in the project when the bodyshell fell from the back of a lorry on the motorway as it was being transported and was destroyed. A completely new widened shell was then produced that allowed the fitting of unaltered Mini subframes without having to resort to large protruding wheel arches, thus giving the new car much cleaner lines than other such conversions. The new car was named the Ibis, though sometimes called the Ibis Berkeley! Mechanically it was all Mini and the cars were in fact registered as 'restored Minis' to avoid new car compliance testing. The Ibis went on sale in either completed or kit form in 1987 and some sixteen to twenty are believed to have been built before the business was sold in 1989 to Replicar Developments Ltd in Auckland, New Zealand. After much work the car remerged three years later with considerable re-styling to resemble the AC Cobra. The new vehicle was called the Wasp and only around six are believed to have been completed before the project was abandoned in 1994, though later the original Ibis shape moulds turned up and were sold to Japan to produce further Mini-based specials there.

CHAPTER THREE

S.E. Opperman Ltd

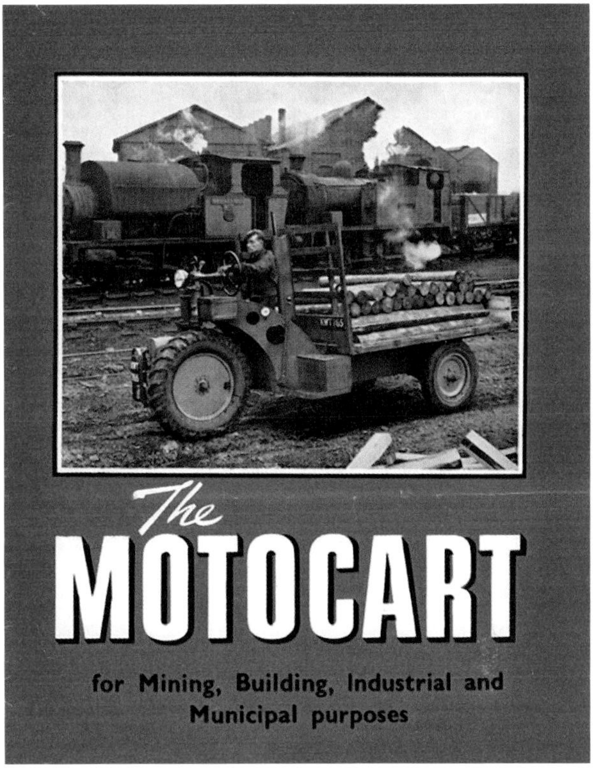
The
MOTOCART
for Mining, Building, Industrial and Municipal purposes

Opperman's only previous vehicle to go into production: The Motocart.

The second Bond design to take to the road in 1956 was announced in October of that year by S.E. Opperman Ltd, located at Stirling Corner, Borehamwood, Elstree, in Hertfordshire. This Company's history can be traced back to 1862 as Opperman Sons & Taskers Ltd, gear cutters and engineers, becoming S.E. Opperman Ltd in 1934, by which time they were also making aircraft components. During the Second World War they became part of the war effort, making beaching gear and anchor-winches for naval vessels, and many parts and control sub-assemblies for aircraft, including the Stirling bomber. Post-war they went on to build, under licence, the Walter Mikron aircraft engine, an in-line, inverted four-cylinder air-cooled motor, used in a variety of light aircraft and originally developed in the 1930s in Czechoslovakia. The Company's only two previous 'vehicular' products had included the Scorpion, a rather odd multi-wheeled, amphibious scout car, developed in secret in 1942 for the Department of Tank Design. Although it compared favourably in tests over extreme terrain conditions against a Daimler Dingo, which was considered its nearest equivalent, it was not accepted and the design was abandoned. Second came the Company's fairly successful Motocart, a three-wheel agricultural vehicle, the prototype of which had been developed in 1945 and which went into production in 1946. Again it was an unconventional vehicle in the form of a Monowheel tractor, with the engine and steering mounted on a large front tractor wheel with the load-carrying body 'towed' behind. The Motocart was powered by an 872cc 8bhp JAP or 630cc 6bhp Douglas single-cylinder air-cooled four-stroke petrol engine, either of which was governed to 1,700 to 1,800rpm with a four forward speed plus reverse gearbox, giving a top speed of approximately 12mph. The Motocart had a unique Opperman exterior control lever, allowing it to be 'driven' by a driver standing or walking alongside the vehicle, very useful for manoeuvring over short distances or for precise loading/unloading operations . Load capacity was stated at 30cwt, but many users found it was quite capable of greater loads and it was available in a variety of body options. The Motocart remained in production until around 1958, with many having been exported, including to the US and Australia.

Opperman Unicar

Opperman's management were looking to diversify and utilise spare capacity at their Borehamwood factory after having been inspired by the growing popularity of the Bond Minicar, and emergence of other lightweight microcars. Having researched the market, they decided there was still room for further producers of this class of new vehicle and Lawrie Bond was commissioned to do the design work. Perhaps surprisingly, Opperman decided to forgo the usual cost-saving route of producing a three-wheeler, with their lower rates of purchase tax and road tax. They believed a small, lightweight, modern four-wheeler would be a much safer and practical proposition, more likely to appeal to working-class families who had perhaps never owned a car before. Price was still going to be a big factor, but by taking this route they must have felt their vehicle would be competing more against smaller conventional cars, than the three-wheelers that were beginning to proliferate on the market.

The new Opperman vehicle was named the Unicar and was a very basic four-wheel vehicle offering limited accommodation for two adults and two children, but priced at just under £400 (£399.10s.0d including

YRO 896
Here comes the incredible
unicar
De Luxe Model £425-17-0 Incl. P.T.
Manufactured by S. E. OPPERMAN LIMITED, BOREHAM WOOD, HERTS.
bringing a new meaning
to light car motoring
75 m.p.g. - 60 m.p.h.
model "t"

Original sales literature for the Model T Unicar, indicating it was powered by the 328cc Excelsior Talisman engine.

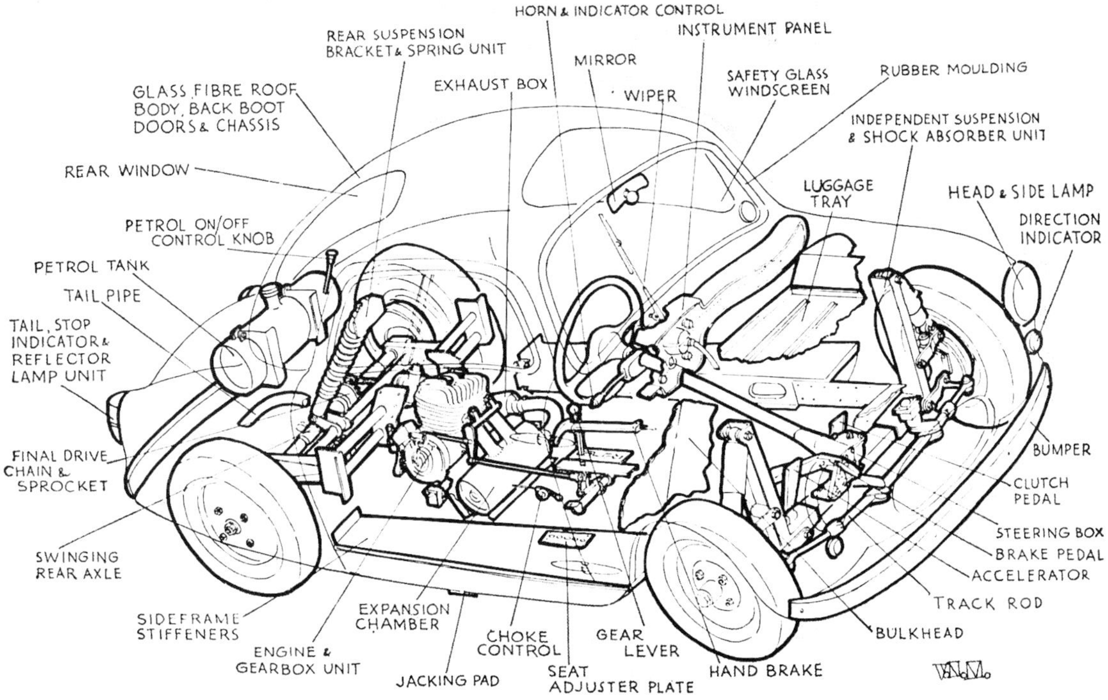
HORN & INDICATOR CONTROL
INSTRUMENT PANEL
REAR SUSPENSION BRACKET & SPRING UNIT
MIRROR
SAFETY GLASS WINDSCREEN
RUBBER MOULDING
EXHAUST BOX
WIPER
GLASS FIBRE ROOF BODY, BACK BOOT DOORS & CHASSIS
INDEPENDENT SUSPENSION & SHOCK ABSORBER UNIT
REAR WINDOW
LUGGAGE TRAY
HEAD & SIDE LAMP
DIRECTION INDICATOR
PETROL ON/OFF CONTROL KNOB
PETROL TANK
TAIL PIPE
TAIL, STOP INDICATOR & REFLECTOR LAMP UNIT
FINAL DRIVE CHAIN & SPROCKET
BUMPER
CLUTCH PEDAL
STEERING BOX
BRAKE PEDAL
ACCELERATOR
SWINGING REAR AXLE
TRACK ROD
SIDEFRAME STIFFENERS
EXPANSION CHAMBER
BULKHEAD
CHOKE CONTROL
GEAR LEVER
ENGINE & GEARBOX UNIT
SEAT ADJUSTER PLATE
HAND BRAKE
JACKING PAD

Cutaway view of the Unicar, showing Lawrie Bond's 'signature' box section stiffeners built into the shell, and details of the suspension and engine location.

purchase tax), it was the cheapest car at the 1956 London Motor Show. Their thinking certainly appeared to pay off as the car received widespread positive coverage in the press at its launch, including a full

Unicar production line at Opperman's Borehamwood factory premises.

road test in *The Motor* magazine. The Company followed up the launch with a series of tests, including economy runs recording up to 76mpg, and even a trip to Spain, covering what were reported to be some of the poorest roads in Europe. According to press reports of these trials, the Unicar took all this in its stride, averaging 38-40mph and a petrol consumption of 71mpg, and the prototype was said to have covered some 35,000 miles in all conditions during its testing.

The Unicar's bodyshell was again of glassfibre construction and formed a semi-monocoque shell made up of several sections bolted and bonded together, with light alloy pressings and tubular steel stiffening members built in to provide rigidity and extra strength at points of stress. The initial version of the Unicar (retrospectively designated the Model A) was powered by a 322cc air-cooled British Anzani, two-stroke, vertical twin engine, as also used on the early Berkeley cars. This was mid-mounted ahead of the rear axle and between the two occasional rear seats, which were in fact little more than padded lids over the battery and tool boxes. It drove the rear wheels via the three forward speed and reverse Albion gearbox using a primary chain direct to the solid rear axle, which was mounted on trailing arms with a single central coil spring and damper unit. The lack of differential in this drive train was compensated for by the rear track being 12in narrower than the front and this layout, although unusual, was noted as being quite effective by various testers and had the added advantage that the vehicle was much less likely to become stuck on soft ground. Front suspension was independent with upper and lower wishbones and combined coil springs with Girling shock absorber units. Steering was quite conventional, being provided by a Burman 'worm and nut' steering

959 GMA

This 1959 Opperman Unicar was bought as a kit by Brian Stephenson of Liverpool who used it as his only car for family transport for many years. It's still owned by the family and is currently on loan to the Hammond Collection (*see appendices*).

43

Somewhat spartan interior of the 1959 Opperman Unicar built from a kit by Brian Stephenson of Liverpool

box and three-piece track rod lining the front wheels, giving two turns lock to lock, though the 30ft turning circle was relatively large for the size of vehicle due to the aforementioned lack of a differential. Brakes were also conventional for the time, being a Girling, cable operated, mechanical system, operating on a finned 6in drum on all wheels - this was found to be well balanced, and adequate for the weight and speed of the vehicle. Finally, electric starting and power for the 12v lighting system was provided by a Siba Dynastart unit.

Inside the Unicar's fully enclosed two-door passenger compartment, it had a basic hammock-style front bench seat suspended on a tubular steel frame, while the rear seats were more basic still as already mentioned. The doors were front hinged and had sliding windows, but were large enough to allow fairly easy access to the rear seats. Neither the 'bonnet' nor 'boot' opened, but there was provision for some luggage and the spare wheel on a deep shelf at the front under the dashboard and over the front passenger's feet. All controls were noted as quite conventional and well placed, if somewhat basic, though it was noted that the fuel cock was awkward to reach from the driver's seat, but that it should always be turned off for anything longer than a short stop. However, early tests of the Unicar did note there was already a problem keeping the Anzani engine cool, especially in standing traffic, and soon overheating was leading to reliability issues that needed to be addressed. As with the Berkeley, which was having similar problems around the same time, the obvious answer appeared to be a change of engine. Opperman chose the same solution as Berkeley and switched to the 328cc Excelsior Talisman twin, two-stroke engine, with the new

In an attempt to revive flagging sales, Opperman came up with the innovative idea of selling the Unicar as a home build kit, which avoided purchase tax and allowed the car to be sold for only £265.

UNICAR
£265
for complete kit.
MADE by one of the oldest engineering firms in the country, the Unicar has been in production for over three years as a complete car and has a fine reputation. This 4-wheeled saloon, with a twin-cylinder, 2-stroke, air-cooled engine, is constructed mainly of glass-reinforced plastic. It comes in kit form with step-by-step instructions. The kit, less engine gearbox assembly, is also a worthwhile buy for the chap with £170 and his own units who can do his own installation, and modify the drive.
Manufacturers : S. E. Opperman Ltd., Boreham Wood, Herts.
The body, engine and main components
Unicar all set for dispatch—a £12 returnable deposit is made on crates
. . . and here is the rest of the kit

vehicle being designated the Model T, indicating the Talisman power unit, and not, as has been suggested in the past, in reference to the original people's car - the Ford Model T. Whilst the power available in the original Model A (indicating Anzani engine) was thought adequate at 15bhp for such a lightweight car, it did not really give the car the

Why not be ready for the Spring . . with a NEW CAR? Use a few of the dark Winter evenings and build one!
75 m.p.g. - 60 m.p.h.
YRO 896
Here comes the incredible
unicar
model "t"
Build-It-Yourself

Opperman's sales literature promoting the possibilities of building your very own new Unicar!

claimed top speed of 65mph, but the new Talisman engine at 18bhp did actually do just that. In fact the testers from *The Scooter* magazine were pleasantly surprised as the car now accelerated quickly up to cruising speed, and could maintain 40 to 50mph easily and tackle uphill gradients without any problem. However, there was a slight downside as enthusiastic driving, and carrying two people and their luggage, did affect the fuel economy, but the Unicar still achieved a very respectable 65mpg. Opperman also offered a new model to the Unicar range, in the form of the Deluxe Model priced at £425.17s.0d including purchase tax, but as the extra cost only seemed to cover chrome-plated bumpers and a few interior refinements, there were probably few takers.

Despite the development work and press acclaim, Unicar sales were disappointing, and during 1958 Opperman began to develop a new more ambitious vehicle, but still a microcar, and again Lawrie Bond was to be responsible for much of the design work. Also at around this time the Company took the bold step to offer the Model T Unicar as a 'Build-It-Yourself' kit, which avoided the dreaded 33 per cent purchase tax and meant the Unicar could be offered for only £265.12s.0d. However, this was not the sign of desperation that it might appear, as the company had clearly thoroughly thought through how they would achieve this. On purchase the car would be delivered in eight separate well-protected crates, together with very detailed and well-illustrated instructions. Once the build was complete, the Company even offered a free inspection service before the car went on the road - no doubt very reassuring for both the builders and their families who would be travelling in the finished car. The Unicar continued in production until 1959 and it is believed that in total around 200 were sold, including those in kit form.

IT'S
NEW!
IN CONCEPT
NEW!
IN DESIGN
NEW!
IN CONSTRUCTION
694 DRM
STIRLING
FAMILY Speed Saloon

Preliminary sales literature from Opperman to announce their new Stirling Coupé.

Opperman Stirling

Meanwhile, Opperman's new car was announced in October 1958 when the prototype Stirling featured on the Company's stand at the Earls Court Motor Show, and immediately the stylish lines of their new 'Mini Grand Tourer' caught the attention of the press. Apart from the car's appearance, there were several important departures from the previous Unicar. The Stirling still featured a glassfibre bodyshell, reinforced with bonded-steel inserts, but this was now produced in two main sections joined around the waistline of the vehicle, and with an opening 'bonnet' for luggage storage and access to the spare wheel. The interior

Possibly the only surviving photo of production work on the Stirling at the Opperman Factory, showing the original body buck nearing completion. The buck is the full-size pattern used to create the mould for the bodyshell. (*J. Hammond.*)

Charles Hunford
The Motor
COPYRIGHT

was still somewhat spartan, but now with wind-down door windows, and the rear seat, which was again only really suitable for two children, could be folded back to give more luggage space. The rear suspension was also largely redesigned and now used a spur-type differential of Opperman's own manufacture - they were gear making experts after all! This allowed the rear track to more conventionally match the front and the car now had independent rear suspension, using radius arms and universally-jointed drive shafts to effectively form a diagonal swing-axle for each wheel, with Armstrong combined spring and shock absorber units forming a third locating point. Armstrong units were also now used at the front of the car and a Burman steering box was still used, but another improvement was fitting of Girling hydraulic brakes all round with 7in drums. The first prototype was fitted with a specially-modified version of the Excelsior Talisman twin, two-stroke engine, with the capacity increased from 328cc to 424cc by increasing the bore by 6mm and the stroke by 4mm. This gave the engine an increase in power output from 18bhp up to 25bhp and a claimed top speed of 70mph, despite an increase in overall weight to 8cwt.

When launched, Opperman declared that production of the Stirling

***Motor* Magazine** certainly felt the Stirling was attractive and innovative enough to warrant their attention, and came up with this cutaway drawing, showing the unusual method of horizontal split shell construction. The drawing depicts the original 328cc Talisman-powered Stirling.

487 FRO

The 1958 Opperman Stirling Coupé prototype, fitted with the 493cc Steyr-Puch engine, the only survivor of the two prototype Stirlings built by Opperman. The front overiders are not believed to be original fittings.

was imminent and an initial batch of fifty cars was planned, but for some reason their plans changed - perhaps they still had misgivings regarding the reliability of the Talisman engine. A second prototype began to be developed, this time in conjunction with Steyr-Puch in Austria. In 1954 Steyr-Puch, whose first car had appeared in 1920, had wanted to build their own small car suited to the post-war austerity conditions prevalent at the time. Development costs proved too costly for the Company to take on alone and they teamed up with Fiat to build their own Puch 500 version of the Fiat 500 in Austria. The heart of this new microcar was a specially-designed two-cylinder, 493cc air-cooled, four-stroke, horizontally-opposed 'boxer' engine, initially producing 16bhp. This was a sophisticated engine, with hemispherical cylinder heads, full-flow oil filtration, a finned oil cooler and well-designed valve train. The result was an exceptionally smooth running engine, perfectly suited to sustained high rpm running, and with considerable scope for future power increases and modification. Racing enthusiasts were not slow to realize the potential of the Puch 500 and later 650 models, and they soon proved most successful on the rally circuit. Steyr-Puch also designed and produced their own transaxle to go with their new engine, comprising: gearbox with Porsche-type synchromesh on the top three gear ratios, differential and drive-shafts. In early 1959 the second prototype Stirling was sent to Austria and by April had been fitted with the new engine (which was now rated at 19.8bhp) and transmission, and began an intensive programme of testing there. The resulting car apparently exceeded expectations and the plan appears to have been for Opperman to build the body shells in the UK and ship them, partly fitted out, to Austria for Steyr-Puch to finish, with the vehicle then being ideally placed for distribution on the European market.

Meanwhile, back in the UK, things were not going well for Opperman, at least in respect of their car production plans, and rumours have long circulated that the British Motor Corporation (BMC) had viewed the Stirling at the Motor Show with growing alarm. BMC had, of course, been working on their own answer to the growing microcar boom for some time and by this time were getting ready to launch their new Mini. It has been alleged that the stalling of Stirling production was due to BMC putting pressure on Opperman's suppliers, meaning the Company could not obtain many of the bought-in parts they required! However, other factors seem far more likely, not least the ongoing and almost complete development work in Austria. But there were also internal divisions within the management of S.E. Opperman Ltd and this led in 1959 to the Company being acquired by E.V. Industrials, who it seems had no interest in continuing car production, and the Company returned to its original main role as manufacturers of power transmission equipment, gear cutting and geared motors. The first prototype Stirling was unceremoniously consigned to the company dump and destroyed, whilst by the time the second car returned

Clean lines and professional appearance of the 1958 Opperman Stirling Coupé prototype.

STIRLING
487 FRO

Interior of the 1958 Opperman Stirling is still somewhat spartan, if a little less 'home-made' looking than the Unicar. This car is left-hand drive as it was sent to Austria for engine installation and development work.

to the UK, the project was forgotten and it was quietly sold off and disappeared, until rediscovered in the early 1980s.

Lawrie Bond's designs, the Berkeley in particular, had by now attracted the attention of a number of other vehicle manufacturers, including, it seems, Jaguar, who were considering entering the small lightweight sports-car market at the time. Sir William Lyons apparently arranged for Lawrie Bond to do some design work at Jaguar's Special Projects and Competitions Department under the direction of F.R.W. 'Lofty' England. Initially the arrangement was on a part-time basis, but when Jaguar began to call for a more permanent commitment this evidently did not suit Bond and he left sometime around 1957/58 to carry on with his own projects.

Chapter Four

Bond Formula Junior Racing Car

BOND

As he had done in the past, Lawrie Bond used the proceeds of his, albeit, brief period of commercial success with Berkeley and Opperman to finance work on a new project connected with his real main interest, that of designing and building racing cars. It seems that he had also exhibited a better business sense in his dealings with the various companies he worked for, or at least had listened to the advice of those closest to him, and he had secured agreements that would hopefully provide a steady income in the future. There followed a period of intense activity at Lawrence Bond Cars Limited in Loxwood, during which all other work was turned away in order to concentrate on the building of a completely new and yet more ambitious racing car.

In addition to his long-time associate, Ray Bristo, who saw to the day-to-day running of the garage premises and the build of the new project, Lawrie Bond now also had the support of a new business partner, Jon Goddard-Watts, with whom he had become acquainted whilst working at Berkeley Cars Limited. Jon Goddard-Watts had in fact raced Berkeley cars for the works with some success and therefore was an obvious candidate to drive the new racing car. The result was the announcement in 1960 of a new Bond racing car, built to compete in the new Formula Junior category which had achieved international status in 1959. Formula Junior had in fact first appeared in 1958, originating from an idea by Count Giovanni 'Johnny' Lurani Cernuschi, a well-known Italian pre-war racing driver and later a motor racing journalist, race organiser and team manager. He had coincidentally managed a team of three Berkeleys which apparently enjoyed some success in Italy. Formula Junior quickly overshadowed

4

Lawrie Bond's vision for his new Formula Junior Racing Car, as depicted in his sales brochure at the time.

The prototype Formula Junior Bond (*Bond 001*) taking shape at Lawrence Bond Cars Ltd at Loxwood.

the existing Formula 3 category in the UK, which used 500cc motorcycle-based power trains and was the class Lawrie Bond's previous Type C racing car had been built for. The new category was intended to provide an entry-level class using components based on those from production vehicles, including engines, gearboxes and brakes. Engine size was 1,000cc for a minimum weight of 792lb for the car or 1100cc for a minimum weight of 880lb, though the latter became almost exclusive and, initially at least, a front-mounted engine layout was widely used.

The Formula Junior class was conceived to not only enable the building of more affordable racing cars to encourage novice drivers, but also to inspire innovation, and in Lawrie Bond's case it certainly succeeded. As with previous Bond designs, Lawrie's new contender was far from conventional, as although it employed the common, at this time, forward-mounted engine layout, it also featured front-wheel drive. This represented an almost unique breakaway from the by-now virtually universally accepted rear-wheel drive layouts used with front, mid-rear and rear-engine locations. In fact, the Peter Emeryson-designed Elfin Mk1 & Mk2 cars built by Emeryson Experimental Ltd (not to be confused with the Elfin Formula Junior cars built by Elfin Sports Cars Ltd in Australia) were the only other such front-wheel drive Formula Junior racing cars at the time. Another departure from the accepted norm was that the basic shell of the Formula Junior Bond was of lightweight, stressed skin monocoque construction in glassfibre with a network of aluminium and steel inserts bonded in to form an extremely strong yet incredibly lightweight structure, weighing only 100lb! Significantly this was two years before the generally accepted first appearance of modern monocoque racing cars with Colin Chapman's lightweight aluminium Lotus 25 Formula One car, which made its debut at the Dutch Grand Prix at Zandvoort in 1962.

The Bond was powered by a forward-mounted, back-to-front,

The Formula Junior Bond made its public debut at the British Racing and Sports Car Club's second Racing Car Show in December 1960 at the Royal Horticultural Hall, Vincent Square, Westminster.

Cosworth-tuned Ford 105E 997cc engine, with two twin-choke Weber carburettors. Transmission was via the Ford four-speed gearbox and a specially-designed alloy differential/transfer box which gave direct drive in top gear to the front wheels. Output from this box was via flanges to take Hardy Spicer drive shafts with universal joints inboard and constant velocity 'pot' joints outboard. The engine position was intended to keep the weight concentrated over the front driving wheels for maximum stability and Lawrie was convinced that the cornering performance would be the key advantage that would give his car the edge in races. Other features included double-wishbone independent front suspension with specially-made alloy uprights, with the coil spring/damper unit mounted above the upper wishbone to allow room for the drive shaft and CV joints. Rear suspension was by low-pivot swing axles, again incorporating coil spring/damper units. Braking was outboard both front and rear, with a Girling hydraulic system featuring twin master cylinders, and all wheels used specially made finned alloy combined hubs and brake drums. Wheels were again specially made, being bolt-on style rims which attached directly to these brake drums via six bolts.

The car had a kerb weight of 796lb in running order, with oil and water, but dry fuel tanks, which was well below that of most Formula

Juniors. In fact, initially the car had been some 60lb underweight for its intended class, allowing further reinforcement of the shell's various built-in chassis members to bring it up to the required minimum weight. It was fitted with a 997cc engine, as specified for lighter weight Formula Junior cars, and extensive development testing was carried out by Jon Goddard-Watts, but press reports noted that the shell had been built to allow the installation of the larger 1.5 litre Coventry Climax engine. This would have brought the car up to Formula 1 standard, but this was to be dependent on anticipated competition success at the Formula Junior level. The Bond made its public debut at the British Racing and Sports Car Club's second Racing Car Show in December 1960, where Lawrie had splashed out and booked a prominent full-size stand near the entrance, which was prepared for the show with the help of his daughter, Viki Bond. One of the visitors to the show was a youthful Chris Featherstone, who although in no position to buy, was certainly taken with the car and impressed by the way Lawrie Bond took the time to explain all the features of the car to him, whereas other manufacturers could be somewhat dismissive due to his young appearance. But apparently no one was tempted by the £1,385 price tag for the, as yet, unraced car and Lawrie's stated aim to build twenty-five machines within a year was clearly more than a little overly ambitious. However, the car did attract an awful lot of attention at the show, and was soon being featured and track tested in a number of motor-racing journals of the time, where the comments were largely favourable despite noting the unconventional design. Both *Motor Clubman* and *Motor Racing* magazines track tested the car, and both noted the low profile and seating position enabled by the engine and transmission layout, giving the car a very low frontal area, a feature sought after by other designers with usually much less success. The front-wheel drive layout did, however, have the disadvantage that the car became very difficult to control if the engine stalled at speed. This, in fact, happened on at least one occasion as a result of a faulty carburettor, causing the car to leave the track, but fortunately without injury to the driver or any serious damage to the car.

Problems with the carburettors also plagued both magazine test runs, one with icing due to extremely cold weather and the other a sticking throttle connecting rod, with each driver experiencing the dreaded loss of power scenario, but managing to cope with it fairly well. Such troubles were easily forgiven as they were clearly rectifiable and the extensive development testing of the car was also noted in these tests, as it had resulted in a very well-finished racing car with particularly well-laid out controls. Both testers considered the suspension set up to be too soft, but again this was something that could be easily remedied. One final noted issue was the unsuitability of the standard gear ratios fitted to the car, but this was due to the fact that Lawrie was still waiting for delivery of a new set. Overall the verdict was that the car certainly had potential, with perhaps a little more development once experience in competition had been gained.

The Formula Junior Bond was initially driven in competition by Jon Goddard-Watts, although the car only competed twice with the official Bond team. Its début was at the 44th British Automobile Racing Club (BARC) Members' Meeting at Goodwood on 11 March 1961, when it was forced to retire at three quarters distance because of engine problems. The second was on Easter Monday, 3 April the same year, again at Goodwood, competing in the XIII Chichester Cup race for Formula Juniors, but it was not placed (DNF - Did Not Finish), though the Bond does not appear to have been involved in the series of crashes that took several other competitors out of the race.

Surprisingly, after all the work, design and development, publicity, and positive reaction to the Bond Formula Junior, the project was suddenly over. Obviously much had been gambled on the car's success in competition, especially with such a capable driver, but teething problems and strong competition, especially from the Lotus and Cooper cars, the former having the added advantage of slightly better Cosworth-tuned engines than were available to other competitors, meant that the Bond failed to live up to expectations. It seems the Bond became caught up in the changing fortunes of motor racing at the time, with the mid-rear-engined cars beginning to really make their mark and component manufacturers giving low priority or even being unwilling to supply smaller racing car manufacturers, especially those with unproven vehicles - hence, possibly, Lawrie's long and fruitless wait for his new gears. No doubt all of Bond's work on the Formula Junior car had also eaten considerably into his finances and with one of his main sources of income, his work for the Berkeley Cars Ltd, drying up as that Company was having serious troubles of their own. It is perhaps inevitable that the project had to be wound up, and with only one complete car and a second partially built, no further racing took place and plans were dropped to upgrade it to Formula One status. Later in 1961 Jon Goddard-Watts ended his association with Lawrence Bond Cars Ltd and left, taking the completed Formula Junior car with him, although he never raced it again and it was soon sold on. Lawrie Bond continued to run the Loxwood premises, as a more conventional garage business, with a new partner, Pat Pearson, and although the second uncompleted racing car remained at the premises, no further work was carried out on it.

The Formula Junior Bond did see action again, however, as by 1963 it was in the hands of John Turner at Guildford, where it once again attracted the attention of Chris Featherstone when it again came up for sale. This time Chris was in a position to buy and so purchased the car and initially raced it as it came to him, but soon found that the suspension was far too soft, as commented on during its track tests. Also he soon found it was still fitted with the unsuitable standard

Chris Featherstone racing the somewhat modified Formula Junior Bond in 1964. Note the slightly wider wheel rims and tyres, and a smaller radiator aperture. *(Photo: via C. Featherstone.)*

Ford gearbox ratios - obviously Lawrie never did get those new gears he ordered! Chris modified the suspension by mounting additional shock absorbers alongside the existing ones, which he felt improved the handling considerably. During the 1963 racing season he raced it at Cadwell Park on 23 June, Mallory Park on 5 August, Brands Hatch on 6 October (but DNF), and Mallory Park again on 14 October.

For the 1964 season there were major changes in the organisation of motor racing in the UK, as Formula Junior was dropped, to be replaced by Formula Two and a reintroduction of Formula Three, which was now to be a one-litre engine formula. Although Formula Junior had indeed proved successful in its aim of encouraging new drivers to take up the sport and develop their skills to move on to higher levels, it had largely failed as an affordable formula for cars designed using production car parts. Perhaps inevitably, the money that the bigger, more serious teams were prepared to put into their machines to gain any advantage, however small, began to spiral out of control, leaving the less-wealthy amateurs with no hope of catching up ,either in their car's specification or on the track. For the 1964 season, Chris Featherstone modified the Bond further, replacing the troublesome gears with a Wooler close ratio set, fitting wider wheel rims and tyres, and altering the car's nose profile to give a smaller radiator aperture. But his 1965 season appears to have been less than successful, with entries for 21 June at Snetterton and 30 August at Brands Hatch both DNS (Did Not

Attend), though the car ran successfully at Cadwell Park on 19 July. By now Chris had become well versed in Lawrie's weight saving almost to the point of failure style of engineering, and the rear suspension on the Bond Formula Junior had given him considerable trouble, often requiring rebuilding/repair after every race, particularly as the anchor plates attached to the shell were not really up to the job. But later in the year at Mallory Park, disaster struck when a rear stub axle failed at the point where it joined the wishbone, causing the car to be pitched tail first into the 'Armco' barrier at speed. The rear end of the monocoque shell disintegrated as far as the back of the driver's seat, but proved much stronger than it looked and absorbed the impact well, leaving Chris completely unscathed, much to the relief of all those who had witnessed his dramatic mishap.

Earlier in 1964 Chris Featherstone had answered an advertisement placed by Lawrie Bond in *Autosport* magazine offering the Bond Formula Junior design as a complete project package. He travelled down to Lawrie's home address at Wormley, not quite sure what to expect, where he discovered the house's garage crammed with the moulds for the bodyshell, wooden patterns for castings and numerous other spare parts. Amongst this treasure trove was the complete, unpainted bodyshell of the second Bond Formula Junior car, with all the aluminium reinforcing sections lying loose inside ready to be laminated into place. Chris found Lawrie to be again very approachable and a deal was quickly struck for much of the collection for relatively little money, though he was conscious that he could only take what would fit in the van and on the trailer he had arrived with. Lawrie seemed happy to have found an appreciative home for his project and even offered to throw in the moulds, but they were simply too large for the trailer, even if it hadn't already been full. In a final parting gesture from Lawrie, he handed over all the detailed technical drawings for the car and the various specially-made components that he had designed for it.

Following his accident, Chris decided not to repair the car immediately and the engine was removed for use in another car, whilst the damaged Bond, the unfinished shell and all the spare parts were placed into storage until such a time as he had the resources and time to repair the car properly. But time moves on quickly and Chris Featherstone was keen to get back out on the track, and by the late 1960s was a regular competitor in Monoposto Racing with his 1966 Lola T60, and went on to win the Monoposto 2000 Class Championship in 1971. Later he competed in Formula 5000 in a McRae GM1, and it was not until the early 1980s that the Bond project was revisited and work started on repairing the damaged car at Lenham Sports Cars. By 1982 the rear of the unfinished shell had been removed and used to repair the damaged car, which was now ready for refitting out, but a change in personal circumstances led to the project once again being put on hold.

Roll on nearly 20 years, and in the late 1990s work on the Formula

Junior Bond once again recommenced. Chris Featherstone's interest in the car seems to have been rekindled by this author's original contact with him in the early 1990s and subsequent correspondence, but it was not until 1997 when Duncan Rabagliati, Chairman of the Formula Junior Historic Racing Association, persuaded Chris to finish the repairs to the car. The aim was to have it ready to run in the second Grand Prix Historique de Monaco due to be held in May 2000. This major event in the historic racing calendar takes place every two years, using the same circuit as the Formula 1 Monaco Grand Prix and includes series for Grand Prix cars from many periods, from pre-war through to the 1970s. The 2000 event saw a strong showing in the series for Formula Junior cars built from1958 to 1963, with some 100 entries forming six representative grids. The Bond was ready in time for the event, now fitted with an 1100cc version of the Ford engine, but its performance on the day is not recorded, though after such a major rebuild and with this being its first racing appearance since its mishap thirty-five years before, it was still a major milestone. The Bond appeared occasionally over the next few years at Historic Formula Junior events, including: Spa in Belgium, the Nurburgring and the Copenhagen Historic Grand Prix. Later it appeared in 2006 at Goodwood and Brands Hatch, as well as in 2008 participating in two races as part of the Historic Formula Junior Golden Jubilee Series.

Team Bond

Meanwhile, Jon Goddard-Watts had done rather well over the years with a hardware supply business which he and his wife Jennie had started and built up, later joined by their two sons, making it a real family-run concern. By 1999 the main part of the business - 'Screwfix Direct' - was still growing, with almost 1,000 employees, and was innovatively making the transition from catalogue-based sales to the internet. At this point the Company attracted the attention of Kingfisher PLC, the owners of B&Q, and was sold, with Jon's sons going on to develop successful new business ventures of their own. This left Jon Goddard-Watts free to pursue his personal interests, initially buying a majority stake in Yeovil Town Football Club, which saw considerable investment and progress under his ownership. By 2005 Jon had achieved what he had set out to do at Yeovil Town FC and decided to move on, this time setting his sights on once again becoming involved in motorsport, though not necessarily as a driver, but rather as an owner. To this end he was introduced by a mutual friend to the renowned historic racing car restoration guru, Andrew Tart, and a visit to his premises was arranged to view the cars being worked on and discuss a list of those that might be available. Although impressed with the workshop and standard of work carried out, Jon soon made it clear that he had his own thoughts on the car he would like to own and run. It seems Jon Goddard-Watts

Jon Goddard-Watts at the wheel of his newly-restored Formula Junior Bond. (*Photo: via A. Tart.*)

believed the Formula Junior Bond he had helped build back in 1959 had never realised its full potential, and asked Andrew Tart if he could track it down and see if its owner would be prepared, part with it. Finding the car was the easy part, as it still belonged to Chris Featherstone, but he had clearly become attached to the car, having owned it for over forty years and it was 2008 before he could be persuaded to sell.

The Formula Junior Bond, together with the unfinished and now incomplete additional shell, the spare parts and original working drawings, were all collected from Chris Featherstone in October 2008 and restoration of the car commenced almost immediately at Andrew Tart's workshop. The car was completely stripped, and the shell checked thoroughly for alignment and integrity, with all necessary repairs being carried out under the watchful eye of its new owner who wanted the car to be as near perfect as possible - though the intention was very much to create a viable racing car and not a museum piece. Every component was checked and replaced or refurbished as required, and it was decided to keep the car in its 1100cc configuration. The Bond was finally ready in April 2009 and its first outing, with Andrew Tart driving

1932 Maserati 4CM
GOODWOOD TROPHY
25

Jon Goddard-Watts (*left*) and Andrew Tart, as work gets underway on the mammoth task of turning the now-repaired second Formula Junior Bond shell into a viable racing car. (*Photo: via A. Tart.*)

at Jon Goddard-Watts' suggestion, was at Mallory Park. Coincidentally this was the venue of its 1965 mishap which was perhaps not a good omen, as the car spun on spilt oil and broke a rear wishbone, ending its race early.

Its next race was in May of that year, at Pau in south-western France, where again the result was DNF (Did Not Finish), this time due to gear linkage problems. However, such results were perhaps hardly surprising so soon after a major rebuild and formed part of the necessary ongoing development of the car, which saw work on improving the steering geometry, addressing the gear linkage problems and strengthening the front and rear wishbones. The Bond competed in a further six races in 2009, finishing all but one and gaining a 1st in class in October at Silverstone. With the car starting to show real promise, the brave decision was taken to build up the second car, and work commenced to rebuild the previously-cannibalised original shell and new moulds were constructed, initially to produce a new rear end, but also to enable repair sections to be accurately produced in case of future mishaps. The second Bond Formula Junior proved to be an even more challenging undertaking than the first, so as the build progressed, the first car continued to be raced, being entered for twenty events in 2010, again with Andrew Tart driving. The Bond was competing in the FJHRA / HSCC (Formula Junior Historic Racing Association / Historic Sports Car Club) 'Millers Oils' UK Championship and continued to

10
23

Bond 001 seen at Cadwell Park in 2015, driven by Mike Walker.

accumulate very respectable results, with only one DNF due to another broken rear wishbone and, by the end of the season, the team had won the front-engined category in the championship and come third overall.

Team Bond planned an even more ambitious season for 2011, which was to see Andrew Tart competing in and winning the front-engined class in the FIA (Federation Internationale de L'Automobile) Lurani Trophy for Formula Junior Cars (named after Count Lurani, the originator of Formula Junior). Also, the 2011 season saw the racing debut of the second Bond Formula Junior car (Bond 002) at Mallory Park for the FJHRA Front Engined Series race on 21 August, again with Andrew Tart driving, finishing a very respectable 2nd in its class and 8th overall. This was the first time both cars had raced together, with Gil Duffy invited to become the second driver and take over Bond 001. Although it had been a long time coming to fruition, being fifty-one years after Bond 001's racing debut, the two-car team now officially adopted the title 'Team Bond'. Bond 002 competed in another six races in 2011, including coming 1st in class and 7th overall at Portimao in Portugal for the final meeting of the FIA Lurani Trophy, whilst Gil Duffy in Bond 001 came 4th in class in the same race. The year was rounded off with Team Bond winning the Spirit of Formula Junior Award and plans began to take shape for both cars to make a concerted effort in 2012 to realise Jon Goddard-Watts' and Lawrie Bond's original dream

Bond 002 seen at Spa in 2014, driven by Andrew Tart. (*Photo: via A. Tart.*)

from 1960, to win the British Formula Junior Championship. Part of the plan involved returning Bond 001 to its original 1000cc specification, and during the car's winter preparations the engine was stripped, fitted with reducing liners and specially-made pistons, to achieve this. This meant that each car would compete in a different class and the team concentrated on the 'Millers Oils' UK Championship and the FJHRA /HSCC 'JMW' Front Engined Series. Both cars raced successfully throughout the season, and Andrew Tart in Bond 002 finished 1st in class and 2nd overall in the Millers Championship, with Gil Duffy in Bond 001 also achieving 1st in his class and 7th overall. Both cars also put up a respectable performance in the FJHRA Front Engined Series. Whilst not an overall win, it was still a pretty impressive result and certainly showed that with some development, Lawrie's design had winning potential, and it was decided that for the following year Team Bond would concentrate on the FIA Lurani Trophy.

Thus the 2013 season saw Team Bond racing at some of the most prestigious circuits throughout Europe in what was to prove an eventful season. The series opened with round one at Hockenheim, in April, with Team Bond's first race in Round 2 at Pau in May, followed by Brands Hatch, Dijon and the Nurburgring, with Jon and Jennie Goddard-Watts attending whenever possible to watch over the Team's progress.

All was going well up to the second race in Round 6 at Jerez in Spain

BOND

Beautifully-prepared engine bay of the Formula Junior Bond.

Further detail of the engine bay of the Formula Junior Bond, showing the reversed Ford gearbox and later-added aluminium alloy bracing the front suspension, as well as airflow deflectors behind the radiator.

Detail shot of the Formula Junior Bond's transmission taken during winter overhaul, with the engine removed. Also the non-original additional stiffeners and airflow deflectors are absent, giving a clear view of Lawrie's original front-wheel drive design features.

'The Office' – cockpit of Bond 002.

in October, when in the second race, Gil Duffy in Bond 001, which had just been upgraded back to 1100cc, spun into the barrier whilst trying to avoid another spinning competitor, once again badly damaging the rear of the shell. This led to some epic repair work to have the car ready for the final round only a week later at the Portimao Circuit in the Algarve region of Portugal. Bond 001 was ready in the nick of time to compete in Race 1, but it was Andrew Tart in Bond 002 that now suffered a mishap, the car losing its oil and damaging the engine. At

10

Close-up rear view of Bond 001 taken during winter overhaul. Note the lack of exhaust and the high ride height due to no engine being fitted.

this point Andrew Tart was looking to be well on the way to securing not only a class win, but to win overall, but was only a few points in the lead, so it was crucial the car could be repaired in time for him to compete in the second race the following day. With Gil already having enough points from his first four races with Bond 001 in its 1000cc form to secure a class win, it was decided to swap the good 1100cc engine now in his car to Bond 002, and Team Bond worked through much of the night to effect the transplant. All the effort proved worthwhile as Andrew Tart drew ahead of his closest rival for the overall title during the race, finishing 1st in class and 13th overall, but becoming the overall FIA Lurani Trophy Champion for 2013.

With Team Bond having by now soundly proved to any doubters

25
10

Both Formula Junior Bonds together, in hibernation at Andrew Tart's workshop, where they undergo an annual inspection and full overhaul in preparation for the new racing season.

that Lawrie Bond's Formula Junior design, with a bit of tweaking, really was capable of winning, it was decided to ease off a little. Also, with Gil Duffy deciding to concentrate on his other motorsport interests, the second Bond would be driven by guest drivers and races chosen for interest rather than any serious attempt to win a championship series. During 2014, these drivers included Duncan Rabagliati and Barrie 'Whizzo' Williams, but by 2015 Mike Walker had become established as the main second Bond driver. Also in 2015, Andrew Tart won the newly-renamed FJHRA / HSCC 'Silverline' UK Championship outright and both cars continue to be used in competition as intended. The team returned to Monaco for the 10th Grand Prix Historique de Monaco held in May 2016.

Lawrie Bond's links with Preston Renewed

By the early 1960s, economic conditions and increasing competition in the three-wheeler market meant that Sharp's Commercials were looking to extend their range of products, and one option which was looked at was that of building a four-wheel specialist sports car. After some consideration and negotiation it was decided to build a high-quality glassfibre-bodied sports coupé, using the chassis and running gear from the contemporary Triumph Herald. Lawrie Bond was commissioned to style the bodywork for the car which was to become the new Bond Equipe GT. The bodyshell of the car combined glassfibre construction, reinforced by a bonded pressed-steel floorpan from

TCK 301

Factory shot of a pre-production Bond Equipe GT, styled by Lawrie Bond.

Early pre-production prototype of the Bond 875 designed by Lawrie Bond.

the Triumph Herald. It also incorporated the Herald's bulkhead and doors, with a one-piece glassfibre forward-hinging bonnet and front wings retaining the Herald's excellent engine accessibility. The result was a smart two-door coupé-style family four-seater (the fastback styling allowed only limited rear headroom, thus making the rear seats suitable only for two children). Again, an enthusiastic reception from the motoring press came when this Bond made its first appearance at the Earls Court International Motor Show in October 1963.

Almost immediately Lawrie Bond began work on another project for Sharp's Commercials, but this time the resulting vehicle was to be more in keeping with his innovative design principles and weight-saving construction techniques. This was to be a completely new Bond three-wheeler, intended to be a complete departure from the earlier spartan economy three-wheel minicars which the Firm had become so well-known for producing. The basis for the new car was to be the complete Hillman Imp power unit (comprising the gearbox and transaxle) with a lightweight glassfibre shell built around it to give adequate accommodation for four adults. This 875cc four-cylinder, water-cooled, four-stroke engine featured a single overhead camshaft, and used aluminium alloy castings for both the block and cylinder head to reduce weight. It had been developed from the single OHC, all-aluminium, Coventry Climax engine, which had been 1220cc, but despite the reduction in capacity the new Rootes 875cc engine produced

39bhp at 5000rpm in 1963, and, with further development, by 1965 was up to 51bhp at 6100rpm.

Due to the light weight of their new three-wheeler, and partly for fuel economy, Sharp's decided to opt for the 34bhp low-compression commercial version of the Imp engine for the production model of the vehicle, which was to be called the Bond 875. The 875's glassfibre bodyshell incorporated a bonded-steel reinforcing frame, with the power unit, including the half-shafts and rear wheels, mounted in a slightly modified Imp subframe that bolted straight onto the Bond shell. Other weight-saving features were incorporated to keep the vehicle within the government's strict 8cwt limit for three-wheelers. These included aluminium-panelled doors and the use of Perspex for all the windows (with the exception of the windscreen). When announced in 1965, the Bond 875 was warmly welcomed and was considered a worthy competitor to Reliant three-wheelers that were starting to dominate the market. However, a series of technical problems and production delays were to have a serious adverse effect on sales.

By 1965 Lawrie Bond had decided to concentrate on his freelance design work. In order to do this he once again moved north, to the Bowes Moor Hotel, near Bowes in Yorkshire, where he intended to combine the roles of both designer and publican. Here he continued his work, and locals who frequented the pub at the time recall seeing many drawings and models of projects scattered around. Details of these projects are sketchy, but it would appear that he had become interested in the design of boats and was working on a design for a new multi-purpose flat-twin air-cooled two-stroke engine. However, for health reasons he moved again in 1974 to stay with his daughter, Viki, in Ansdell, near Lytham, in Lancashire. Shortly afterwards in September of that year he became ill and died at the age of 67.

Although over the years many different vehicles carried the Bond name, Lawrence 'Lawrie' Bond is undoubtedly best remembered for the little three-wheel Minicar which paved the way for a new concept in motoring in post-war Britain. The Minicar, which provided so many people with a basic, but affordable means of personal motor transport, has all but passed into history as millions of people now take this privilege for granted. But perhaps with continually increasing fuel costs and evermore congested roads, especially in our towns and cities, the future may see a revival of such economy personal transport. In fact, in many cities in Europe, small lightweight vehicles are already appearing in significant numbers. In recent years an additional factor has emerged, namely environmental considerations, leading to many such vehicles being electrically powered and therefore opening up a whole new area for development.

CHAPTER FIVE

Development of the Bond Minicar

Bond

Post-War Austerity

In order to understand the success of what today seems to be such an unlikely little vehicle, it is important first to have an understanding of the economic situation prevalent in Great Britain immediately following the end of the Second World War. Despite the apparent crudity and unconventional design of the original Bond Minicar, there was a certain amount of sound business sense behind the decision to put such a vehicle into production. In the austere post-war era of the late 1940s, a combination of factors effectively put the ownership and running of private motor cars out of the reach of most people in Britain. Although ultra-lightweight economy vehicles had existed before the war, by the 1930s they had all but disappeared with the advent of small, relatively cheap, more conventional cars such as the Austin Seven and Morris Eight. Such vehicles costing little more than £100 had become known as 'People's Cars' and had put the ownership of a motor car within the reach of more people than ever before.

The end of the Second World War saw the economic structures of many countries severely disrupted. During the war Britain had been totally committed to the war effort, leaving a post-war situation where the country's industry, roads, railways and so on, were all run down and worn out. Britain had also incurred huge debts, mainly with the United States of America and Canada, and only further loans enabled payment for urgently needed imports of food and raw materials. This led the Government to take drastic measures, including the continuation of rationing of petrol until 1950 and of some foods until 1954. Import quotas were also enforced and the allocation of scarce raw materials, such as steel, was mostly to industries that could guarantee export potential. This situation obviously had a serious effect on private motoring as well as on new car production. The shortage of materials, together with heavy taxation, led manufacturing costs to increase to

Very early example of the production version of the Bond Minicar built by Sharp's Commercials Ltd.

three or four times their 1939 values. Although many car manufacturers had been carrying out design work during the latter part of the war with a view towards the post-war market, it soon became clear that any vehicle production was likely to be severely limited. In the case of Rover it is recorded that their initial steel allocation was calculated to allow for the production of only around 1,100 cars. Vehicle manufacturers were also encouraged by the-then President of the Board of Trade, Sir Stafford Cripps, to pursue a one-model policy, ie that a company's range of vehicles should share as many components as possible, and this led many manufacturers to continue with a 'one-chassis' policy, using familiar pre-war designs and closely related model ranges.

By 1946 the first new models were just beginning to appear on the market, but production remained limited at only 220,000 vehicles, which only just matched 1933 figures. In 1948 the first Motor Show for nearly ten years was held, attracting more than half a million visitors, but they had little chance of buying anything, even if they could afford to do so, because over 60 per cent of motor vehicle production was directed by the Government for export. Those who were able to place orders were told that they would have to wait up to three years for delivery, as well as being liable for the high levels of purchase tax levied on new cars. This tax had been introduced in 1940 at the rate of 33.3 per cent, with an increase in 1947 for cars over 1,000cc to 66 per cent, (the higher rate then being applied to all new cars in 1951 and falling to 55 per cent only in 1955). This meant that even the most basic post-war equivalents of the Austin Seven or Morris Eight now cost around £400 if you could buy a new one. The petrol allowance for such a car was around eighteen gallons for six months, but the cost was between four to five times the pre-war price and then only low-quality 'Pool' petrol was available, so economy was the order of the day and many existing larger cars remained laid up whilst the values of smaller second-hand vehicles rose dramatically.

It was soon recognised that there was a need for a very basic type of vehicle and much discussion was had in the motoring press as to the required specifications of such a car. It would need to have as small an engine as possible and therefore very light overall weight in order to achieve the maximum possible fuel economy. Other desirable features would include construction in a relatively cheap and plentiful material which was not subject to any restrictions, and also that the new vehicle should preferably have only three wheels in order to take advantage of the new road tax laws which were brought into force on the 1 January 1948. These new regulations saw the replacement of the old RAC horsepower rating system with a flat-rate annual fee of £10, but with three-wheelers liable only for half that amount.

Early Progress

Such basic ultra-lightweight vehicles had previously achieved popularity immediately prior to the First World War in the form of the cyclecar class of motor cars of that period. Development of this basic

Two of Sharp's employees demonstrating the lightweight construction of the production version of the Bond Minicar.

form of motor transport had been limited, partly by the technology available at the time and also by the advent of the true light car in the 1920s. However, by the late 1940s technical advances now allowed for this concept to be developed further, particularly as regards advances in small engine design. The original cyclecars used engines of around 500-1,000cc capacity producing around 4-15bhp, but by the late 1940s similar output could be expected of the new 100-400cc engines now available. This, together with advances in lightweight construction techniques and materials, allowed for better performance coupled with comparatively lower running costs. Despite its limitations the prototype Bond Minicar fitted these requirements perfectly and it is little wonder that it aroused considerable interest when it was first announced early in 1948. This new generation of cyclecar was initially designed to provide reliable and reasonably comfortable local transport for two adults, with luggage, at up to 40mph and with petrol consumption of up to 100mpg. The advantages of such a vehicle at this time were numerous, for it attracted not only half the new flat-rate road tax, but a much lower rate of purchase tax as well. The mainly aluminium construction gave the prototype its incredibly low dry weight of 195lb besides ensuring that there would be no problems with the supply of materials for construction. Finally, at 100mpg it gave the possibility of up to 1,800 miles motoring on the 18-gallon allowance for cars of up to 9hp, as compared to around 540 miles for a conventional vehicle at the time.

As already outlined, the original prototype Bond Minicar was quite different in appearance from the eventual production model, with a streamlined bodyshell that could even be termed quite stylish for its time. Lawrie Bond, with the help of his wife Pauline, arranged publicity for the new vehicle and the motoring press responded enthusiastically, proving that there was indeed considerable interest in such a vehicle and that it had commercial potential. Before long Lawrie Bond had a number of prospective customers, but it was clear that the production rate of several cars a week that had been promised was not possible at his existing works. The space available at Towneley Works was severely restricted and the first prototype had in fact been built on the first floor and then lowered through a trap door - clearly demonstrating that alternative premises were required! It was at this time when the first approach was made by Lawrie Bond to Lieutenant Colonel C.R. Gray in order to try to rent suitable premises to put the Minicar into production. Colonel Gray was the Managing Director of Sharp's Commercials Limited in nearby Preston, and in order to fully understand how this Firm became involved in the production of the Minicar and went on to turn it into such a success, we need briefly to examine something of the background of the Company.

BOND
MINICAR
MANUFACTURED BY
Sharp's Commercials Limited
PRESTON ENGLAND

Sharp's Commercials Ltd

The history of Sharp's Commercials Limited can be traced back to 1922 when Paul Sharp, a motor engineer in Preston, set up a motor car repair business under the title Sharp and Company at Lea Garage, on Long Lane in Ashton, Preston. The Company changed its name in 1924 to Paul Sharp Limited, and remained in business until about 1938 when it was bought by Ewart Bradshaw and became part of Loxhams Garages Limited, which in turn was part of the Bradshaw Group of companies. Bradshaw's Motor House Limited itself was situated on Marsh Lane in Preston. As main Ford agents they could not undertake work on other makes of motor vehicles, therefore all such work was done by Loxhams Garages to keep within the conditions laid down by Ford. The new Company was bought in anticipation of the Bradshaw Group negotiating an agreement with General Motors in America to import, assemble and distribute Chevrolet Commercial vehicles. General Motors had agreed to an eight-year abstinence on imports of these vehicles into Great Britain in order to allow time for their subsidiary, Bedford, to become established. This period was now coming to an end and an agreement was secured for the renamed Sharp's Commercials Limited to handle this work, as well as take over all the commercial vehicle work for Loxhams Garages. The new American vehicles were imported in completely knocked down (CKD) form, ie fully disassembled, as assembly and possible local manufacture of some parts such as bodywork would provide employment, thus they attracted a lower rate of import duty than fully-assembled vehicles. The Company had barely become established when war broke out and any relatively new civilian vehicles considered suitable for military use began to be requisitioned. At first this increased the civilian demand for Sharp's imported vehicles, as initially only British-made vehicles were being considered for requisition, to avoid possible maintenance problems. But after the fall of France in 1940, so many vehicles were destroyed or had to be left behind that the War Office began to extend their scope and also bought up stocks of vehicles from pretty well any manufacturer able to deliver, including American-made vehicles, such as those under assembly at Sharp's, which could be more easily converted for military use. In early 1941 Britain signed the Lease/Lend Agreement with the United States, and Sharp's Commercials were now formally contracted to assemble and supply Chevrolet vehicles directly for the British Army for the duration of the conflict.

By 1942 the Company was assembling some 40 vehicles per week. In addition, the Ministry of Supply were appointing civilian contractors to form a network of Auxiliary Army Workshops to repair vehicles for the Army, and Sharp's received such a contract. The Company soon found that the additional work meant that they needed larger premises, and a redundant rope works on Gosford Street, off Ribbleton Lane in Preston, was purchased. By the end of the war Sharp's import agreement with General Motors had expired, but the Company had plenty of work to occupy their workforce, as they concentrated on the repair of military vehicles, including the complete reconditioning of war-weary vehicles to resupply the British Army under a Ministry of Supply contract. In order to ensure a full workload, Sharp's also entered into the lucrative business of buying, refurbishing or converting and selling surplus military vehicles. This proved extremely successful - the demand for such vehicles was enormous because virtually no new commercial vehicles were being built, and with many requisitioned vehicles never returned, this only left a few existing vehicles that were invariably worn out. Col. Charles Reginald Gray had served with the Royal Artillery throughout the war, during which time he had married Miss Anne Bradshaw, daughter of Ewart Bradshaw, Chairman of the Bradshaw Group of companies. He returned to Lancashire in 1946 and had become Managing Director of Sharp's Commercials Limited, but in 1948 he was informed that the Ministry of Supply contracts would come to an end in December of that year, therefore he would have to find alternative work for the Company to do. At this time Lawrie Bond and his wife Pauline were acquainted with Colonel Gray and his wife, as they lived quite close to his house in Longridge, so Lawrie learned of Sharp's predicament. Although his first approach to try to lease Sharp's Commercials' Ribbleton Lane premises was not taken seriously by Colonel Gray, Lawrie Bond persisted and a meeting was arranged to view the new Bond Shopping Car and to discuss its commercial potential. Apparently Colonel Gray was not completely convinced as regards the strength and reliability of the little microcar, but he did recognise the sound thinking around the economic factors behind the design and agreed to consider the matter further - no doubt also encouraged by the favourable reaction shown by the motoring press so far. A further meeting was arranged and Ewart Bradshaw himself came to see the Minicar (apparently he took some convincing), and a formal arrangement was entered into under which Sharp's Commercials Ltd would build what would be called the Minicar under the Bond name.

Although Sharp's are reputed to have completed a first batch of twenty-five vehicles at Ribbleton Lane in order to fulfil the orders taken by Lawrie Bond, first they had the challenge of turning the Minicar into a practical, reliable, commercial proposition.

Colonel Gray was a businessman and realist, and realising that whilst Bond's innovative design work and enthusiasm were all well and good, he needed to ensure his Company were producing a product that would live up to the claims made about it. The Minicar had to be marketable and reliable, so it could be given a warranty and would develop a reputation that would encourage dealers to stock it and help build a nationwide servicing network. To achieve this, considerable development work was required before full production could proceed. Work began on this immediately with the help of Lawrie and two of his employees from Longridge, Alan Pearson and Fred Atkinson, who now joined Sharp's Commercials. In November 1948 the remodelled, much stronger and substantially improved production version of the Bond Minicar was announced to the motoring press, and again the response was very encouraging. The revolutionary little car was now beginning to be taken seriously, especially as it was the first such vehicle to go into production, although many others would soon follow. This media coverage started a flood of enquiries arriving at Sharp's Ribbleton Lane premises and Colonel Gray soon realised that he was on to a potential winner.

Production Begins

Full production of the Bond Minicar at Ribbleton Lane began early in 1949, with some fifteen vehicles a week being built initially -

Early Minicar production, circa 1950, at Sharp's Ribbleton Lane premises, showing the bodyshell jigs for the new Minicars.

Assembly line, showing newly-built Bond Minicar bodyshells receiving their additional body panels prior to paint, circa 1950, at Sharp's Ribbleton Lane Factory.

somewhat less than the fifty a week predicted when the model was announced. The workforce in Sharp's factory at this time amounted to some sixty to seventy individuals, most with engineering skills, but few with manufacturing experience, though no doubt some had worked in the north-west's predominant aircraft industry during the Second World War. It would have been a steep learning curve as they adapted to the Firm's new direction, hence this seemingly low production figure actually shows they were willing to adapt and learnt fast. By this time most of the problems identified with the initial prototype had been sorted out and Lawrie Bond began to lose interest in the Minicar, possibly as it had evolved into quite a different vehicle from his original design. Under the arrangement he had agreed with Sharp's Commercials, Lawrie received a small 'royalty' payment on each car produced. However, he was now tempted to sell the design and manufacturing rights outright. Although he was to regret it later, Lawrie Bond accepted an offer from Sharp's, probably because it gave him ready cash to spend on his other projects without having to wait for the Minicars to sell. He did, however, remain in contact with the Company in the capacity of an informal consultant designer and occasional trouble-shooter when things went wrong. This led to frequent telephone calls to his Longridge Workshop asking him to go to the Ribbleton Lane Works to help sort out the various problems which arose during the early production.

The Mk A Bond Minicar, as it was later retrospectively designated, basically retained the extremely lightweight monocoque construction bodyshell of Lawrie's prototype, which was fabricated from sheet aluminium giving the vehicle a remarkably low dry-weight of only 308lb. Although considerably remodelled, the Minicar was still in the form of an open two-seat tourer with limited luggage space behind the bench front seat which, it was claimed, could accommodate a third person at a squeeze. In order to ensure the rigidity of this bodyshell there were no doors fitted, just a slight curvature of the cockpit side to provide a lower section for getting in and out - which was alright when the hood was lowered, but made entry and exit from the vehicle quite a strenuous feat when the hood was raised. Power was provided by a 122cc Villiers Mk 10 D single-cylinder two-stroke motorcycle engine with an integral three-speed gearbox, which was claimed to produce 5bhp at 4,400rpm and, according to C.P. Read of *Motor Cycling,* gave the vehicle an unladen power/weight ratio of 57bhp per ton! The manufacturers were slightly less optimistic, claiming only 49bhp per ton unladen. Also, as this engine's gearbox did not incorporate a reverse gear, there was the added advantage that the holder of a Group 3 or motorcycle licence was entitled to drive the Minicar without supervision and without having to pass a car driving test. This might not be seen as a big deal today, but at that time many of the Minicar's potential customers had never owned a car and were more likely to have gained their motoring experience on the only form of transport they could afford - a motorcycle. This left a significant market of older motorcycle riders, now with families of their own, riding pillion or squeezed into sidecars.The engine unit was mounted together with the front wheel on the lower cast aluminium section of the front steering 'fork', with the suspension achieved using a single coil spring and André Hartford friction-type shock absorber. Later a double-acting hydraulic-type shock absorber was used, giving considerably improved and easier

You too ought to own a
BOND MINICAR
The world's most economical car

Early advertising brochure for the first model of Bond Minicar, heralding 'The World's Most Economical Car'.

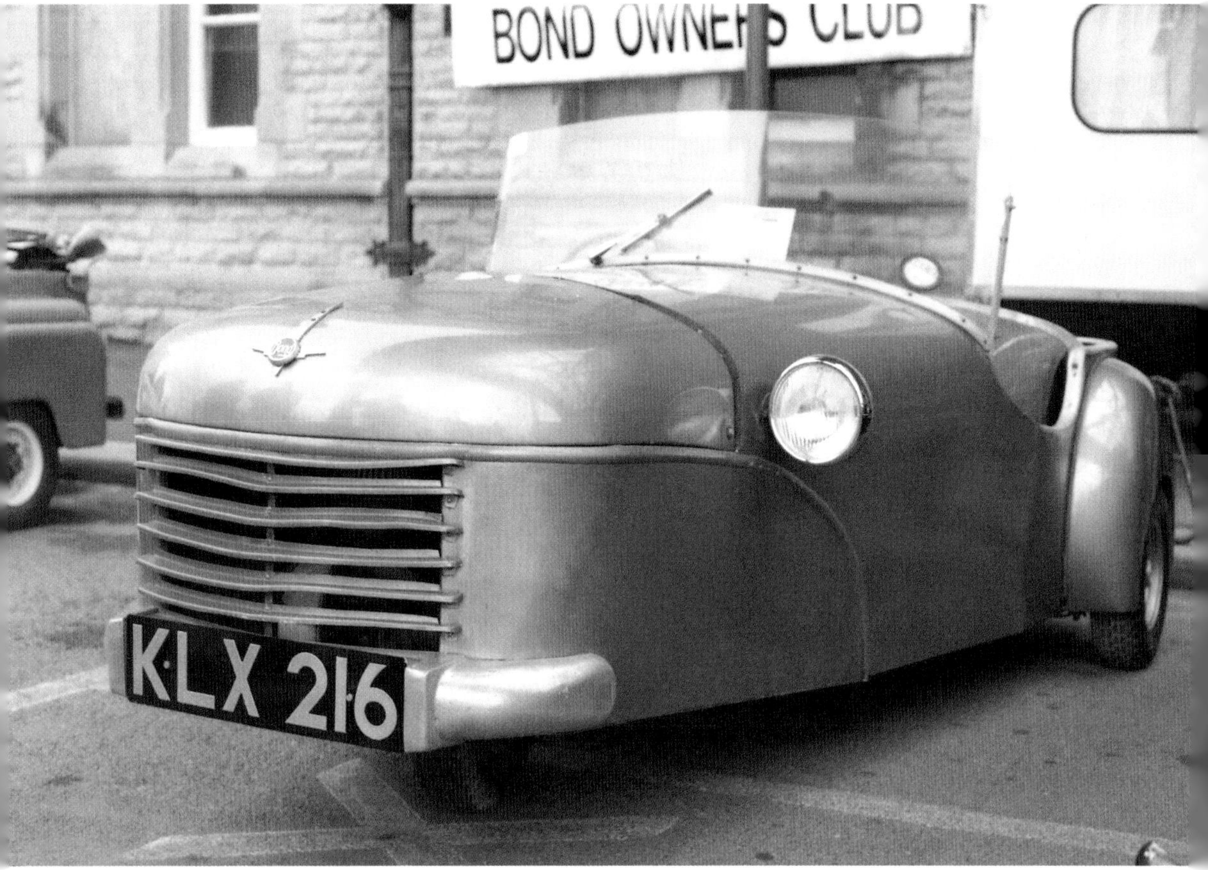
BOND OWNERS CLUB
KLX 216

Believed to be the earliest known surviving Bond Minicar, built in May 1949 and within the first fifty built according to the official production figures. This car is in unrestored original condition, with less than 5,000 miles recorded.

to maintain front suspension - many early cars were converted to this system. Rear suspension was succinctly summed up in the owners' handbook as 'Nil', although some cushioning effect was provided by the 16.00 x 4.00 low-pressure tyres. All three wheels were the same size and featured split steel rims bolted directly to the hubs, using six nuts, and with an additional steel stiffening rim on the front driving wheel. In use these wheels soon proved somewhat fragile as well as requiring the tyre to be completely deflated before removal. Most were replaced by the stronger wheels of the later models of Minicar when these became available. Brakes were provided on the rear wheels only, and were cable and rod operated, with internal expanding shoes operating on cast aluminium combined rear hubs/brake drums which incorporated a cast-iron liner.

One feature that the early Minicar shared with many of its cyclecar predecessors was the use of the 'cable and bobbin' method of steering, where a steel cable was wound around a central drum (bobbin) connected directly to the steering wheel, and with the outer ends of the cable in turn passing thorough pulleys and being connected to the steering arms on the front-wheel assembly. Surprisingly this set up proved quite effective when new and correctly set up, but required frequent maintenance to keep the cable tensioned, and soon wore out, or worse still failed altogether. This problem was quickly recognised and Sharp's Commercials set to work on solving the problem, coming up with a simple rack and pinion system which was substituted. They also realised that such developments in the design of the Minicar were of considerable interest to existing owners as well as potential ones, and that because of the nature of the vehicle (which had been designed with home maintenance in mind) it was well within the capacity of many owners to carry out modifications to existing vehicles themselves. Therefore they were not surprised when there was considerable demand for information regarding this conversion and, in response to the many enquiries received, the Company put together a complete home conversion kit with full instructions. This was a policy that would

NYA 538

Lancashire Museums Services' 1951 Mk A Minicar, converted to Triplex glass windscreen, and rack and pinion steering.

Shelf h

Under the bonnet view of Lancashire Museums Services' 1951 Mk A Minicar, which is fitted with the Villiers Mk 6E 197cc engine, as used on the Deluxe model.

Passenger compartment view of Lancashire Museums Services' 1951 Mk A Minicar, showing the basic controls, including gear selector above the steering wheel, engine starting lever mounted centrally on the floor, and the 'umbrella stick'-type handbrake tucked away to the right of the driver's legs.

be continued with later developments to the Minicar and it enabled owners to update their vehicles at least to a limited degree, but it was a trend that few other vehicle manufacturers were likely to emulate.

The electrical system of the Mk A Minicar was provided for by the Villiers flywheel combined magneto generator, with a selenium-type rectifier to convert the AC current into six-volt DC current. The combined front side/head lamps were mounted on either side of the rounded front grille and set back behind the small bonnet opening with 12/3 watt double-filament bulbs. Rear lighting was provided by a tiny single centrally-mounted lamp with a 3/3 watt double-filament bulb so that it remained lit whether the side lamp or separate headlamp circuits were in operation. The controls and instruments of the Minicar featured a fairly conventional car-style layout, but were somewhat basic. The floor-mounted clutch, footbrake and accelerator pedals were arranged from left to right, with an additional decompressor pedal mounted centrally on the bulkhead. A pistol-grip-type handbrake lever was supplied and was situated on the extreme right, just below the dashboard, and the gear-change lever protruded through a bracket immediately above the steering wheel and incorporated an indicator to show which gear was selected. The ignition was operated by a simple dash-mounted toggle switch and starting was achieved with a central floor-mounted starter handle which was connected to the engine unit's 'kick-start' lever by a strong steel cable, allowing the engine to be started from inside the vehicle. The only instrument provided was the small speedometer which incorporated a total mileage indicator, although the lack of a fuel gauge was partly compensated for by a reserve tap system on the two and a half gallon fuel tank, which could be operated from inside the car (as long as you had remembered to switch it back off after its last use!).

Almost as soon as the production version of the Minicar began appearing on the roads, the motoring press responded with a spate of articles about this revolutionary miniature runabout. Perhaps the most important of these appeared in March 1949 in *Motor Cycling*

Erla
præsenterer:
DEN POPULÆRE ENGELSKE
BOND MINICAR
CCK 919
Verdens billigste Vogn
35 km pr. Liter — 65 km i Timen
BOND »Minicar« med Forhjulstræk er konstrueret og udviklet af en af Englands førende Aeroingeniører og Teknikere, Mr. Lawrence Bond.
Resultatet af hans Indsats er blevet et Køretøj, hvori Minimums Vægt er forbundet med Maximums Styrke for derigennem at sikre den største Ydeevne af en lille Motor samt et minimalt Benzinforbrug.
Den første virkelige „Folkevogn"
LIGESAA BILLIG I ANSKAFFELSE OG DRIFT SOM EN MOTORCYKLE

In Denmark Erla Auto Import were appointed as agents for the Minicar. They offered it at 3,685 Krone, describing it as the 'World's Cheapest Car', designed and developed by one of England's foremost aero-engineers.

when their well-known tester and assistant editor, C.P. Read, accepted the invitation of Colonel Gray to visit the Bond production line and to put the Minicar through its paces. This testing involved trying out two vehicles. The first was a works 'hack' which had already covered 15,000 miles and this was used for a 66-mile round trip from Preston to Bolton and back, over some fairly testing terrain including moorland roads and cobbled streets. Apparently even the representatives of Sharp's were surprised at the duration of this initial test as it was Mr Read's first drive in a Bond Minicar! On returning this vehicle to the factory, C.P. Read found Lawrie Bond awaiting him with their transport back to London - a brand-new Minicar straight from the production line. The only modification made to this vehicle was the fitting of an already 'run-in' cylinder barrel and piston for what was to be a 228-mile journey that was to provide independently-proven figures which were widely used by the motoring press at the time. Coming as they did from such a well-respected source, these figures undoubtedly did much to enhance the reputation of the Minicar. The final results from this road test were: 228 miles covered at an average speed of 22.8mph and an overall fuel consumption of 97mpg, with the car carrying two eleven-stone adults and over seven stone of luggage. Cruising speed was recorded as around 30mph. The financial statistics given also make interesting reading - with the total cost for fuel at 7s.6d as opposed to £4.5s.6d for the same journey by train, third class for two people. The 1949 price of the Minicar was £198.16s.1d including purchase tax.

This publicity run to London also attracted the attention of Pathé News, which resulted in Lawrie and the Minicar appearing in one of their Newsreels, the vehicle being heralded as Britain's cheapest car at under £200. The piece somewhat surprisingly included the bold statement that the maker had '4,000 export orders already lined up'. Although the Minicar was largely unaffected by the restrictions that forced other vehicle manufacturers to reserve most of their production for export, it seems that Sharp's still had export aspirations for the Minicar from an early stage. In Denmark they appointed Erla Auto Import as agents for the Minicar, who offered it at 3,685 Krone. They even recruited an agent in the United States: Constance I. Rushton, located on Fifth Avenue, New York, who offered a 197cc model with an unusual split-glass windscreen for $850 dollars, delivered to New York with all duties paid within four to six weeks of order! However, the American agent did appear somewhat less ambitious in his recommendations for uses for the Minicar, stating it was most suitable for short-distance use and non-road uses, such as a golf cart, camp runabout, holiday resort transport and country estate use. An important feature of the way in which Sharp's Commercials went about the business of producing and marketing the Minicar, which was undoubtedly significant in its success, was that they were always prepared to listen to their customers and respond to criticism. This can be seen in the constant development and upgrading of the various models of Minicar throughout its production life. At the outset the design work for such improvements was done on a fairly informal basis by a small group of Sharp's employees who also worked on the production line. These included Roy Atkinson, who was responsible for many of the mechanical modifications - including those made to the steering and rear suspension of later models of Minicar; also Fred Atkinson (no relation), who had originally worked for Lawrie Bond at Longridge and was a skilled sheet-metal worker. His work included restyling the bodywork of the later models and eventually redesigning the bodyshell altogether. Some design work was also carried out by individuals outside of the Company such as Lawrie Bond himself, who remained a design consultant, and helped with some work on the development of the Mk A and also the transition to the Mk B Minicar. Another well-known figure who became involved with some design work was Granville Bradshaw, a designer of some considerable reputation, though not always a commercial success, whose work included the design of the ABC flat-twin motorcycle engine and the Bradshaw oil-cooled engines, as well as work on Panther motorcycles in the 1920s. Coincidentally Bradshaw oil-cooled engines were used in the Preston-built Matador and Toreador motorcycles built by Bert Houlding between 1922 and 1927. One of these motorcycles was restored at Sharp's and was retained by Colonel Gray. Granville Bradshaw became involved with Sharp's Commercials as he was related to Sharp's Ewart Bradshaw, Chairman of Loxhams Garages, and he occasionally did work for the Firm, including the design of the rear suspension for the Mk B Minicar. He also carried out other work at Sharp's premises such as the design and building of a prototype single-seater motorcycle-engined vehicle nicknamed the 'Bug', intended as a cheap form of transport for getting around on large airfields. Also, while he was at Sharp's, Granville Bradshaw was working on his final and perhaps most intriguing design, the Omega rotary engine. This was a toroidal internal combustion engine incorporating an annular cylinder and four double-ended pistons that reciprocated in pairs, while the cylinder rotated around them, carrying around the spark plug and inlet/exhaust ports - though apparently it was hard to see how this could work at all. But despite difficulties in machining the components to Granville Bradshaw's specifications, and problems with sealing the two halves of the annular cylinder, a prototype engine was actually completed at the factory in 1955 and in fact ran for several minutes. Bradshaw believed his new engine would eliminate the friction normally caused by the crankshaft and be perfectly balanced, thereby being vibration free, with a claimed output of up to 380bhp at 6,000rpm for a 1,250cc engine! However, it was incredibly difficult and expensive to build, and during later testing it not only failed to live up to its claimed performance figures, but actually disintegrated catastrophically!

CONTRACT
BLACKPOOL
SCOUT
PRIVATE

Workers at Sharp's Commercials were proud of their new product and a sense of community quickly built up. By 1951 things were obviously going well enough that the management organised this day trip to Blackpool for the workers – a common treat for workers in northern factories at the time. The location is believed to be Gosford Street off Ribbleton Lane, Preston, in front of the Minicar Factory, with the row of houses being initially used as offices by Sharp's, but later demolished. The Bond Minicar shown is a Mk A featuring a non-standard chromed rear bumper, with externally-mounted spare wheel and a fuel can. Seated in it are Charlie Hollins (*passenger seat*) who ran the Spares /Stores Department, and Fred Atkinson (driver) who was in charge of the Body Shop. (Photo: collection of the late Ronald Richardson.)

Overall, most of the design work for the development of the Minicar was done 'in-house', and there was a policy of constant discussion and improvement. This was soon demonstrated by the introduction of a new model, the Deluxe, in 1950. Because more and more owners were using their Minicars for considerably more than local travelling, this model featured a larger 197cc Villiers Mk 6E engine. The Deluxe model was priced at £262.13s.11d and also featured an electric windscreen wiper as well as the improvements already made to the standard Mk A, namely the aforementioned rack and pinion steering and hydraulic front shock-absorber. Although production by now had reached around forty vehicles per week, the demand was such that delivery time was quoted at five to six months and Sharp's planned to increase production as soon as possible to alleviate this delay. However, the use of an electric windscreen wiper brought about an unforeseen problem, which was noted in a road test conducted by *Autosport* that year, when the Perspex windscreen became gradually more and more opaque. This in turn gave rise to another significant improvement, as the problem was soon solved by fitting a curved 'Triplex' safety-glass windscreen with improved cast aluminium windscreen pillars to take the extra weight. As with the rack-and-pinion steering conversion, these improvements were also soon available from the factory in the form of kits enabling existing owners to upgrade their vehicles.

Also around this time the Company marketed the first of what was to become an extensive range of custom-made accessories for the Minicar. This was in the form of an interesting device that was designed to enable the driver to reverse his Minicar into a parking space without having to leave the driving seat. The usual procedure involved the driver having to get out and manhandle the vehicle into position. The new device simply comprised an extended ratchet spanner handle, the socket end of which fitted onto a square boss on the driver's side rear wheel, allowing it to be turned about a third of a revolution at a time, thereby propelling the Minicar backwards by hand! Apparently this simple and unlikely device actually worked quite effectively, and was a practical solution to the problem of having no reverse gear, being especially useful in wet weather!

The 'New' Mk B Minicar

The Bond Minicar had caused a sensation at the Motorcycle Show when it first appeared in October 1949 because it was the first such vehicle to go into production and the only three-wheeler at the Show. Again in 1951 the Bond still had the market largely to itself, and considerable interest was aroused with Sharp's new Mk B Minicar when it was first launched on 1 July that year. The Mk B now superseded both previous models, which between them had reached a production total of almost 2,000 vehicles. This new Minicar naturally incorporated all the improvements made as standard during the production of its predecessors, but perhaps the most important feature of the Mk B was the adoption of rudimentary rear suspension. The design of this had been mainly the work of Granville Bradshaw and consisted of a cast light-alloy casing bolted to each side of the body; this contained two pillars on which was mounted a sliding block that carried the stub axle. The movement of this block was controlled by a coil spring that took the load of the vehicle, and two smaller coil springs to damp the rebound. The rear units were also provided with a screw adjustment for the main spring to accommodate varying loads. This system gave the Minicar a basic form of all-round independent suspension.

The Mk B was very similar in appearance to the earlier model. The only real change to the bodyshell was a re-profiled rear section that gave additional luggage space. Power was provided by the 197cc Villiers Mk 6E engine which had been used on the Deluxe version of the Mk A, now fitted with an improved automatic decompressor valve in the cylinder head to aid starting. This engine produced 8.4bhp at 4,000rpm, giving a cruising speed of around 40mph and a top speed of 50mph, with fuel consumption recorded during a road test by *Light Car and Car* of 76.8mpg. This was slightly less than the manufacturer's claim of

DRN 919

Preliminary leaflet giving abridged specification of

The Bond Minicar

(MARK B)

The following improvements have been incorporated in this model to be delivered after July 1st. 1951.

(1) **REAR SPRINGING.**
This is of coil spring design and, in conjunction with a hydraulic shock absorber around which is fitted a new type suspension spring on the front suspension unit, gives independent springing on all wheels, so ensuring a comfortable and untiring ride.

(2) **EASY STARTING.**
A newly designed automatic decompressor (Prov. Pat. No. 12007), making starting very easy for lady drivers.

(3) **BETTER VISIBILITY.**
Carefully designed and strengthened windscreen brackets into which a TRIPLEX curved glass windscreen is mounted on rubber, greatly enhancing the appearance of the car and giving better visibility in all weather.

(4) **IMPROVED BODY DESIGN.**
Alterations to the rear luggage boot which not only improves the appearance of the car but offers sufficient room for an extra seat for a child or additional luggage space.

(5) **ALL WEATHER PROTECTION.**
A re-designed hood which fits snugly on top of the windscreen on a sorbo rubber pad, and sidescreens which fasten on the inside of the windscreen pillars, making the car waterproof.

Sole Manufacturers

Sharps Commercials Ltd.

Ribbleton Lane Preston

Telephone 1002.3.4

Telegrams Autosharp Preston

Advanced notice from the factory of the specification for the new Mk B Bond Minicar.

85-90mpg, although the test route did include a section through heavy traffic and it was driven flat out. Other features included the Triplex safety-glass windscreen as standard, but now rubber mounted in an improved rigid frame, and an improved redesigned hood that gave extra headroom and better weather protection. Also incorporated were improved all-cast-iron brake drums and redesigned split-rim wheels

MYL 461

A

1951 Mk B Bond Minicar in the yard of Towneley Works at Longridge during filming for the BBC *Inside Out North West* programme, who produced a short documentary on Bond Cars in 2009. Left to right: Clive Steggel, Andrea Steggel, Nick Steggel and the author. (*Photo: C. & A. Steggel.*)

that could now be removed in one piece without the need to deflate the tyres first. The Mk B was still offered in only one body configuration, as with the earlier Mk A models, ie a 2/3-seater open tourer, now weighing in at a slightly heavier 420lb and at an ex-works price of £215 plus £120.18s.10d purchase tax (£335.18s.10d in total).

The motoring press were eager to test the new model of Minicar to compare it with the previous one. Generally the new model received a warm reception, and favourable comments were made regarding the increased power available and the improved ride from the new rear suspension. As before, one of the most enthusiastic reports came from *Motor Cycling*'s tester, C.P. Read, although he did have reservations about the omission of front-wheel braking. He had felt that this feature would have been advantageous on the previous model and now felt that it was absolutely essential considering the increased power available, together with the improved luggage-carrying capacity of the Minicar.

The Minicar Goes Forth

Soon after the Minicar's introduction in 1949 many owners had realised the little vehicle's potential as a means of making their extra holiday petrol rations go further and had begun to make longer trips in their vehicles for this purpose, especially as for such leisure driving, a high top speed was no longer of prime importance. Although by May 1950 this consideration was no longer as paramount because petrol rationing finally ceased, economy was still uppermost in many drivers' thoughts, as fuel prices remained high. The option of Continental touring on the other hand remained severely limited because of restrictions on the amount of currency, no more than £25 per person, that could be taken out of the country. This factor, together with the high price of petrol on the Continent, made the little Minicar seem the ideal transport for such a holiday. A number of enthusiastic and adventurous owners were soon crossing the Channel and subjecting their vehicles to road conditions and distances never envisaged by the builders of the Bond Minicar. It is now a matter of record that the Minicar stood up to this treatment remarkably well and the experiences of many such expeditions abroad were recorded in the motoring journals of the time. Perhaps the best known of these appeared in *Motor Cycling* in June 1950 and related the experiences of, again, C.P. Read, who together with his wife and a 'lavish' amount of luggage and spare parts, travelled to Geneva and back in a Mk A Deluxe Bond Minicar. The vehicle, powered by the 197cc Villiers engine, was provided by Sharp's Commercials for the trip and was completely unmodified. The spare parts were Mr Read's idea and so were also provided by the Company, although they were confident that no parts would be needed. Sharp's were subsequently proved right as none were needed throughout the 1,581 miles covered. The vehicle, loaded with 80lb of luggage and spares, made the first part of the journey via a Silver City Airways Bristol Freighter from Lympne Airport in Kent to Le Touquet. The outward journey was made via Paris and despite experiencing the notorious 'pavé' road surfaces, good time was made and an 'honest' 45mph cruising speed was maintained. Following an enthusiastic reception in both Paris and Geneva by representatives of the appropriate country's motoring journals, the return trip was made via Reims. Along the way Mr Read was surprised to meet a fellow Bond Minicar driver at Abbeville and after the two owners had swopped experiences the other Minicar continued southwards. Apart from a minor accident in Paris (which obviously reinforced Mr Read's view that a front brake was needed), the journey was without incident or mechanical breakdown. In later years Colonel Gray often light-heartedly blamed C.P. Read for inciting the many other Minicar owners who subsequently subjected their vehicles to progressively longer and more challenging trips on the Continent

LEEDS
BOND
MINICAR
OWNERS
CLUB

- accounts of which became almost regular features in the various motoring and motorcycling journals.

Perhaps the most ambitious of these early expeditions was reported in *Motor Cycling* in November 1952. This described the adventures of a Mr Tipper, who had covered some 9,200 miles that summer in a 197cc Mk B Bond Minicar. This mammoth Continental tour took in some nine countries from Spain in the south to Sweden in the north, and again the simplicity of the Bond resulted in surprisingly few mechanical mishaps. Along the way many international motor racing meetings were attended and the Minicar was reported as attracting large crowds wherever it went. The final cost in petrol for the whole journey was only £33. Fuel consumption averaged between 68-72mpg and the only parts changed were the front stub axle, wheel bearings and a new driving chain. Clearly the Minicar was rapidly gaining an enthusiastic following and this may be illustrated by the announcement in September 1951 that the Bond Minicar Owners' Club now had north-western, midland and southern area regional secretaries, making this Club one of the earliest national one-make owners' clubs - and it's still going strong today!

Ultra-Light Commercial Travelling

Towards the end of 1951 Sharp's announced an additional version of the Minicar at the Earls Court Motorcycle Show in November. This took the form of a single-seater light-utility vehicle known as the Sharp's Commercial 3cwt - its name reflecting the load-carrying capacity of the vehicle, which was powered by a 250cc single-cylinder Indian Brave motorcycle engine, manufactured by the Brockhouse Engineering Company at nearby Southport, Lancashire. The design for this vehicle was largely the work of Granville Bradshaw, and it featured a strengthened bodyshell which closely resembled that of the Minicar, but with a squared-off front end and headlamps mounted further forward. The single driver's seat was centrally mounted, as was the steering wheel, and the driver entered via deep square cut-outs in the body sides. All three wheels were provided with 5-inch brake drums and a new 'worm-and-wheel' type steering mechanism was used, giving 180 degrees lock-to-lock and exceptional manoeuvrability. The load area behind the driver's seat was fitted with a wooden-slatted floor and the vehicle was claimed to be capable of cruising at 40-50mph with a full load, yet still return 70-80mpg. Classed as a commercial vehicle, the Sharp's Commercial 3-cwt attracted a lower rate of purchase tax than other models of the Minicar. It was offered at £255.13s.14d in standard

Sales literature for the odd-looking Sharp's Commercial 3cwt. Note the central driving position and no mention of the Bond brand for this ultimately abandoned project.

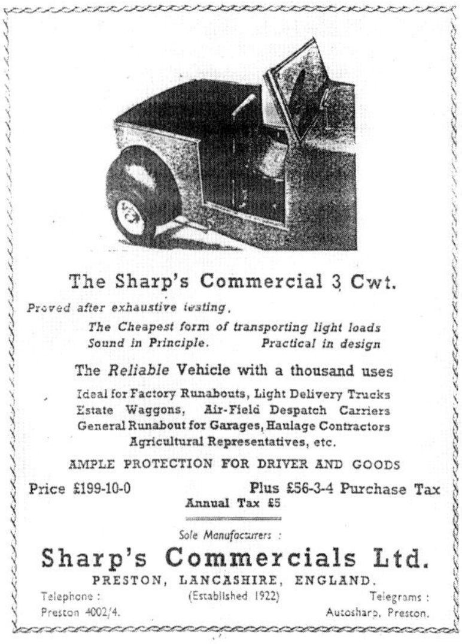
The Sharp's Commercial 3 Cwt.
Proved after exhaustive testing.
The Cheapest form of transporting light loads
Sound in Principle. Practical in design
The Reliable Vehicle with a thousand uses
Ideal for Factory Runabouts, Light Delivery Trucks
Estate Waggons, Air-Field Despatch Carriers
General Runabout for Garages, Haulage Contractors
Agricultural Representatives, etc.
AMPLE PROTECTION FOR DRIVER AND GOODS
Price £199-10-0 Plus £56-3-4 Purchase Tax
Annual Tax £5
Sole Manufacturers :
Sharp's Commercials Ltd.
PRESTON, LANCASHIRE, ENGLAND.
Telephone : Preston 4002/4.
(Established 1922)
Telegrams : Autosharp, Preston.

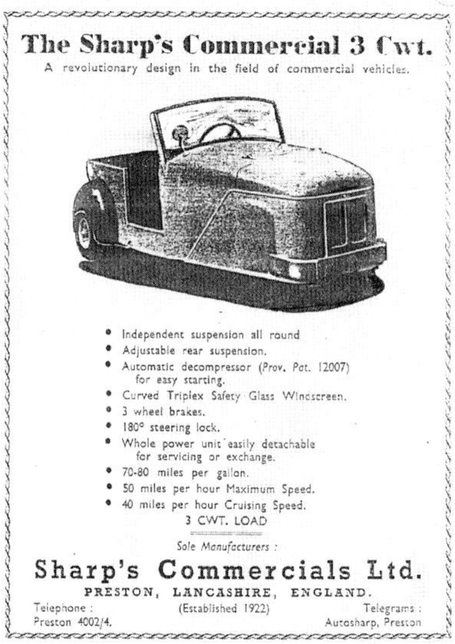
The Sharp's Commercial 3 Cwt.
A revolutionary design in the field of commercial vehicles.
• Independent suspension all round
• Adjustable rear suspension.
• Automatic decompressor (Prov. Pat. 12007) for easy starting.
• Curved Triplex Safety Glass Windscreen.
• 3 wheel brakes.
• 180° steering lock.
• Whole power unit easily detachable for servicing or exchange.
• 70-80 miles per gallon.
• 50 miles per hour Maximum Speed.
• 40 miles per hour Cruising Speed.
3 CWT. LOAD
Sole Manufacturers :
Sharp's Commercials Ltd.
PRESTON, LANCASHIRE, ENGLAND.
Telephone : Preston 4002/4.
(Established 1922)
Telegrams : Autosharp, Preston

Sharp's Motorised Unicycle was another unsuccessful attempt by the Company to capitalise on their products for an ultra-light commercial vehicle market that seemingly did not exist!

open form with a detachable hood, with a van body version due to follow shortly after production commenced. In spite of widespread publicity, the Sharp's Commercial 3-cwt never reached the production stage - just one prototype is believed to have been built and the project faded into obscurity following the show.

At around the same time Sharp's introduced an even more extraordinary vehicle in the form of their Motorised Unicycle. This was not strictly a 'vehicle', for it was a completely self-contained power-unit which was designed to be attached, using only four bolts, to any existing unpowered wheeled platform or body. The Unicycle comprised a 250cc single-cylinder Indian Brave motorcycle engine mounted on a Minicar-style tubular steel fork, attached to an alloy bulkhead which incorporated the 'worm and wheel' steering mechanism from the Commercial 3-cwt, and provided the means of attachment to the vehicle to be powered. Also incorporated were a fuel tank, flywheel magneto dynamo and rectifier, three-speed gearbox, coil spring suspension and brakes. Electric headlamps, horn, windscreen wipers and a six-volt battery were all offered as optional extras. The Motorised Unicycle was claimed to be ideal as a power unit for everything from a factory platform truck to an invalid carriage or rickshaw. Perhaps not surprisingly the idea failed

Sharp's Commercials Motorised "Unicycle"
(Prov. Patent 27629).

This immaculately-restored 1952 Mk B Minitruck ultra-light commercial vehicle is a rare survivor, Note the extended rear bodyshell and larger squared-off hood with roll-up rear flap for access. (*Photo: C. & A. Steggel.*)

to catch on. Production is believed not to have even reached double figures.

Sharp's ultra-light commercial vehicle concept did, in fact, reappear in June 1952, with the introduction of the Mk B Minitruck - exhibited at the Motorcycle Show later that year. On this occasion the vehicle was fitted with a more straightforward modified Mk B Minicar bodyshell, using the latter's rack-and-pinion steering, and Villiers 197cc engine. The Minitruck still featured a single driver's seat, this time more

The interior of the 1952 Mk B Minitruck. Note the single driver's seat and the extended load area where the passenger seat would normally be sited.

NYP 960

1952 Bond Mk B Family Safety Saloon in unrestored condition. One of only a handful believed to have been built, it is likely this vehicle was originally sold as a Minivan to avoid purchase tax, and converted later.

conveniently fitted to the right-hand side, with the luggage platform extending forward over the normal passenger seat location, and a specially-designed hood with a roll-up rear flap to facilitate loading. Also in June 1952 Sharp's introduced a further model of the Mk B, known as the Bond Minivan. This model was created by removing the rear panel of the existing bodyshell and replacing it with a vertical extended panel with a rear side-hinged door for access, which formed the rear of an aluminium-panelled 'box' built onto the rear of the Minicar. All-

The interior of the 1952 Mk B Family Safety Saloon is remarkably original, though it would still take a lot of work to restore to show standard, and some might see such work as ruining the integrity of such a rare survivor. Note the typical breakdown of the early plastic used to cover the steering wheel, which is a common problem on many cars of the period.

NYP 960

The aluminium rear Minivan bodyshell of the 1952 Mk B Family Safety Saloon is also remarkably intact, and whilst it is thought that the side windows are likely to be later additions, they do correspond to contemporary illustrations of the Family model.

weather protection was provided by a short hood that bridged the gap between this structure and the top of the windscreen frame. This odd-looking vehicle was soon followed by a similar machine named the Bond Family Safety Saloon. It shared the Minivan's rear bodyshell, this time with side windows fitted and two sideways-facing hammock-style seats in the rear to accommodate two children. The 'safety' part of the title was apparently derived from the fact that the rear access door could be opened only from the outside. This was to give the parents in the front passenger compartment the reassurance that small hands could not open this door and cause an unfortunate accident without their noticing. The Minitruck and Minivan were priced at £225 and £255 respectively plus purchase tax of £42.8s.4d. It is interesting to note that both vehicles attracted the same figure since the tax on commercial vehicles was based only on the chassis price. Sharp's clearly expected these ultra-lightweight commercial vehicles to prove popular with a whole range of customers, and they were vigorously advertised as suitable for butchers, bakers, farmers, veterinary surgeons and so on, under the bold slogan 'Can you afford to walk?' However, judging by the production figures for these models, low sales must have seriously undermined the Company's expectations. In total some 240 Mk B Minitrucks, 80 Minivans, and only a handful of Family Safety Saloons were built. The latter vehicle apparently proved unpopular because of its relatively high price when compared to the almost-identical Minivan - the only visible difference was the fitting of windows to the rear

1951 Mk A Bond Minicar De Luxe 2/3 seater Tourer, with 197cc engine fitted with early electric start conversion as outlined in the text. (*Photo: C. & A. Steggel.*)

'saloon' body and its small rear seats, but this was sufficient enough to make the model liable for the full rate of purchase tax.

As the Minicar gained popularity, a number of firms began to market 'bolt-on goodies' for owners to buy and an early example of this was an electric starter conversion offered by GBR Motors Ltd. This used a Ford Eight starter motor mounted behind the front steering fork, which was fitted with a sprocket and chain drive to a drum mounted on the engine's flywheel. The drum was driven via a flyweight device with friction linings on the weights that engaged on the inside of the drum by centrifugal force when the motor was operated. As the Minicar's battery was not up to the job of operating this system, it was replaced by a conventional car-type six-volt battery which had to be mounted in the luggage compartment. Although ingenious, this conversion obviously came with a considerable weight penalty of between 40-50lb. Before long Sharp's came up with their own somewhat similar solution to the problem, again using a small car-type starter motor mounted above the engine and operating via a V-belt onto the rim of the flywheel magneto, using the modified Bendix gear to engage the motor. Electric starting was apparently a major improvement over the old manual system which (even with the automatic decompressor) required considerable effort to operate. The Firm's own conversion kit was soon available and was considerably cheaper as well as lighter than the competition, although the Villiers flywheel magneto was not always up to the task of charging the small battery sufficiently to allow its use, especially following a night drive during which all the lights had been in use.

Competition in the Three-Wheeler Market

The 1951 Motorcycle Show had seen another important event that was eventually to have serious implications for Sharp's Commercials Limited: the Bond Minicar was no longer the only three-wheeler exhibited at the show. The new contender in the three-wheeler market

Bond
Minicar
"MARK C"
The worlds most economical car

Company sales brochure announcing the new Mk C Bond Minicar in late 1952 – initially offered as one basic model, a 2/3 seater Tourer in either Standard or Deluxe specification. The Mk C featured a reshaped body with more conventional-looking front wings with headlamps mounted in them, which also allowed room for the new worm-and-sector steering to turn the front-wheel drive unit through a full 180 degrees.

TIME IS MONEY—Can you afford to walk?
Going to work—taking children to school—long or short journeys, doctors, midwives, commercial travellers and tradesmen generally.
A BOND MINICAR gives the comfort and weather protection, speed and performance of a larger car.
Standard Model £269-8-4 Including P.T.
De Luxe Model £285-14-7 Including P.T. complete with self starter
Ample room for two adults and one junior.
Good luggage capacity.
MOTOR CAR COMFORT FOR 3 AT MOTOR CYCLING COST

Further promotional material for the new Mk C Minicar, emphasising the practicality of the vehicle as a realistic alternative to more conventional vehicles, whilst still extolling the economic advantages under the slogan 'Can you afford to walk?'

was an early prototype of what was to become the Regal saloon and had been built by Reliant, who, for some time, had been producing light three-wheel commercial vehicles, powered by their version of the Austin Seven's side-valve 747cc four-cylinder water-cooled engine. This new Reliant four-seat passenger vehicle was said to be due to go into production in 1952 and although it was considerably heavier than the Bond, it claimed a top speed of 65mph and fuel consumption at the rate of 50mpg. The vehicle was based on the Firm's existing light three-wheel van, with traditional bodywork of aluminium panels mounted on an ash frame and with a separate steel box-section chassis. The engine was set well back in the body for stability and projected quite obtrusively into the passenger compartment, with conventional drive to the rear wheels. But the new Reliant was overweight and the Company had a lot more work to do to get it within the Government's 8cwt weight taxation limit. Bond did not lose all the limelight at the 1951 show, however, for their stand featured a prototype with a new proposed 'streamlined' body style for the Minicar that attracted considerable attention and favourable comment from the motoring press. It was still built around Lawrie Bond's aluminium monocoque body tub, but featured a much more conventional car-like appearance with mock front wings that housed the headlamps, an elongated bonnet, front valance and bumper, and front 'radiator' grille.

The following year this prototype had developed into the new Mk C Minicar, announced in September 1952 with limited production commencing in October. At the 1952 Motorcycle Show there were now three manufacturers of three-wheelers exhibiting: Reliant had slimmed down their prototype from the previous year and now presented it as the Regal 4 Seater Coupé (eventually to become the Regal Mk 1), but still not quite ready for production, and the new two-seater AC Petite was announced. A brief comparison of the three vehicles shows that the Bond Minicar still held the price advantage and remained competitive overall.

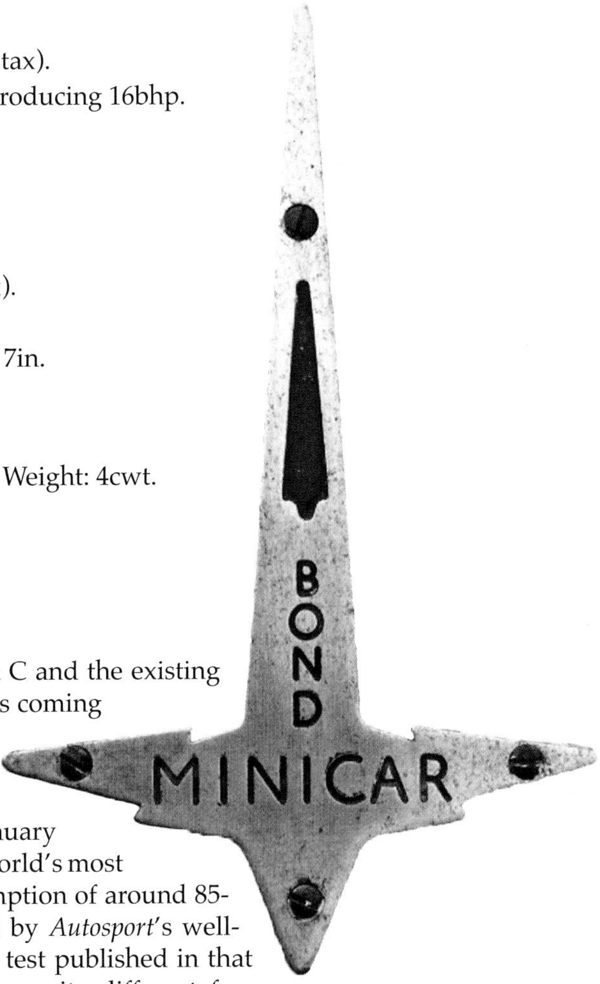
BOND
MINICAR

Reliant Regal

Price: £467.7s.10d (including purchase tax).
Engine: 747cc water-cooled, side-valve producing 16bhp.
Weight: 8cwt.
Length: 11ft 4in.
Width: 4ft 10in.

AC Petite

Price: £398.10s (including purchase tax).
Engine: 346cc Villiers producing 8.1bhp.
Weight: 7cwt. Length: 10ft 3in.Width: 4ft 7in.

Bond Mk C

Price: £355 (including purchase tax).
Engine: 197cc Villiers producing 8.4bhp. Weight: 4cwt.
Length: 9ft 3in.
Width: 5ft

The Minicar Grows Up

During late 1951 production of the new Mk C and the existing Mk B models had overlapped, the last Mk Bs coming off the production line in December (with just over 3,000 having been built), probably to satisfy the backlog of orders. Full-scale production of the new Minicar began in January 1952 and it was heralded by Sharp's as the 'world's most economical car', with a claimed fuel consumption of around 85-90mpg. These figures were soon confirmed by *Autosport*'s well-known vehicle tester John Bolster in a road test published in that journal. The appearance of the vehicle was quite different from the previous models and although, as stated, it inherited the original body tub designed by Lawrie Bond, a number of major improvements

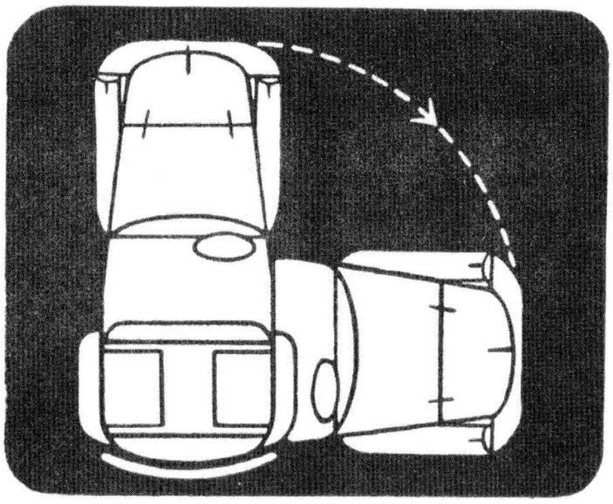

The BOND MINICAR is the only three-wheeler with front wheel drive and the ONLY CAR IN THE WORLD which can turn round in its own length.

made the Mk C an altogether different and more practical proposition. The most obvious difference at first sight was the frontal appearance - this now featured large conventional car-like dummy front wings which incorporated the headlamps. These were added not for purely decorative purposes, but to allow for sufficient room underneath for the front-wheel-drive unit to turn 180 degrees from lock to lock. This amazing steering ability was achieved through the use of a completely new type of steering mechanism using the worm-and-sector principle, which had been experimented with on Sharp's abandoned 3cwt ultra-light commercial vehicle project already mentioned. It gave the Mk C the ability to be literally turned round in its own diagonal length, a feature that was to become a trade mark of the Bond Minicars and is

A Bond Mk C Minicar demonstrating the advantages of the new steering system when parking.

often demonstrated to amazed onlookers at classic car rallies today! Sharp's also made much of this feature in their sales literature for the Minicar because it overcame, in their eyes, the need for a reverse gear that continued to be omitted mainly in order that the Minicar could continue to be driven on a motorcycle licence. A less visible, but major change was made to the basic bodyshell, with a completely new bulkhead assembly comprising a full-width aluminium casting in place of the old braced aluminium sheet. This considerably strengthened the basic structure of the vehicle and provided a more durable support for the newly-redesigned front suspension. Other features of the new body design included the inclusion of a small opening passenger side door (as also fitted to a few of the last Mk Bs) and the use of glassfibre for the first time for the rear wings. These rear wings also incorporated the new separate twin rear lights that were now required by law.

The early models of the Mk C used the same 197cc Villiers Mk 6E engine from the previous model, but this was now mounted on a completely redesigned tubular-steel front steering fork, carried on the steering-head bracket which in turn was bolted to the new strengthened bulkhead. Front-wheel braking was finally provided as advocated by C.P. Read - and even Sharp's admitted that previous experience had proved this necessary. The engine was also now provided with a rubber insulated torque stay to prevent vibration reaching the occupants. The front wheel was carried on a trailing arm that pivoted in line with the drive sprocket, in order that the correct chain tension was maintained. The troublesome rear suspension of the earlier Minicar, which had required frequent maintenance, had also been replaced by a completely redesigned system. This employed independent trailing arms carried on 6-inch spindles that were bonded into cylindrical rubber 'Flexitor' units. These rubber units were in turn bonded into steel housings which were then bolted to each side of the rear cross-bracing member under the rear of the car body. The main advantage of these Flexitor units - unique to the Minicar at that time - was that they required no maintenance or lubrication.

Expanding the Range

During the production of the Mk C Minicar, a number of different models were developed and offered as options in order to cater for the needs of a wide range of potential users. To begin with only three models were available: a three-seat standard model at £269.8s.4d (including purchase tax), a Deluxe model with electric starter, and front and rear chrome bumpers at £285.14s.7d (including purchase tax), and finally the Mk C Minitruck, a light commercial version of the current Minicar with a single seat and a hood that featured a roll-up flap at the rear to facilitate loading. As with the previous Minitruck models, this was intended to provide an economical alternative for businesses

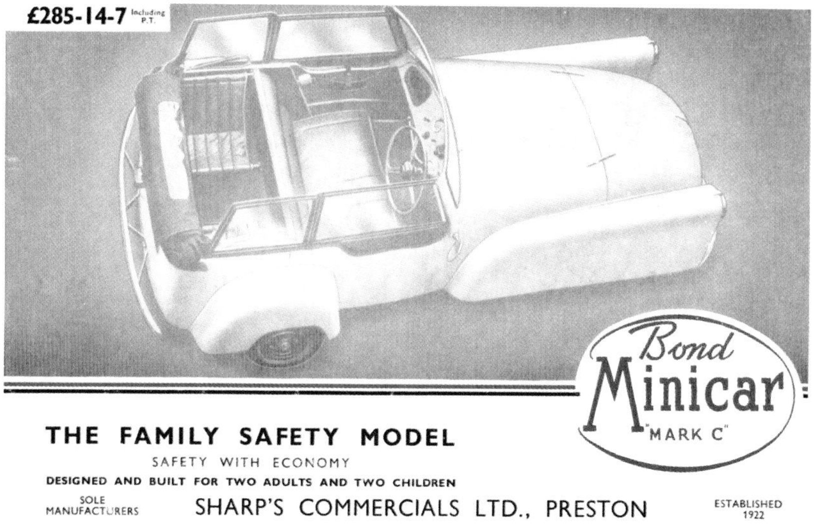
£285-14-7 Including P.T.
Bond
Minicar
"MARK C"
THE FAMILY SAFETY MODEL
SAFETY WITH ECONOMY
DESIGNED AND BUILT FOR TWO ADULTS AND TWO CHILDREN
SOLE MANUFACTURERS
SHARP'S COMMERCIALS LTD., PRESTON
ESTABLISHED 1922

Company sales leaflet announcing the new Family Safety Model and clearly showing the arrangement of the two sideways facing 'hammock type' rear seats for children.

that required frequent local transportation for light deliveries and was priced at £274.12s.6d (including purchase tax). Because Sharp's believed that many customers for the Minicar were former motorcyclists who now had families to transport, they decided to produce a new family model based on the Mk C. This featured the same extended rear-body section as the Minitruck which was fitted with two sideways-facing hammock-type seats suitable for two young children. The new Family Safety Model also incorporated the Minitruck's extended hood, modified to give sufficient rear headroom and with the roll-up flap now giving access to the rear seats. Though now the Company's advertising carried no explanation as to exactly what feature the 'Safety' aspect referred to. As the Family model also used the same front-bench seat as fitted in the Standard and Deluxe models (which in those models it was claimed could accommodate three people), the new model was advertised as a five-seater! The Family model could be purchased in either Standard or Deluxe form at £284.10s.5d and £299.15s.0d respectively in 1953 with both prices inclusive of purchase tax. As with previous models, there was still a process of ongoing development and various minor modifications were made to the Mk C during production, including improvements to the front suspension and steering to reduce maintenance, and the use of later improved models of the 197cc Villiers Mk 8E engine. One problem, which had been experienced for some time, was that of providing sufficient power for the electrical system, and this was at least partly overcome in late 1953 with the fitting of a new high-output generator and magneto unit. This also included the fitting of a charge-rate control switch on the dashboard, with a high rate for night driving and a low rate for daytime to avoid overcharging (and therefore damaging) the battery. As with previous modifications, Sharp's capitalised on the market potential of this conversion by offering a kit to update existing owners' vehicles fitted with earlier Mk 8E and Mk 6E engines.

Selling the Minicar

Marketing the new Mk C Minicars became much more sophisticated, involving a widespread advertising campaign with professionally

Bond
Minicar
"MARK C"
MARK C
The worlds most economical car

Multiple page, full colour (*albeit using artist colour-tinted black and white photographs*), sales brochures were now the norm for marketing Bond Minicars, such as this example for the Mk C Family Safety Model.

CAR COMFORT FOR 5
at a total running cost of less than 1d. per mile
STANDARD FAMILY MODEL
£284 10s. 5d. complete
(inc. P.T.)
THE FAMILY SAFETY MODEL
Designed and Built for 2 adults and 3 children with full weather protection for all
DE LUXE FAMILY MODEL
£299 15s. complete
(inc. P.T.)
The service behind the now well established Bond Minicar ensures security
Distributors, Dealers and Service Agents throughout the British Isles
Manufactured by
SHARP'S COMMERCIALS LTD., (Est. 1922) PRESTON, LANCASHIRE

Illustration from the 1952 Mk C Family Safety Model Minicar sales brochure still emphasising the economy advantages of the Minicar, but the Company's claims for 'Car Comfort for 5' may have been stretching the truth just a little!

produced full-colour sales brochures replacing the old single-colour leaflet-style literature used previously. Sharp's still maintained export aspirations for the Minicar and 1953 saw the start of a marketing campaign in the United States, where the Mk C was sold as the Sharp's Bear Cub by the US distributors - Craven & Hedrick Inc., located on Fifth Avenue in New York. The Bear Cub was priced at $895 delivered to New York and this time was promoted as an economical alternative to more conventional cars, with its distinctive 'Continental' look and projected savings of some $500 a year in driving costs over a standard car. Copy for the US adverts was imaginative to say the least, with the Minicar described as 'nimble and quick' with the climbing ability of a 'goat', and went on to liken the car to a 'sports car', but only in so much as it had more luggage space and leg room apparently.

Meanwhile, back in the UK, Sharp's new marketing was a little more restrained, concentrating on the practicality of the Minicar as a realistic alternative to the more conventional small car, with the added advantages of its low initial purchase price and almost unbeatable running costs. The sales literature also included excerpts from the media that stressed the virtues of the Minicar as a practical and reliable form of transport that had by now proved itself to be much more than simply an amusing novelty. Much was also made of the various long-distance runs made by owners of Minicars, which continued to become more and more ambitious with each successive model. In fact, 1954 saw a much publicised unofficial 'entry' in the Monte Carlo Rally of a Bond Minicar which completed the same gruelling 2,000-mile rally course

SILVER CITY
AIR FERRY
GCK 83

Lieutenant Colonel M. Crosby and Captain T. Mills in their 1953 Mk C Tourer following their 'Monte Carlo Run' in 1954.

and then made the 1,000-mile trip home! This run was undertaken by two Regular Army officers, Lieutenant Colonel M. Crosby and Captain T. Mills, in a cream-coloured Mk C, and followed the exact route taken by the official competitors, with Glasgow as their starting point. The outgoing journey to Monte Carlo was completed in three and a half days and included arduous sections over the peaks of the Massif Central and the French Alps. Petrol consumption was recorded at 63mpg on the rally route and 75mpg on the more relaxed homeward journey, during which the 771 miles from Monte Carlo to Le Touquet Airport were covered in 34 hours (including stops), despite heavy snowfalls and freezing conditions.

Although it was often emphasised in such accounts that few, if any, repairs were required on such extended tours, it was also realised that most owners would prefer to be prepared for such an eventuality. Therefore in 1955 Sharp's followed the lead of many Sports and Grand Tourer car manufacturers, and offered a Continental Touring Kit for the more adventurous owners of the various models of Minicar. This could be borrowed from the factory in return for a non-returnable £1 service charge plus the cost of any spares used, providing that the kit was returned within two months. The complete kit was also available at £4.16s.4d and contained: a set of light bulbs, a set of clutch corks, a clutch cable, a starter cable, an accelerator cable, a drive chain, two hub bearings and fuses.

Another ambitious Continental trip in a Mk C Minicar that caught the imagination of many enthusiastic owners of these little vehicles took place as late as 1963. The car was a 1955 Mk C model, in which David Orchard and his fiancée made a 2,000-mile journey behind the 'Iron Curtain', visiting Hungary and Czechoslovakia, and taking in the cities of Ulm, Salzburg, Vienna, Budapest, Prague and Nuremberg. Clearly, considering the political climate of the time, this was a very unusual tour for any car to make and Sharp's were not slow to capitalise on the interest generated. On his return, Mr Orchard and his companion, by now his wife, were presented with a silver trophy by Tom Gratrix, who had now become the Managing Director of the recently re-named Bond Cars Limited. The vehicle used was slightly modified by fitment of various extras including a spot lamp, twin horns, windscreen washers and a chain oiler. Overall the journey was reported as being relatively trouble free, despite the age of the vehicle, and the only serious repair carried out was the replacement of the cylinder head gasket, which cured a recurrent starting problem. An average fuel consumption of 70mpg was apparently maintained despite the poor condition of many of the roads covered. Clearly it is not possible to include details of all such expeditions undertaken and those selected merely provide a flavour of the sense of adventure that many Minicar owners seemed to

NUTSHELL
FOLDING
CARAVAN
THE PINES
CAMPSITE
TENTS 1/6d
CARAVANS 3/-

1955 Mk C Bond Tourer in the Bubblecar Museum (*see appendices*) in a scene typical of Minicar ownership by the mid-1950s – set up for a holiday stay on a campsite having towed its own caravan! The caravan in question is the Nutshell manufactured by W.R. Stewart and Sons of Dundee, weighing under 2cwt and priced at £86.

WHAT STIRLING MOSS SAYS

"More people these days are turning to three-wheelers as an economical means of transport so I jumped at the opportunity to find out for myself exactly what made them so attractive to so many. My first surprise came immediately— what a lot of room there is for both driver and passenger, and there is room for a child in between them, though in the Family Model which I borrowed there are two seats at the rear which comfortably accommodate two children. Not a scrap of space has been wasted. The leather covered facia panel is neat and the controls are within easy reach.

I switched on, eased the starter knob, and the engine started at once. I then got surprise No. 2. It seemed incredible that the two-stroke engine was of only 197 c.c. The pulling power was very good and in London's congested streets its liveliness was handy in the extreme. Travelling between my Kensington flat and West End office took no longer than in the average sports model due to the three-wheeler's ability to weave its way through the queues of traffic. It was in doing this that I got the third surprise—I discovered the fantastic steering lock. The provision of a front wheel which turns through 180 degrees enables all manner of interesting and useful manoeuvres to be executed —most, if not all, outside the capabilities of other double tracked vehicles. In a town with limited parking space, to park a Minicar is bliss and, driven in the normal way, the car behaves perfectly. It is, of course inadvisable to use too much lock when travelling at a fast speed.

The Minicar cruises happily at around 40 m.p.h. and has a maximum in the region of 50 m.p.h. On average, it covers 70-80 miles to a gallon. In town, of course, due to excessive low gear work it uses a little more and conversely on a long run the figure increases to over 90 m.p.g. The wheels are independently sprung and provide a very smooth ride on all but the roughest of surfaces. This, in conjunction with the well padded bench seat, gives an excellent standard of comfort, way out of the Minicar's price range. The standard of weather protection too, is high, the Vynide hood and side screens effectively eliminate draughts, and all-too-common rivulets which penetrate the coverings of many open cars. When one considers the light weight of the Minicar the retarding effect of the brakes is very good indeed. Even when using heavy pedal pressure there is no deviation from a straight line.

One pleasing facet of motoring in a Bond Minicar is the courteous manner in which other drivers treated me—this compact three-wheeler seems to generate good feeling! Indeed, it is a very likeable little car."

Stirling Moss.

exhibit. By the late 1950s, the quarterly magazine of the Bond Minicar Owners' Club was publishing such accounts in almost every issue. In addition similar articles appeared in the motoring and motorcycling journals of the time almost as frequently.

Production of the Mk C continued until 1956, with around 6,700 having been built. This relatively long production run allowed Sharp's to continue to become more professional in their approach to marketing the Minicar, including further improvements to the sales literature which now included a personal testimonial from Stirling Moss describing his experiences driving a Family Model Minicar through

Mk D Minicar production gets underway at Ribbleton Lane circa 1956.

heavy London traffic! The Company also now produced an additional brochure advertising its own exchange service parts scheme and a full range of Minicar accessories which included tonneau covers, bolt-on chrome embellishments and a very useful glassfibre winter hard top priced at £25.

The Mk D Minicar

In May 1956 an improved version of the Minicar was announced which, although very similar in appearance to the earlier model, was considered different enough to be given the designation Mk D Bond Minicar. The initial success of this new model was almost guaranteed as a result of a turn in world events in 1956. The Suez Crisis of that year led to a steep rise in petrol prices and by December there was even the re-introduction of petrol rationing in Britain. Economy once again became the order of the day and although rationing was lifted by May 1957, prices remained high. At first sight there was very little to distinguish the new model from its predecessor, and the situation is further confused as there was again a slight overlap in production of the two models. The main differences were to the mechanical components, although a restyled front grille and larger glassfibre rear wings were used for the family model, providing some external identification cues.

The Mk D was powered by the newly-introduced 197cc Villiers Mk

749 AKO

Nicely-restored 1957 Mk D Tourer. Note the new shape radiator grille (*the sidelight/indictor clusters are non-original*).

9E engine, now rated at 8.4bhp at 4,000rpm, but the main improvement was a new four-plate clutch for easier and smoother gear changing. At first this engine retained the older unit's three-speed gearbox, but in 1957 this was replaced by a four-speed one. The standard model of Minicar now had 12-volt electrics, although it still used a Villiers flywheel unit, but the Deluxe model now featured a SIBA Dynastart unit. This at last gave the Minicar a reliable lighting system and practical lightweight push- button electric starting. The Dynastart unit was built onto the engine, driven directly from the crankshaft, and it combined a generator, starter, and ignition all in one with an automatic voltage-controlled DC output, which meant that a rectifier was no longer required. SIBA Dynastart units were available in two versions, designated Unidirectional and Reversing. The first of these allowed the engine to start in only one direction, (ie: the forward one), as the two-stroke engine could in fact run in either direction as some owners had discovered in the past (much to their surprise when setting off!). The Reversing Dynastart used this ability by allowing the direction in which the engine was started to be controlled, and therefore providing an effective reverse gear. The direction of starting was controlled by a dash-mounted switch operated by the driver, and it was possible to use all the gears in reverse - a feature that was no doubt tried out by

Interior view of the restored 1957 Mk D Tourer, with side-screens in place. Note the single door on the passenger side and basic control/instrumentation reminiscent of earlier models.

some intrepid owners. Other improvements on the Mk D included modifications to the transmission to make it harder wearing and to allow for easier chain adjustment. Also, the rear suspension was redesigned with improved larger Flexitor units and trailing arms, making it more robust and reliable.

The same basic range of models was offered for the new Mk D

VFD
455

The new Mk D Family Safety Model also differed in appearance from the previous Mk C Family model with larger glassfibre rear wings that accommodated the revised rear suspension, as on this 1958 vehicle. (*Photo: C. & A. Steggel.*)

London Press
Preview of the Mk D Family Safety Model in 1956, with TV actress Gay McGregor in the driving seat, though one has to wonder if she was in fact selected for the role due to her petite stature?

Minicar as for the previous Mk C, with the new 2/3-seater Standard model costing £278.13s.2d and the Deluxe version £304.7s.8d. The Family Safety Model was now more realistically advertised as a four-seater offering 'car comfort' for two adults and two children at £304.7s.8d and £320.4s.1d respectively. The Minitruck was apparently discontinued, as despite a prototype Mk D model being built, it never went into production. Although the introduction of the new glassfibre hardtop already mentioned effectively gave two further models to the range. These were the hardtop convertible Coupé at £293.1s.10d and a Deluxe version at £318.16s.10d. These prices were for 1957 and all inclusive of purchase tax.

The new 'Streamlined' Bond Minicar

Sharp's certainly seem to have perfected the design of the Minicar with the Mk D and it is probably hardly surprising that it should prove to be the most popular so far, so popular in fact, that it led to the postponement of a new model of Minicar designated the Mk E, which had been announced in December 1956 at the Motorcycle Show. But the Company knew it could not rest on its laurels and in order to stay competitive they continually needed to move forward with

JRN 263

Early Company publicity photo of the prototype Mk E Minicar. Note the longer wheelbase and narrow track, which were to lead to major handling problems.

the times. It was also becoming obvious that the original aluminium monocoque body tub designed by Lawrie Bond had reached the limit of what could be developed around it and, in order to move on, a new approach was going to be required. Although based on the proven mechanical components of the existing Mk D, the new Mk E was a complete departure from the previous Minicars in its appearance and

JRN 263

Rear view of the prototype Mk E Minicar shows neat new 'conventional car' styling, but unfortunately the effect on the car's handling hadn't been taken into account.

bodyshell design. Initially only a couple of prototypes were built for Sharp's stand at the Motorcycle Show in December 1956, but the demand for the existing Mk D range was such that the decision was taken to exploit this popularity and to defer the expense of tooling up for a completely new model. The handful of Mk E Minicars produced so far were therefore put into storage at the factory, with the exception of one, which became the everyday transport of Fred Atkinson, who had been largely responsible for the styling of the new bodyshell.

Eventually, instructions arrived from Colonel Gray that the Mk E was to go into production, to coincide with the 1957 Motorcycle Show in December of that year. One of the laid-up prototypes was now taken out of store for the customary road testing of new models, usually carried out in the Longsands area just outside Preston. According to John Woods, who was Works Manager at the time, this led to something of a shock, for the new vehicle handled terribly, especially when cornering hard where it went on to two wheels and threatened to overturn. Clearly something had to be done. After further testing it was realised that the car's basic geometry was to blame: the rear wheels were set too far back, thus altering the centre of gravity of the vehicle. Fortunately this proved fairly straightforward to rectify by shortening the wheelbase and increasing the rear track width slightly, and full production commenced in January 1958 after the existing vehicles had been rebuilt to the new specification.

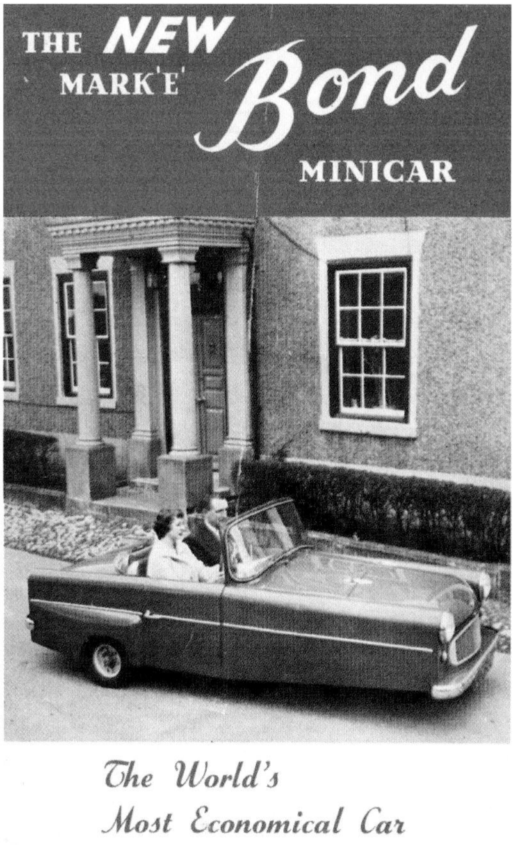
THE NEW MARK 'E' Bond MINICAR
The World's Most Economical Car

Sales brochure for the new Mk E Minicar from circa October 1957, when production finally commenced. Note the redesigned protruding rear wheel arches to allow for modifications to the vehicle's track.

The design of this new Bond Minicar abandoned the stressed skin monocoque construction principles of earlier models in favour of a new steel box-section chassis, which was riveted to the underside of the new aluminium panelled bodyshell. This provided sufficient strength and rigidity to allow the vehicle to incorporate full-size opening doors for easier access, as well as allowing the production of a much more streamlined and conventional-looking vehicle. However, there was a weight penalty to these construction techniques and the overall weight of the new Minicar was approximately 620lb. This was found to seriously affect the performance of the vehicle, which was still powered by the 197cc Villiers Mk 9E engine used on the Mk D Minicar, though now fitted with a four-speed gearbox. The Mk E Minicar was intended

the car you can afford—motor car comfort at motor cycle cost!
1957
The Bond Minicar Three-Seater Solves your Problem
The family man can now leave his motor cycle behind and travel in comfort and safety, wet or fine at motor cycle cost.
For long or short journeys, holidays, shopping or taking the children to school—the Bond Minicar is truly the people's car.

Centre-page illustration from the 1957 Mk E brochure still shows the prototype model with its narrower rear track width. Sharp's were still promoting the Minicar to former motorcycle riders now with a family to transport.

to complement the existing Mk D range which, because of continued demand, remained in production. Therefore the Mk E was available only as a three-seater convertible, priced at £399.10.6d and replacing its equivalent Mk D model, which was discontinued from February 1958. A glassfibre hardtop was also made available for the Mk E which could be fitted to provide a three-seater coupé, and the larger body meant that there now really was room for three on the split-bench front seat.

LCK 562

This 1956 Mk E Tourer is in fact one of the early prototype vehicles originally constructed in November 1956, but not finally approved as tested until January 1958! Like many of Sharp's pre-production, development and show vehicles, it later went on to be sold as just another production vehicle.

The new body design also provided ample luggage space with access gained via the forward-tipping hinged seat backs as no opening boot lid was provided. The SIBA Dynastart system was fitted as standard to the Mk E, though reverse was still optional, and this powered a much improved lighting system incorporating larger 7-inch headlamps with built in sidelights and allowing the use of higher wattage bulbs.

Always keen to exploit events that could help to promote the Minicar, the Company saw the opening of the Preston bypass, Britain's first motorway, on 5 December 1958 as an ideal opportunity for a publicity stunt. The opening ceremony was to be performed by Prime Minister Harold Macmillan, and knowing there would be considerable press and even television coverage, Sharp's arrived early to be at the front of the queue when traffic was allowed on to the new road. To ensure a Bond featured prominently, and as the bypass was only two lanes in each direction initially, they used two Mk E Minicars fitted with standard 197cc engines to slow the other traffic. A third Mk E, fitted with a new Villiers 31A 247cc engine that the Company was testing, would pull away and thus be the focus of attention. However, their scheme did not go according to plan, as either the film crew were not ready when the lone Minicar sped past or they were waiting for a fuller shot showing the rest of the traffic and that is what the public saw when the newsreel was shown. The opening of the new road was said to mark the beginning of a new era of motoring in Britain, but it was to be one without the Mk E Minicar as the short-lived model had already ceased production in November 1958 after some 1,180 had been built.

BOND

Bond Build Scooters

We take a break from the Minicar story at this point, as earlier in 1958, Sharp's Commercials had announced a completely new product to the motoring public in the form of the new Bond Scooter, unveiled on 15 January that year. At the Motorcycle Show later in 1958, the Bond Scooter was considered one of the Show's highlights, where the centrepiece of Sharp's stand was an impressive scooter in full Police livery complete with radio installation. Colonel Gray took a very keen interest in this project and preparations had been in progress for some time at Sharp's Commercials. There was a certain amount of sound business sense behind the new Bond Scooter, as Britain at this time was importing some 1,000 foreign machines every week, and even the so-called British scooters available were often little more than foreign designs built under licence. The theory behind the Bond Scooter was

Bright and upbeat sales literature for the launch of the new Bond Scooters.

THE NEW ALL BRITISH
Bond
SCOOTER
Model P1 - 150cc (3 Speed)
Model P2 - 197cc (4 Speed)

to create a 'superior' all-British rival to these foreign machines at a highly competitive price and secure a place in this extremely lucrative worldwide market. Col. Gray believed that the key to keeping his new machines competitive lay in efficient mass production to help keep costs to a minimum.

Sharp's invested heavily in the Bond Scooter, both initially in the design work (which involved analysing many of the imported scooters available on the market) and also in setting up sufficient production capacity to allow mass production to commence immediately on the model's announcement. In order to increase production capacity, Sharp's had recently purchased new premises on nearby New Hall Lane in Preston, in the form of a redundant cotton mill known as India Mill; this gave an additional 80,000 square feet of floor space. Much of the design work for the scooter was carried out here under the utmost secrecy and initial plans were drawn up for the new machines to be produced at the rate of one every eight minutes. With full production it was estimated a rate of one machine every four and a half minutes could be achieved, for it was believed that only with such volume production could Sharp's hope to capture any significant share of the market.

For some time Sharp's had been making limited use of glassfibre as the ideal lightweight material for some of the external panels on their Minicars, starting with rear wings and bonnets on some later Mk C vehicles. This developed into more complex mouldings such as hardtops for various models of Minicar and some experimentation with boatbuilding, covered elsewhere in this work. Now, with the acquisition of new premises and plans for mass production of their scooters, which would feature glassfibre to a greater extent, Sharp's looked to set up a new specialised, larger, scale workshop for this material at India

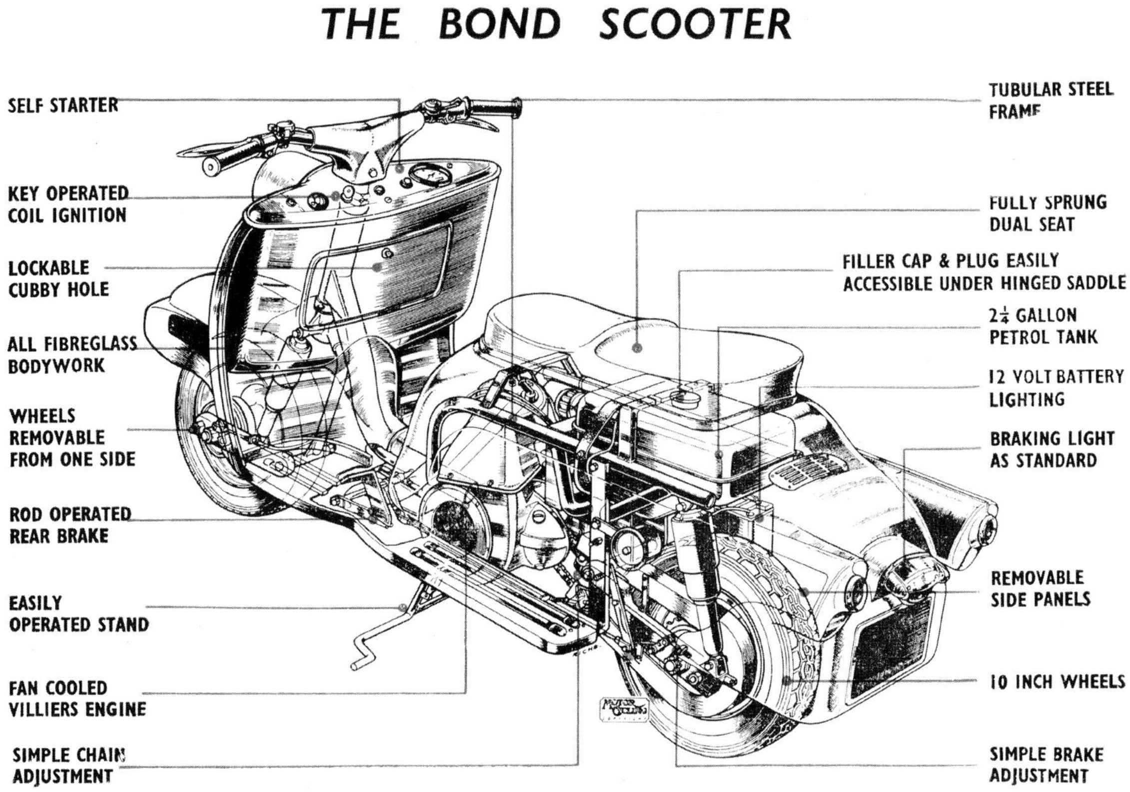
THE BOND SCOOTER
SELF STARTER
KEY OPERATED COIL IGNITION
LOCKABLE CUBBY HOLE
ALL FIBREGLASS BODYWORK
WHEELS REMOVABLE FROM ONE SIDE
ROD OPERATED REAR BRAKE
EASILY OPERATED STAND
FAN COOLED VILLIERS ENGINE
SIMPLE CHAIN ADJUSTMENT
TUBULAR STEEL FRAME
FULLY SPRUNG DUAL SEAT
FILLER CAP & PLUG EASILY ACCESSIBLE UNDER HINGED SADDLE
2¼ GALLON PETROL TANK
12 VOLT BATTERY LIGHTING
BRAKING LIGHT AS STANDARD
REMOVABLE SIDE PANELS
10 INCH WHEELS
SIMPLE BRAKE ADJUSTMENT

Cutaway drawing of the Bond P1/P2 Scooter used in the Company's sales literature to illustrate the main features of the new machines.

Mill. Already the management at Sharp's had found that their female employees seemed to be particularly proficient at working in this relatively new material and, unusually at that time for what was mainly an engineering company, they sought to recruit female employees to staff this new department. This policy certainly paid off and as the use of glassfibre in their products grew, the Company became particularly noted, for the quality and innovative use of the material, particularly in the later Bond 875 and Equipes.

The first Bond Scooter model was designated the P1, and was powered by a 148cc Villiers Mk 31C engine and a three-speed gearbox that gave 6.3bhp at 5,000rpm with a top speed of 50/55mph, and a claimed fuel consumption of 110mpg. An innovative feature of the Bond Scooter was the fan cooling of the engine, which was fully enclosed in a specially designed 'streamlined' glassfibre body. This method of construction was said to save around 40lb in weight over the pressed steel used by some of the machine's rivals. Engine access was achieved by removable body side panels, and the fuel tank was reached by lifting the dual seat. A small lockable luggage compartment was also provided, built into the front weathershield. The Bond Scooter featured a strong (and heavy) tubular steel frame with front suspension by a single pivoted

VXF 257

Circa 1958 P1 Scooter with side panels removed to show engine and rear wheel access. (*Photo: N. Kelly.*)

leading arm and the rear by a single trailing arm, both with coil springs and hydraulic shock absorbers. Wheels were 10in steel bolt-on Minicar-type items that could be removed without disturbing the drive chain or brakes. Push-button electric starting was provided as standard via a SIBA Dynastart unit that also provided power for the 12-volt electrical system. The P1 was fairly well received with favourable reports in many motorcycling journals, and was considered to be an advanced design for its time and competitively priced at £184.12s.6d including

THE
BOND
SCOOTER
models
P.3. 150 c.c. and
P.4. 197 c.c.

Colourful Company sales literature for the new 'improved' P3 and P4 model Bond Scooters, circa 1959.

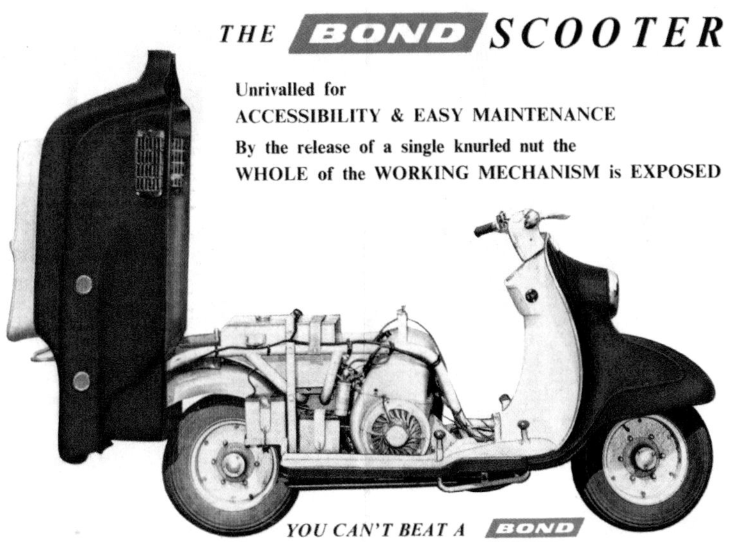
THE BOND SCOOTER
Unrivalled for
ACCESSIBILITY & EASY MAINTENANCE
By the release of a single knurled nut the
WHOLE of the WORKING MECHANISM is EXPOSED
YOU CAN'T BEAT A BOND

One of the main improvements on the new P3 and P4 model Bond Scooters was the redesign of the glassfibre bodyshell to allow easier access to the mechanical components for adjustment and maintenance.

purchase tax. However, all these features and the cumbersome frame and suspension added up to a hefty 262lb dry weight compared to only 165lb.for one of its main foreign competitors, the similarly engine sized 150cc Lambretta LD.

Before long the P1 was joined by the very similar looking P2, the difference being that the latter was powered by a 197cc Villiers Mk 9E engine with a four-speed gearbox and priced at £199.12s. Extras included a windscreen, luggage carrier, spare wheel and a tailored plastic protective cover to meet the needs of the garage-less owner. Both models continued in production until late in 1959 when they were superseded by the improved P3 and P4 models, respectively. The main changes were to the bodyshell for improved engine access, and to the frame for improved handling. The new bodyshell featured a restyled front apron with a fixed-front mudguard and a rear body section that pivoted from a point behind the rear wheel. The whole unit now lifted in one to give exceptional engine access. The two new scooters retained the same engines as their predecessors, but these were positioned some two inches lower in a redesigned frame intended to lower the centre of gravity and therefore improve handling. Production of the new models started early in 1960, and the P3 was priced at £178.10s.6d and the P4 at £193.0s.0d, both inclusive of purchase tax.

The Bond Scooters continued in production until 1962, but never achieved the anticipated popularity, and sales were always slow despite a vigorous advertising campaign and favourable reports in the motoring press. Bond Scooters even appeared in the 1958, 1959 and 1960 Isle of Man Scooter Rallies, and achieved limited success. In 1960 a 'Works Team' with riders supplied by Lancashire County Constabulary achieved particularly impressive results, including first place in the 24-

This 1961 Bond P3 148cc Scooter is certainly a striking machine, with its American-inspired fins and chrome trim.

hour endurance race, with only two marks lost for timekeeping, as well as several trophies. But the Bond Scooter was widely regarded as too heavy and too slow, and although it was not expensive in comparison with the competition, it was not cheap either. From the start profits had been cut to the minimum and when the anticipated volume of sales failed to materialise there was little scope for price-cutting tactics.

66
61
56
OCK 301

The official Bond Works Team for the 1960 Isle of Man Scooter Rallies, with riders from Lancashire County Constabulary.

Production problems further aggravated this situation and the project began a downward slide as attempts were made to cut production costs, which then resulted in a poorer-quality product. Eventually Sharp's abandoned the Bond Scooter altogether.

BOND

The new Mk F Minicar Range

In late 1958 it was decided that it was time to completely update and rationalise the Minicar range, with the ending of production of the final Mk D models and the Mk E. Three new models were announced at the London Motorcycle Show in November, all now based on the highly regarded modern appearance of the Mk E's larger bodyshell. Firstly, a three-seat Tourer - very similar to the previous Mk E - at £379.13s.9d. Secondly, a four-seat Family Saloon with a glassfibre roof and two small hammock-type seats in the rear, suitable for two children, at £389.14s.6d, and finally there was a three-seat Saloon Coupé, again

669 KKJ

A nicely-restored 1960 Mk F 2/3 seat Tourer – externally almost identical to the equivalent Mk E Minicar.

Interior of a 1959 Mk F Tourer. Note the split back rest of the seat, allowing access to the luggage compartment.

very similar to the previous Mk E model and also priced at £379.13s.9d. Surprisingly, also seen on the Company's show stand was a new Mk D model, the Family Four Saloon, priced at £339.10.6d (with all prices inclusive of purchase tax), which Sharp's claimed had been produced to meet popular demand and would continue to be offered as 'available', though no more are thought to have been built. As the main problem of the Mk E had already been recognised - that at 620lb with only a 197cc engine it was somewhat under-powered - it was already obvious that something needed to be done, and with the new Mk F Family model now even heavier at 672lb there was a definite need for more power. This was provided by fitting the range with the 246cc Villiers Mk 31A engine with its four-speed gearbox, giving the Mk F Minicars a respectable top speed of 55mph. All models were now fitted with the SIBA Dynastart unit as standard, with an optional reverse, depending on the type of unit fitted, at an extra £9.17.0d.

The new Mk F Minicar was an immediate success and production at Sharp's Commercials' Ribbleton Lane Works and India Mill Premises (where most of the glassfibre moulding was carried out), was up some 150 per cent. By April 1959 production had reached almost 100 Minicars a week and orders were said to be very good. There was, however, a minor setback that month with a strike by some 60 of the Firm's 200-strong workforce. This was in support of a sacked colleague

669 KKJ

Rear view of a 1960 Mk F Tourer. Note the lack of opening boot lid, meaning there was no external access to the luggage compartment.

who had allegedly taken leave without permission. The industrial action was short-lived because it coincided with the workers' payday, although the Sheet Metal Workers and Braziers Union were involved in the negotiations with the management.

The potential of the Minicar as offering a realistic economical alternative to more conventional vehicles had been a feature of Sharp's advertising literature for some time. This had mainly taken the form of reprints of independent road tests and accounts from owners who had taken their vehicles on ambitious extended Continental tours. However, 1959 saw a publicity stunt specifically arranged by Sharp's to promote the new improved range of Minicars, in the form of a timed endurance run from Land's End to John O'Groats. This was undertaken by Company employee Douglas Ferreira in his Mk F Family Saloon named *Boanerges IV*, which, apart from a thorough service in preparation for the run, was unmodified. The intention was to cover the 889 miles within 24 hours, including stops, which would require an average speed of 37mph. The run started at 14:00 hours on 19 March, which was timed to avoid rush-hour traffic in Bristol and to ensure that the busy Lancashire section of the route would be covered at night, when traffic was at its lightest. *Boanerges IV* reached Preston at 00:48 am on the 20th, 32 minutes behind time following delays caused by road works, sheep on the road and unpunctual cameramen. Following a quick check-up and refuelling at the Bond Works, more time was lost and Carlisle was reached 43 minutes behind schedule. Despite this, the remainder of the run saw lost time quickly caught up, with few incidents to impede progress and arrival at John O'Groats was at 13:40 pm - 23 hours and 40 minutes since leaving Land's End. Figures for the trial, published in *Motor Cycling* in April 1959, record an average speed of 36.89mph - 35.34mph up to Carlisle and 39.11mph from then on,

THE
BOND
MAGAZINE
Volume 6
September, 1960
No. 2
IT'S HERE!!
THE NEW
BOND RANGER
AT £295
FOR BOND MINICAR
AND SCOOTER OWNERS
PRICE
1/-
EVERY QUARTER

The launch of the Mk F Ranger Van in 1960, as announced in the Company's in-house magazine for Bond owners.

with fuel consumption at 60mpg overall. Doug Ferreira's time record remained intact, despite many attempts to better it, until August 1967 when it was beaten by 38 minutes by Brian Thomas and Doug Barnes from the Berkshire section of the Bond Minicar Owner's Club. Their vehicle was a 1956 model Mk D Minicar fitted with a 250cc engine and a special six-gallon fuel tank to minimise the number of stops required. This time the 889-mile journey was tackled in the opposite direction, starting at John O'Groats at 10:00 am on 16 August and arriving at Lands End at 09.02 am the following morning.

An additional model of the Mk F Minicar was announced in March 1960, when the Company decided to revisit their ultra-lightweight commercial vehicle offering and came up with the new Bond Ranger Van. This used the same basic body as the four-seat Family Saloon, but without the rear side windows. The Ranger Van was fitted with two front seats only, to allow maximum floor space for load carrying, and also featured an opening rear window section for loading and unloading. However, there was some sound business thinking behind this new model, as in fact its main advantage was that as a commercial vehicle it was no longer subject to purchase tax and it was offered at £295 in primer or £305 in colour finish. Sharp's also then marketed a conversion kit which included the rear side windows and rear seats necessary to convert the Ranger into a Family Saloon Model once the obligatory two years since purchase had elapsed. However, it seems that although this became a widely-adopted practice at the time for vans from many manufacturers, owners could technically find themselves liable for the purchase tax at a later date if a Customs and Excise inspector saw fit to check! Two variants of the commercial model of the Mk F were eventually offered - the Ranger (which had a front passenger seat fitted), and slightly later the Minivan (identical, but with no passenger seat fitted). The difference was apparently based on a point of law - the Minivan was able to be driven legally by an unaccompanied learner driver with a motorcycle licence, effectively allowing a sixteen-year-old to drive it. But, the concept of this 'modern-day' delivery boy's bicycle failed to catch on and just some 40 were built in the three years of production, compared with over 1,100 Mk F Ranger Vans. The Mk F Ranger, in fact, proved to be the most popular of all Sharp's ultra-lightweight commercials and became a common sight on Britain's roads. Not only were they popular among small business users, but also larger companies - for instance the Cooperative Society in Reading, who ran a small fleet of them for local grocery deliveries.

The 'New Line' Bond Minicar

Sharp's continued with their policy of constantly updating the Minicar in August 1961 with yet another 'new' variation on the theme, somewhat unsurprisingly designated the Mk G Minicar. With the introduction of this new model, production of the Mk F range ceased with exception of the Ranger Van, which continued through to mid-1962 (although it was fitted with the Mk G's 246cc Villiers Mk 35A engine). In total some 7,000 Mk Fs were built, and it was probably the most popular and practical Minicar that Sharp's built. It was, and in many respects still is,

Bright new full-colour sales brochures accompanied the launch of Bond's New Line Minicar in 1961, with a new Bond logo and even a hint of glamour in an attempt to help boost sales!

The BOND 250 G
You can't beat the NEW LINE BOND

Bold graphics also started to be used to market the Minicar, especially in magazine adverts, though the underlying themes were still very much practical family transport and economy.

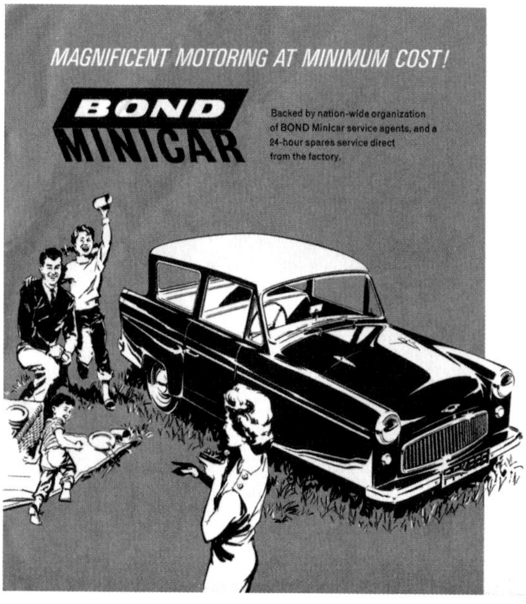
MAGNIFICENT MOTORING AT MINIMUM COST!
BOND MINICAR
Backed by nation-wide organization of BOND Minicar service agents, and a 24-hour spares service direct from the factory.

quite capable of providing an economical reliable means of everyday transport. The Mk G range of Minicars were to be the last of the line for Sharp's Commercials, since by the late 1950s the economic factors and various restrictions that had given the earlier models such a boost had by now almost completely disappeared.

The first signs of what was to be a new era in motoring for Britain could be seen at the 1959 Motor Show, which was one of the most important since the war because it saw the introduction of a number of totally new models, replacing the large and expensive export-motivated cars of the 1950s with the lightweight, small-engined, economical and fashionable cars for the 1960s. Perhaps the most important contributor to the demise of the Minicar also made its début at this show in the form of the revolutionary Mini, heralding a new chapter in the story of the light car. Apart from the obvious threat from the compact and economical Mini, buyers were also

918 DXU

tempted by such new cars as the 'ultra-modern' competitively-priced offerings from Ford and Triumph in the new Anglia and Herald. The Minicar therefore now had to compete in a far more competitive market, not only against similar three-wheelers, but also to some degree against the new cheaper economy-conscious lightweight conventional cars that had been inspired by the earlier Suez Crisis.

Although basically the same bodyshell as previous Mk E and F Minicars, the Mk G's appearance is greatly altered by moving the windscreen forward, adding quarter lights and providing a 'cut-back' rear window, as seen on this 1962 Bond 250 G model.

918 DXU

Rear view of the 1962 Bond 250 G Minicar reveals new American-style fins and the cut-back rear window, but surprisingly, still no opening bootlid.

The three-wheeler did, however, still have one advantage over such competition, in the form of concessions on road tax, as well as being liable to only around half the rate of purchase tax levied on conventional four-wheel cars. This meant that the Bond's chief rival at this time was Reliant, whose Regal three-wheeler, though now glassfibre-bodied, was considerably heavier than the Bond and was still powered by a 747cc four-cylinder side-valve unit based on the old Austin Seven engine. The Regal did have one advantage over the Bond, in that it had a full four-seater body, but the introduction of the new Mk G Minicar was soon to put this right. The Mk G used the same basic bodyshell as the previous Mks E and F, but modified and with the windscreen moved further forward to give a larger passenger compartment, allowing the fitment of a full-width rear seat that could just about accommodate two adults. The roof was redesigned with a 'cut-back' rear windscreen, as on Ford's Anglia, to improve rearward vision and give sufficient headroom over the rear seats. Other refinements, such as opening quarter lights, wind-up door windows, modernised interior trim and larger 10-inch wheels, were all included to enhance the 'real-car' feel of the 'New Line' Bond Minicar. The improvements were not all cosmetic, either, for many of the Minicar's mechanical components were also brought up to date as well. The rear suspension was redesigned and the old bonded-rubber Flexitor units were replaced by independent assemblies using a trailing arm with a coil spring and double-acting hydraulic shock

Engine compartment of a 1963 250 G Minicar, showing the single-cylinder 246cc Villiers Mk 35A engine mounted on its front-wheel drive unit.

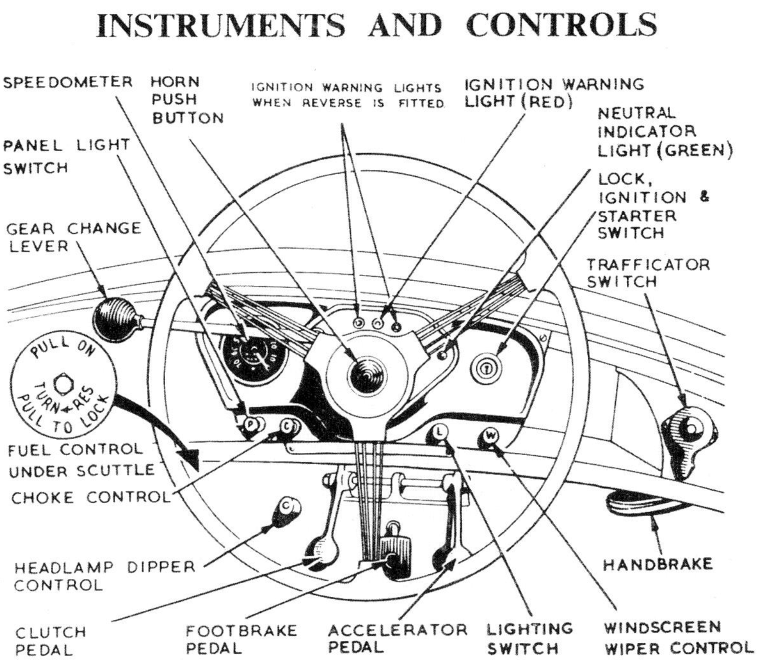
INSTRUMENTS AND CONTROLS
SPEEDOMETER
HORN PUSH BUTTON
IGNITION WARNING LIGHTS WHEN REVERSE IS FITTED
IGNITION WARNING LIGHT (RED)
NEUTRAL INDICATOR LIGHT (GREEN)
PANEL LIGHT SWITCH
LOCK, IGNITION & STARTER SWITCH
GEAR CHANGE LEVER
TRAFFICATOR SWITCH
PULL ON
TURN-RES
PULL TO LOCK
FUEL CONTROL UNDER SCUTTLE
CHOKE CONTROL
HEADLAMP DIPPER CONTROL
HANDBRAKE
CLUTCH PEDAL
FOOTBRAKE PEDAL
ACCELERATOR PEDAL
LIGHTING SWITCH
WINDSCREEN WIPER CONTROL

Bond 250 G Minicar dash and controls.

absorber. Perhaps the most important improvement was the use of Lockheed hydraulic brakes, employing hydraulically-operated brake shoes at the front and mechanically-operated brake shoes at the rear. The mechanical linkage operating these rear brake shoes was actuated by means of a hydraulic frame cylinder and stirrup mounted beneath the floor of the vehicle, so effectively all three brakes were hydraulically operated. The engine was updated to the new Villiers 246cc Mk35A engine, rated at 11.5bhp at 4,500rpm, which gave the 250 G a claimed top speed of 55mph and up to 70mpg.

At first only the four-seat 250 G model of the new Minicar was available, at £395.8.4d, but the range was expanded during 1962 with the introduction of the new 250 G Estate at £394.12.6d and 250 G Ranger Van at £325 (in primer). The Estate model featured a large top-hinged tailgate giving excellent access to the rear which had a folding dual-purpose rear seat giving extra versatility for passenger or load carrying. The 250 G Estate achieved the distinction of being one of the few three-wheelers to become the subject of a full *Autocar* Road Test, published in November 1962. *Autocar*'s impressions of this Bond Minicar were certainly favourable and few faults were found that were worthy of comment. One impression noted was the enthusiasm and loyalty of other Bond owners encountered during the testing - there were apparently frequent wavings and thumbs-up signs for encouragement. (It's good to see that some things have not changed!) Performance figures recorded during this road test give the maximum

THE NEW EXCITING
BOND
ESTATE
EASY FOR PARKING...IDEAL FOR SHOPPING...PERFECT FOR TOURING
The first of its kind—the BOND ESTATE is the most exciting development in light-weight vehicle design yet achieved in the history of motoring.
Incorporating fully opening rear door and folding dual-purpose rear seating giving complete versatility for passenger/luggage carrying.
THE SAFEST AND MOST ECONOMICAL ESTATE CAR ON THE ROAD

Promoted as a realistic alternative to more expensive conventional cars, the 250 G Estate was available in 1963 in single or twin-cylinder forms.

mean top speed at 50.5mph, 52mph being the best obtained during the test. The mean acceleration figure recorded a respectable 0-20mph time of 5.4 seconds, but 0-40mph took 26.6 seconds. Finally, the overall fuel consumption for the 438 miles covered was 45.5mpg - rather less than Sharp's claims, but still not bad considering the very varied types of driving required for the purpose of testing the vehicle.

The Beginning of the End for the Minicar

Just as the new Mk G range of Minicars was becoming established, the Government dealt a serious blow to Sharp's Commercials as well as to all other manufacturers of three-wheel vehicles. This came just before the Motorcycle Show in November 1962 with the announcement by the Chancellor of the Exchequer, Reginald Maudling, of a major reduction in the rate of purchase tax on cars. There had been considerable pressure on the Government for some time to make such a move, as there had been a revival of export markets, due to improved world economic conditions, which had also boosted domestic markets. Hence

With the launch of the 250 G Estate in 1962, it seemed that Sharp's had indeed found a new niche for the Minicar, with a very positive initial reaction from the motoring press.

it was now felt that the purchase tax on new vehicles was now actually holding the British motor industry back and in 1961 production had actually begun to fall, despite still being way below the industry's capacity. An initial cut in the rate of 10 per cent in April of that year, down to 45 per cent for four-wheel vehicles, had failed to alleviate the situation and Maudling realised that more drastic action was required to remove this relic of the post-war austerity era. There was a further reduction on 5 November, bringing the rate of purchase tax on cars down to 25 per cent.

Although the motoring press rejoiced at this (in their opinion) somewhat overdue return to reason, it left manufacturers of three-wheel vehicles with a serious problem. For some time the main advantage that such vehicles had enjoyed over their four-wheeled competition was the differing rates of purchase tax levied on each type of vehicle. The newly-announced tax concession had made no mention of two- or three-wheeled vehicles and it soon became obvious that the cut was specific to four-wheel vehicles. This made the new rate of purchase tax a flat rate and three-wheel vehicles were to remain the same at 25 per cent, effectively removing overnight one of the main attractions to the motoring public of such a vehicle. Protests were immediately made to the Chancellor by the Director of the Cycle and Motorcycle Industries Association, Hugh Palin, but without success. Tom Gratrix, who was by now Managing Director of Sharp's Commercials, announced that the absence of a similar concession for the Bond Minicar was likely to cause a collapse of the market for the firm's products, and he added that should the factory be forced to close, the jobs of the 300-strong workforce would be lost. Colonel Gray had by this time left Sharp's Commercials to become Chairman of Loxhams Garages following the death of Ewart Bradshaw, although he retained an interest in Sharp's as chairman of the Company.

Bond Trailer Tent

The situation appeared somewhat improved following the Motorcycle Show at the end of November, with continued interest in the Minicar evident, as well as the Company's new product announced at the show - the Bond Trailer Tent. This new product was apparently the focus of attention at the show for it was the first such British trailer tent on the market. It was described as providing 'full family holiday accommodation' with 60 square feet of floor area and requiring only a claimed 90 seconds to erect ready for use. The Bond Trailer Tent was designed to complement the Minicar and utilised a number of Minicar components in its construction, including the 8-inch wheels and bonded-rubber Flexitor suspension units from the earlier models. Since the trailer weighed only 260lb, the Minicar was quite capable of towing it, and there was the additional advantage that the tent itself could

NEW
FROM
BOND
THE INSTANT TRAILER TENT
ERECTED IN 90 SECONDS

Sales leaflets for the Bond Trailer Tent launched in 1962 surprisingly featured a towing Mini, not a Minicar, on the cover.

LIGHT & EASY TO HANDLE
STANDS FIRM & LEVEL
READY TO GET INTO
RIGHT OFF THE GROUND- SO SNUG SO DRAUGHT-PROOF
See the new BOND Trailer Tent for yourself - it's especially designed for discerning campers and tourists. Ideal to take behind the car - it has the well-known BOND Mini-car independent suspension incorporating 8 in. wheels with trailing arms and bonded rubber suspension units. The strong timber floor puts a barrier between you and ground draughts or damp, while wind and rain won't worry you when you're protected by the heavy tent canvas on its rigid tubular frame. The air space between the sturdy aluminium base and the timber floor provides ideal insulation. If desired, you can easily remove the upper section of the unit and use the lower half only as a general purpose trailer. To combine beauty with utility, BOND Trailers are available in a choice of high gloss, hard-wearing finishes in attractive colours.
SPECIFICATION
LENGTH (closed excluding tow bar) 7′ 6″
WIDTH OVERALL 5′ 0″
HEIGHT (closed) 2′ 9″
LENGTH (open) 15′ 0″
GROSS WEIGHT 260 lbs.
TRAILER ONLY 150 lbs.
LUGGAGE SPACE 40 cu. ft.
FLOOR AREA 15′ × 4′
HEADROOM 6′ 8′
1½″ BALL & SOCKET.
Manufactured by: SHARP'S COMMERCIALS LIMITED, PRESTON, LANCS. (Tel: PRESTON 4002/3/4)

It was claimed that the Bond Trailer Tent could be erected in 90 seconds!

be detached if required, leaving a useful trailer. Two models of trailer tent were produced, the earlier 1962 model opening lengthways and the later 'Trek' version, introduced in 1964, opening to one side. The earlier model featured aluminium construction with a wooden floor and a canvas cover on a folding tubular-steel frame, which opened to give 15ft length, 6ft 8in headroom and 5ft width. It was priced at £98 for green or green/white canvas, with red, yellow or blue tent canvas listed as optional for £5 more. Also there was the advantage of space within the trailer when the tent was folded and the lid closed for additional luggage or camping equipment, such as chairs and a table, etc. that could not easily fit in the towing vehicle. With the rise in the popularity of camping holidays around this time and especially a growing trend for continental touring holidays of this type, Sharp's seemed to have done their homework and clearly hoped the Bond Trailer Tent would be a success. But despite the interest generated, production was limited and only some 100-200 are thought to have been sold. One likely reason is that although the Bond was indeed the first British trailer tent, others were very close behind, such as the well-known Dandy in 1963, and two years previously in 1960 the first British folding caravans had appeared, complete with built-in seating and furniture etc. As other products appeared they tended to include things we now would take for granted, such as built-in cupboards and cookers, and maybe

Company promotional photo from the launch of the Bond Trailer Tent – but a pretty model and a few props could not hide the fact that despite its innovative design, it was actually a very basic product.

even a sink, but more importantly, built-in bed platforms with their own mattresses became pretty much standard - all making the Bond look very basic indeed. Another issue with the Bond Trailer Tent was its long, narrow and relatively tall configuration, which owners soon found made it susceptible to strong winds, especially if inadvertently placed across the direction of gusts.

Sharp's clearly still believed there was a niche in the market for their Trailer Tent and set to work redesigning it, no doubt in light of owners' experiences, this time coming up with the Bond Trek Trailer Tent in

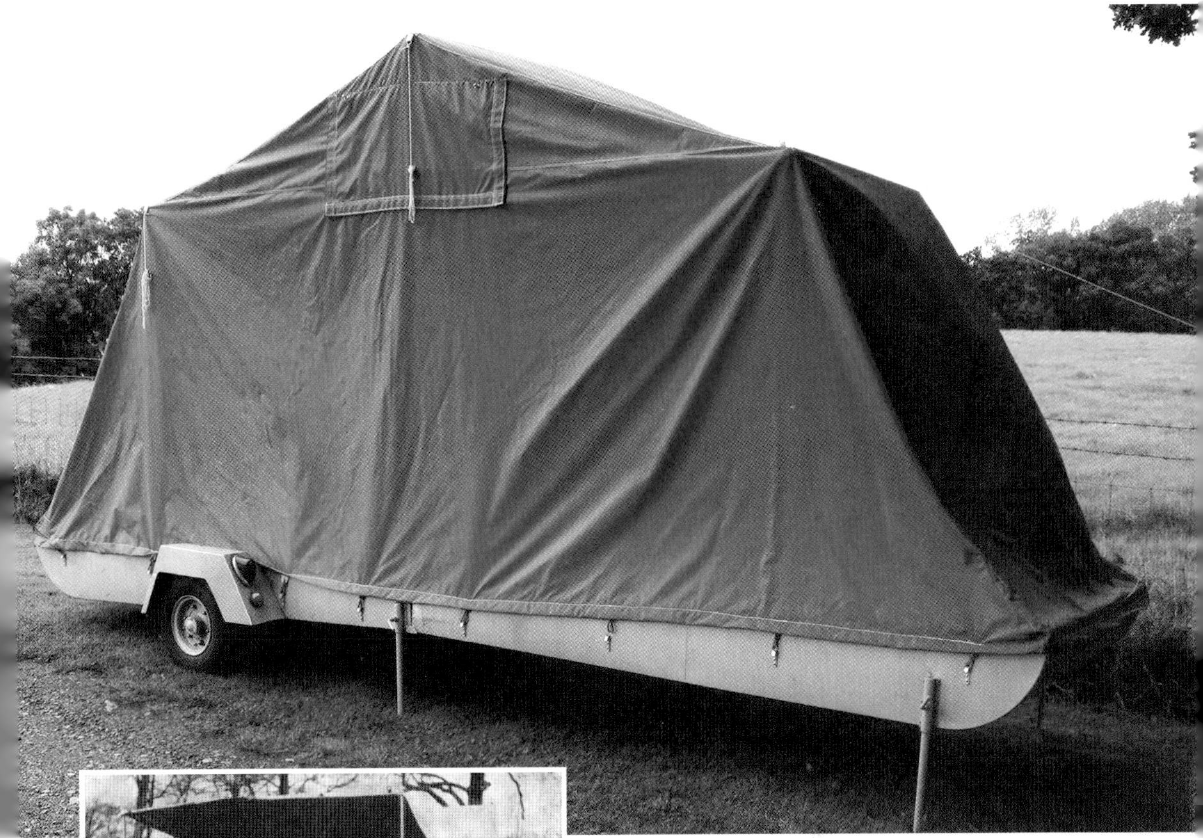

A restored Bond Trailer Tent shows the long narrow profile, coupled with relatively high sides which led to problems in windy conditions. (*Photo: C. & A. Steggel.*)

The later (*Inset*) 'Trek' sideways-opening version of the Bond Trailer Tent overcame the stability issues, but was still very basic compared to other products at the time.

autumn 1964. The main focus of the new design was to alter the layout by building a completely new trailer base, now with a glassfibre lid, which hinged sideways to provide 70 square feet of floor space in a more stable square format. The folding tent frame was also reconfigured and now had its opening on the lower 'lid' floor side of the erected tent, which was also now provided with a useful sun/rain canopy. Claimed set-up time was increased to a more realistic two minutes and the complete Trek Trailer Tent was offered at £118. Additionally the trailer base could be bought on its own at £85, complete with glassfibre lid, or £65 without. Although Sharp's had indeed addressed the main issue identified with their Trailer Tent design, the result was still very basic, with none of the built-in equipment and comforts now being offered by competitors for similar or not a lot more money. By the summer of 1964, sales had remained slow, and with just under 100 Trek Trailer Tents built, the Company discontinued production.

Following the favourable response from the public at the Motorcycle Show it had been announced that Sharp's Commercials would continue production of the Minicar, but before long the Company began to experience a fall in demand. This led to the decision to cut production, and at the end of November 1962 there was the announcement of 100 jobs to be lost at the Factory. The losses were partly blamed on the normal seasonal fall in orders. Reassurances were given to the rest of the workforce that the Factory would remain open, and also that assistance would be given to those made redundant to find new jobs.

Bond Motor Boats and Skis

Perhaps anticipating that the Minicar era was coming to an end, Sharp's Commercials had become involved in another attempt at diversification late in 1961. Following negotiations with an American company, Power/Ski Inc. in Sausalito, California, Sharp's gained exclusive European rights to manufacture and market a self-powered water ski, to become known as the Bond Power Ski. The new product was unveiled at the International Boat Show at Earls Court in January 1962, offered at £95. Sharp's had high hopes for volume sales and plans were set in motion for an initial production run of 1,000 units. Also during 1962 came

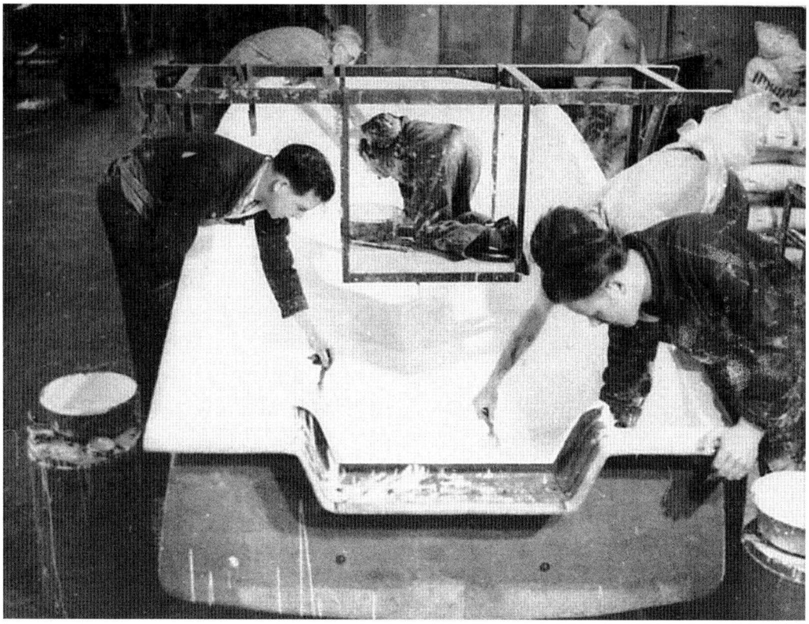

Moulding the hull for the Bond Sea Ranger was apparently a labour intensive job.

another opportunity to produce a waterborne product in the form of the Bond Sea Ranger, a motor-boat design first constructed as a one-off at Sharp's in the late 1950s from moulds bought by Alan Pounder. This new version was now regarded as a more serious commercial proposition, but the market for such a boat was already overcrowded, and with little demand few were actually built. Meanwhile, trials of the prototype Power Ski were carried out on Fairhaven Lake at Lytham St Annes and it was claimed that the machine could top 35mph, although Sharp's did not supply the outboard engines required - they only advised which were most suitable. Despite various significant export

Although the original 1950s Bond Sea Ranger never went into production, the later 1962 Bond Sea Ranger was a more serious commercial proposition, but relatively few were built.

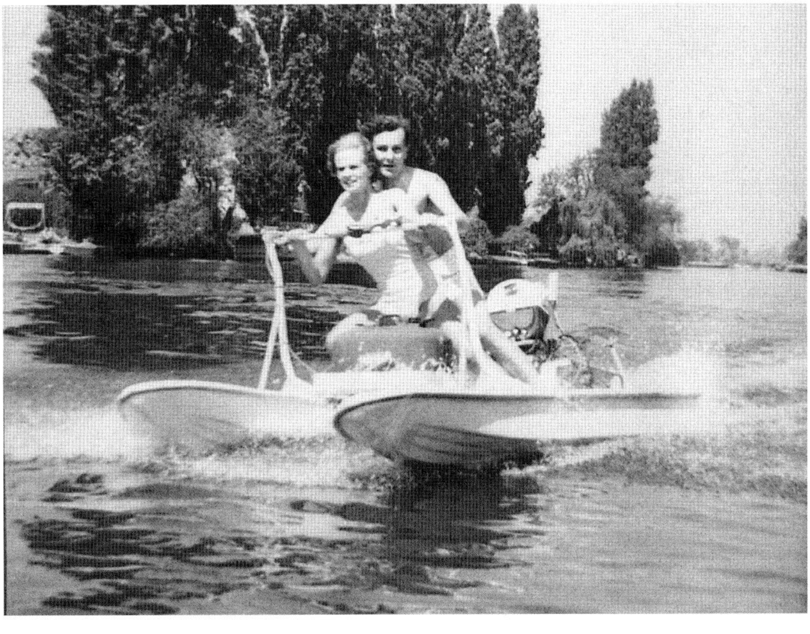

The ideal – a Power Ski at speed on Florida waterways circa 1960. It was certainly a novel product and no doubt immense fun in the right conditions, but the Bond Power Ski failed to find a market in the UK and as such was short lived.

The reality – the prototype Bond Power Ski during obviously chilly trials on Fairhaven Lake, Lytham St Anne's, in 1961.

orders being reported in the press, in reality just over 100 Power Ski were actually built by Sharp's. It was realised that, with this country's climate and chilly waters, there was simply not the demand for such a product so production was discontinued.

Some years later an enquiry was received from a company named Kirkham's Marine Limited who were looking to export self-powered water-ski craft for hire use to the many tourists now filling the hotels in the coastal resorts on the Mediterranean. They placed an initial order

A surviving Bond Power Ski seen at a recent Bond Owners' Club event. Note the folded-up Bond Trailer Tent to its right. (*Photo: C. & A. Steggel.*)

for 200 Power Skis in late 1966, with a slightly altered specification that required the twin 15ft hulls of the Power-Ski to incorporate polyurethane, closed cell, foam-filled buoyancy sections. This made the machine virtually unsinkable and prevented the accumulation of water that had been a problem with the original design. Initial production of 150 units began in mid-1967, with a further instruction that the floats should be coloured signal red. Expected further orders sadly never materialised and the Bond Power Ski finally faded into obscurity, although there was a revival of the concept of individual self-powered water craft in 1969 when the Preston Factory began production of a completely different machine known as the Scooter Ski for Bond's new owners, Reliant.

The End of the Road for the Bond Minicar

The 1962 Motorcycle Show saw the announcement by Reliant of a development which was to have serious consequences for Sharp's Commercials: the unveiling of the new Regal 3/25. After years of selling similarly bulbous-looking three-wheelers, with their wood floors, narrow windscreens and powered by a pre-war side-valve engine, Reliant seemed to have taken stock and realised they had to move with the times. Their new model was completely updated with a new, roomier, modern-styled body with a full-size windscreen, wind down door windows and again with that 'fashionable' cut-back rear window as on the Ford Anglia. This bodyshell was all glassfibre, moulded in two main sections, joined together and mounted on a steel chassis. But the most important change, however, was the introduction of Reliant's own, specially-designed all-alloy 598cc overhead-valve engine for this new three-wheeler. Production of the new Reliant Regal began in early 1963 and before long Sharp's responded with the announcement of a new engine for the Bond Minicar. This was the 249cc Villiers Mk 4T twin-cylinder, producing 14.6bhp at 5,500rpm as compared to 11.5bhp at 4,500rpm from the Mk 35A single-cylinder engine. This gave the 'new' 250 G Twin Bond Minicar a top speed of 60mph and, it was hoped, a boost to flagging sales. The standard 250 G models with their Mk 35A engine remained in production and were offered as an alternative to the 250 G Twin. This, together with the other options available that now included Unidirectional or Reversing Dynastart units and single-colour or dual-tone paintwork (primer or colour finish on the Ranger), etc. meant that the prospective buyer was faced with an almost bewildering choice of 24 different versions of the three basic models available on the 1963 price list! The Standard four-seater saloon was priced at £387.4s.7d, the Estate at £393.5s.5d (all inclusive of purchase tax) and the Ranger at £325 in primer, with the twin-engine adding some £18, and with reverse for approximately £10 extra. When compared to the Regal at £442, the motorcycle-engined four-seat 250 G Twin Minicar

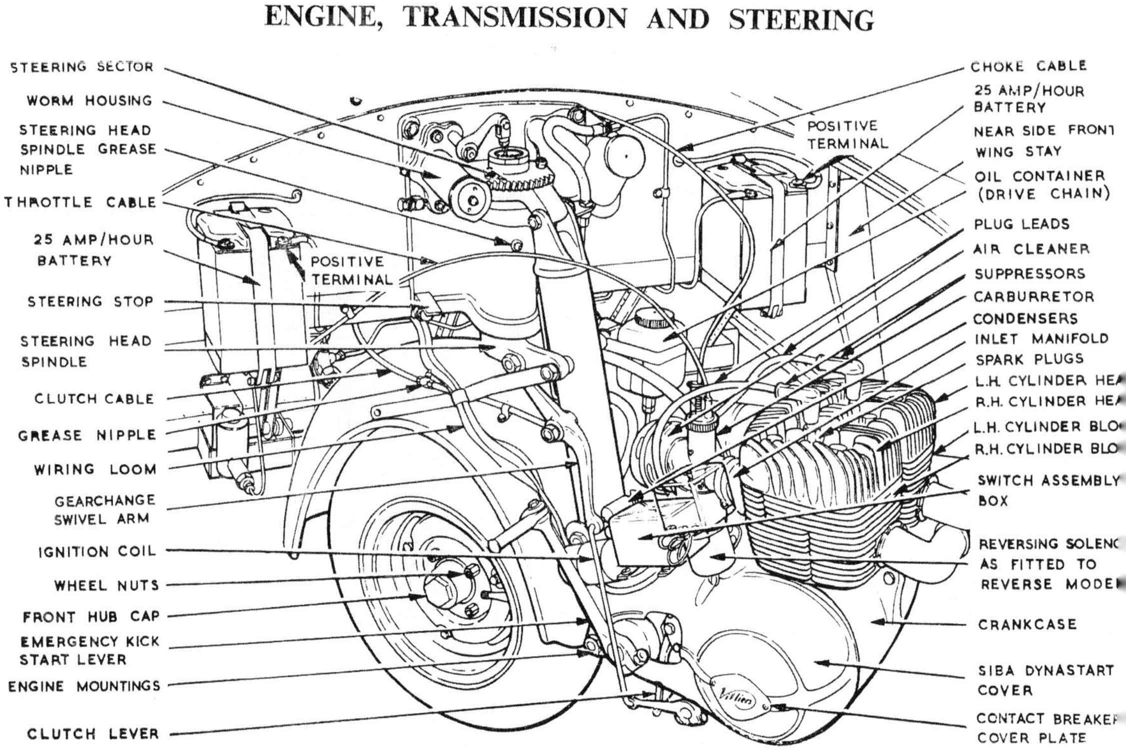

ENGINE, TRANSMISSION AND STEERING
STEERING SECTOR
WORM HOUSING
STEERING HEAD SPINDLE GREASE NIPPLE
THROTTLE CABLE
25 AMP/HOUR BATTERY
POSITIVE TERMINAL
STEERING STOP
STEERING HEAD SPINDLE
CLUTCH CABLE
GREASE NIPPLE
WIRING LOOM
GEARCHANGE SWIVEL ARM
IGNITION COIL
WHEEL NUTS
FRONT HUB CAP
EMERGENCY KICK START LEVER
ENGINE MOUNTINGS
CLUTCH LEVER
CHOKE CABLE
25 AMP/HOUR BATTERY
POSITIVE TERMINAL
NEAR SIDE FRONT
WING STAY
OIL CONTAINER (DRIVE CHAIN)
PLUG LEADS
AIR CLEANER
SUPPRESSORS
CARBURRETOR
CONDENSERS
INLET MANIFOLD
SPARK PLUGS
L.H. CYLINDER HE
R.H. CYLINDER HE
L.H. CYLINDER BL
R.H. CYLINDER BL
SWITCH ASSEMBLY BOX
REVERSING SOLEN
AS FITTED TO
REVERSE MODE
CRANKCASE
SIBA DYNASTART COVER
CONTACT BREAKE
COVER PLATE
Villiers

Details of the 249cc Villiers Mk 4T twin-cylinder engine, as fitted to 250 G Twin models from late 1962, showing the various components of the engine, transmission and steering.

with reverse at £415.0s.5d was clearly losing ground to the new Reliant at an alarming rate.

Sales of the 250 G and 250 G Twin remained slow, and Sharp's realised that further changes were required if they were to retain a share of the market. Although many of Sharp's employees by now realised that what was really required was a completely new product, a last-ditch attempt was made to try to revive sales of the Minicar. There

Under-bonnet view of the 249cc Villiers twin-cylinder engine fitted to a 1964 250 G Twin Estate. (*Photo: C. & A. Steggel.*)

Rear view of the final model of Minicar – the prototype 250 G Tourer, showing the neat provision of an opening bootlid.

was now intensive research into how production costs could most effectively be cut, which resulted in a predicted saving of some 25 per cent through the production of a basic no-frills model. This final version of the Minicar was announced at the 1964 Motorcycle Show as the 250 G Tourer and was promoted as an economy version, fitted with the single-cylinder Mk 35A engine as standard, with Twin versions built only to special order. Further savings were made by down-grading the interior trim with plain door panels and non-opening quarter lights. It was recognised, however, that the model still had to be attractive to potential customers and it was decided after some discussion to include the proposed opening bootlid, which was also incorporated into the existing Saloon models.

By this time Bond's share of the three-wheeler market was slipping fast as the Minicar concept had ceased to be relevant to the economic climate and the Firm's products began to look dated when compared to the competition, namely Reliant. The economy Tourer model unsurprisingly failed to revive sales, although production of Mk G Minicars did continue as late as 1966, but only to order, and with just over 3,000 Mk G vehicles built the Minicar story came to a close. After fifteen years of continuous production, with some 24,500 (Bond Owners Club figures) Minicars rolling off the production line, it was now time for some major changes at the Preston Factory. The recently-appointed new Managing Director of Sharp's Commercials, Tom Gratrix, had already seen the danger signs and as early as 1962 plans were being discussed not only for a replacement three-wheeler, but also the possibility of diversification by entering the four-wheel specialist sports car market. Therefore, as the 'New Line Minicar' became the end of the line for both the Minicar and Sharp's Commercials, the company, now newly re-named Bond Cars Limited, looked set to enter a new era of vehicle manufacture.

The Bond 875

In the early 1960s the Company became involved in a complete change of direction by entering the four-wheel specialist sportscar market. This resulted in the announcement in May 1963 of the first of the Bond Equipe range, the Equipe GT Coupé. It was the heavy investment in

THE POWER BEHIND THE BOND

Rootes 875 c.c. Power Unit

- ✳ Compression ratio 8:1 ✳ Develops 34 b.h.p. at 4,900 r.p.m.
- ✳ Aluminium die cast construction ✳ Overhead camshaft
- ✳ Solex downdraught carburettor
- ✳ Synchromesh on all 4 forward gears
- ✳ $6\frac{1}{4}$" diaphragm hydraulically operated clutch

this vehicle, both financially and in terms of manpower, that had led to the postponement of the development of a new Bond three-wheeler to replace the Minicar. Therefore, it was not until early 1964 that serious discussion began on the design of a new three-wheel vehicle. By this time it was realised that a completely new design concept was required and that the Minicar's traditional motorcycle-type Villiers engine and gearbox units were no longer a satisfactory means of powering such a vehicle. The three-wheeler-buying motorist was now demanding something considerably more up-to-date and sophisticated, and it appeared that this was just what the competition - ie Reliant - was now providing.

Hillman Imp Power Unit

It is known that whilst they were considering the specification for their own new three-wheeler, Bond actually went to the trouble of examining the current Reliant model in some detail with the intention from the start that the new vehicle would compete directly with the three-wheeler giants from Tamworth. After some discussion on the best power unit for the new Bond, it was obvious that there could be only one really suitable contender - the lightweight alloy water-cooled four-stroke 875cc Hillman Imp engine. This engine had already caused something of a sensation in the motoring press of the time with its light-alloy construction and overhead camshaft, features usually found only on expensive sportscar engines at the time. Negotiations were soon under way with Rootes, through their Special Products Division, Tilling Stevens Limited, based in Maidstone, who agreed in principle since the proposed vehicle would not be in competition with any of Rootes' existing products. Rootes at this time were keen to boost sales of their parts and so they readily agreed to a three-year renewable contract with the newly-renamed Bond Cars Limited in 1964. This contract did, however, include the right to examine the prototype of the vehicle, which Rootes would have to approve before production commenced. Work now began in earnest on the new Bond 875 project, as it became known, and Lawrie Bond was commissioned as a consultant to help with the design of the vehicle. He soon came up with a series of drawings that depicted three proposed basic models: a Saloon, a GT model, and an Estate car or van. These were to be derived from the same basic monocoque glassfibre shell designed around the complete Imp engine, gearbox and axle unit, complete with its semi-trailing arm suspension, with coil springs and separately-mounted hydraulic shock absorbers - all mounted on a steel cross member that bolted directly to the Bond shell. But the front suspension was to be to Lawrie Bond's own design, comprising an offset tubular-steel steering stanchion, turned by a Burman steering gear using the worm-and-nut principle. From this the front wheel was mounted on a leading arm with a Woodhead Monroe spring and shock absorber unit. Unusually this steering set-up featured progressive cambering of the front wheel intended to improve handling at higher speeds. As soon as the design had been approved and work got under way, it was stressed to all Bond employees involved in the project that there was a need for complete secrecy so that Bond's competitors should have no knowledge of the vehicle before it was ready to be announced. Throughout the design work for the 875, Lawrie Bond worked closely with Alan Pounder, the company's chief design and development engineer, to turn the initial Concept into a practical production model. The target date for the 875 launch was somewhat optimistically set for the Motorcycle Show in November 1964, but in the event the only new model announced was the spartan, economy, Mk G Tourer version of the old Minicar.

Designing a completely new vehicle from scratch was never going to be easy, but the 875 project seemed to be beset by problems from the start, and by October 1964 it had become obvious that the target date could not possibly be met because of delays in the production of the prototype bodyshell. The prototype 875 did not, in fact, run until February 1965 and there immediately followed an intensive and rigorous testing programme, much of which was carried out in the Lake District, and included the challenging Hardknott Pass between Eskdale and the Duddon Valley, officially one of the two steepest roads in England. This testing was carried out almost to destruction in

HARDKNOTT PASS
ACUTE S BENDS
STEEPEST GRADIENT

The first prototype Bond 875 during testing in the Lake District in 1965. Note the small fins at rear, narrow bumper line (*later widened to increase headroom inside*) and separate aluminium rear wings, all to be altered on the production version.

order to evaluate the structural strength and handling qualities of the vehicle and the resulting information was used to construct a second prototype. This latter vehicle was intended to provide the production standard for the Bond 875 and was somewhat altered in appearance from the first prototype. The most obvious change was the widening of the bumper strip where the two sections of the glassfibre shell joined, by some two to three inches, in order to increase the headroom in the vehicle without major alteration to the shell or moulds. Minor detailed

Prototype Bond 875 during testing in the Lake District, with companion early GT4S Equipe.

Second Bond 875 prototype early 1965, now closely resembling the final production model, with increased bumper line depth and rear wings now part of moulded bodyshell, but still with aluminium doors and bonnet.

changes were also made to the rear wings, now incorporated into the bodyshell instead of separate aluminium fixtures, and the sloping rear end of the vehicle was cleaned up with the removal of the small fin-like projections incorporated in the original design. The new prototype Bond 875 featured an all-glassfibre construction, monocoque bodyshell, with shaped aluminium doors and a bonded-in U-shaped steel chassis members for added strength.

Problems with the 875

Once completed, this second prototype was sent to Tilling Stevens in Maidstone for evaluation and approval, and a revised announcement date for the new model was set for April 1965. But again things did not run smoothly, as Rootes were not happy with the high-running temperature of their engine in the 875 and would not pass the prototype. Other problems were also becoming apparent with keeping the 875 within the Government's 8cwt weight limit for three-wheelers. This latter problem led to a general down-grading of the vehicle's specification, especially with regard to the interior trim, as almost every component was assessed for suitability according to its weight. Other weight-saving changes included the replacement of the original steel U-shaped bonded-in strengthening members in the floor, with

Testing a later prototype of the Bond 875. Note the aluminium front bumper, similar to that used on the Equipes, which didn't make it on to the production.

BP

lightweight aluminium channel section alternatives, which in turn led to problems with the lack of rigidity of the bodyshell. Further delays resulted from problems with the supply of the specially-manufactured front suspension components and it was not until October 1965 that Bond Cars Limited felt confident enough to resubmit the prototype to Tilling Stevens. Anticipating that this would be little more than a formality, it was decided to finally announce the Bond 875 to the public late in August 1965, with production to commence as soon as approval was received from Rootes.

Releasing a Bond 875 bodyshell from its mould at the Company's India Mill Factory. (*Photo: Peter G. Reed.*)

Bond's advertising campaign was understandably somewhat restrained to begin with, but the response from the motoring press was enthusiastic. Reports were soon appearing relating the 100mph speeds attained during testing and the unofficial beating of the equivalent saloon car lap record at Brands Hatch with John Surtees at the wheel; this certainly caught the motoring public's attention! The prototype was, in fact, deemed to be too fast, so the production model was fitted with the low-compression Hillman Imp Van version of the 875cc engine. Even in this detuned form the engine still produced 34bhp, giving the Bond 875 a 0-60mph time of sixteen seconds, a quite respectable figure for the time. The 875 had a top speed of 80mph and could provide quite

CCK 875C

John Surtees (*with Tom Gratrix – left*) at Brands Hatch with Bond 875, prior to his test drive and unofficial lap record with the car!

economical motoring at 50mpg on the lower three-wheeler rate of road tax.

Despite the supposedly successful weight-saving policy which it was claimed had brought the overall weight of the vehicle to 19lb under the 8cwt limit, even with a heater fitted, the Bond 875 was still having trouble keeping within the limit. This, together with further technical problems, led to further delays in putting the car into production. Even when production did finally get under way in June 1966, only some fifteen vehicles a week were being produced - the resulting delays in fulfilling orders meant that many customers simply cancelled and bought alternative vehicles. Also, by the time the production models began to appear, many potential customers (who had been impressed by the high standard of the prototypes displayed at the 875's launch at the Brighton Show the previous year) were now disappointed to find a quite different level of finish on the new vehicles. The overall weight of the vehicle had in fact remained a considerable problem, which had led to the re-assessment (from the point of view of weight) of every part of the interior trim The new interior was now fitted with smaller, more basic, seats, door trim panels had been omitted, sound proofing had been removed and all the windows, with the exception of the windscreen, were fitted with Perspex.

CCK 875C

John Surtees demonstrating the dramatic cornering ability of an early-production Bond 875 at Brands Hatch.

In September 1966 *Autocar* once again departed from their norm of testing only conventional four-wheel cars and published a full road test on the 875 three-wheeler. They were apparently quite impressed with the vehicle's performance, said to be similar to BMC's Mini-Cooper! The brakes were also found to be especially good, and the steering light and positive. Some reservations were held about the stability of the 875 at high speeds, but under normal driving conditions this was not

Full production of the Bond 875 underway at Ribbleton Lane, circa 1967, with the first Ranger Vans being visible as well as GT4S and 2-Litre Equipes. (*Photo: Peter G. Reed.*)

GND 901E

Immaculately-restored 1967 Bond 875 Mk 1.

found to be a problem. *Autocar* did, however, find the 875 somewhat expensive at £505.13s.6d including purchase tax. Even this price was only achieved by Bond Cars Ltd offering the heater at £9.4s.5d and the spare wheel at £9.4s.6d as optional extras! Considerable criticism was also directed towards the standard of finish - especially with regard to the interior trim. The doors were said to slam with a 'deafening crash' and the seats were considered to be 'more appropriate for a child's pedal car'! Engine noise was unacceptably high because of the lack of sound proofing and a number of sharp edges noted were said to be the result of poor workmanship. Certainly such scathing remarks were not in Bond's interests and they must have been the cause for some considerable concern at the Preston Factory. Development of the 875 continued during production in an attempt to address at least some of these problems and particularly to provide a more acceptable standard of interior finish. This included work on new lightweight glassfibre seat-shells to give improved back support, improved door seals and even an optional, removable, contoured roof-mounted luggage compartment that doubled as a suitcase when not fitted, offered at £12.10s.4d.

Further Development

From the conception of the 875 project it had been the intention to produce a complete range of models sharing the same basic bodyshell and mechanical components. Unforeseen problems in keeping even the basic saloon models within the 8cwt limit, and later in maintaining the rigidity of the lightened bodyshell, meant that it was not until April

This specially-designed roof mounted detachable carrier for the Bond 875 overcame the fact that the vehicle had no boot for carrying luggage.

1967 that a second model of the 875 was announced. This was the 875 Ranger Van, again exploiting the vehicle's commercial-vehicle status to avoid purchase tax and offered at £417.10s.0d in primer, though still with the heater and spare wheel as optional extras. The 875 Ranger used a slightly modified saloon bodyshell with a revised roofline to incorporate a top-hinged rear tailgate that gave access to the 40-cubic feet load area. As with some previous Minicar-based Ranger Van models, only a driver's seat was fitted; the load-area floor therefore being extended over the site of the passenger seat. Rear side windows were also omitted, which must have gone some way to solving the problems with the lack of rigidity of the bodyshell that had proved troublesome in the development of the tail-gate for this model and the proposed Estate version. In fact, Bond Cars Limited had by now realised that their 875 bodyshell design was not going to be as versatile as they had anticipated. This led to plans for the 875 Estate, an open two-seat tourer, and work on a left-hand-drive version, all to be abandoned. Some work was done on a stronger 'universal' 875 chassis that would allow such a range of models to be built, but this never reached the production stage.

In an attempt to boost sales of the Bond 875, the saloon model was given a facelift with a more modern-style nose section, incorporating rectangular headlamps, a dummy radiator grill and a larger squared-off

BIG NEWS FROM BOND
...the 875 Ranger...

Company sales material for the launch of the Bond 875 Ranger Van model.

opening bonnet. This became the Bond 875 Mk II and was introduced during March 1968, with the intention being that the changes gave the vehicle a far more conventional car-like frontal appearance. Which, coupled with improvements to the interior trim, was hoped to make the 875 more attractive to potential customers. Indeed, Bond Cars Limited must have felt fairly confident that the problems had now finally been ironed out and that sales were set to increase, as a new agreement was signed with Rootes in September of that year to ensure the supply of their components for a further three years.

Unexpected Demise of the 875

The 875 remained in production and although sales were never to reach the anticipated levels when the model was launched, some forty-five vehicles a week were being built by late 1968. By 1969, however, events were set to overtake the 875, with the takeover of Bond Cars Limited

875 MKII

Idyllic publicity shot for the new 'facelift' 875 Mk II taken at Fairhaven Lake, Lytham St Annes, with the original 1950s Bond Sea Ranger.

by their old rivals, the Reliant Motor Company. Clearly, since the 875 design originated from the desire to produce a direct competitor to Reliant's own three-wheeler, it was hardly surprising that Bond's new owners did not wish to continue production of the 875 models. No

T.T. RESCUE CAR
GRN 297F

Bond 875 Mk II Isle of Man TT rescue car!

doubt this factor alone would probably have seen the demise of the model, but Reliant did not have to look far for more acceptable excuses to end production, citing the car's troubled production history and, later, rumours of weakness in the 875's steering-gear attachment to the bulkhead. Almost immediately production of the 875 was cut back to the minimum required to fulfil existing orders and to use up the supplies of major components already in stock at the Preston Factory. From early 1969, only two to six vehicles a week were being built and in February 1970 the last 875 left the Bond Factory. Throughout its four years of troubled production only some 3,400 Bond 875s had been built, compared to Reliant's 15,000 three-wheel vehicles per year. Clearly Bond's 875 must have had an almost insignificant effect on the three-wheeler giant's sales figures and the somewhat over-simplified view that Reliant were 'silencing the opposition' when they took over Bond seems unlikely. As we shall see, the reasons behind the sale of Bond Cars Limited by its parent company, Loxhams, and Reliant's own reasons for acquiring the Company, were far more complex, and the 875 was merely an unfortunate pawn in the game.

The sad fate of many Bond 875s. Note the full set of new, unused, radiator hoses lying on the parcel shelf, perhaps indicating that the owner's intended attention to an overheating problem came too late! For many years the model seemed largely ignored by enthusiasts, though today they are far more likely to be sought out and restored.

LKO 557F

Chapter Six

The Bond Equipe

Following a serious re-appraisal of Sharp's Commercials' position as a vehicle manufacturer in light of the events of the early 1960s, it had become clear that in order to remain in business a completely new product was required. Both Sharp's Managing Director Tom Gratrix and Colonel Gray, who remained Chairman of the Company, were keen on the idea of moving into the four-wheel car market. They realised that in order for a small company such as Sharp's to compete in this market, a substantially different vehicle from anything else available was required in order to attract customers. This led to the decision to enter the specialist sportscar market and it was decided to produce a sports-style vehicle that would make use of the Company's expertise and experience in glassfibre construction techniques. It was realised that this material was the only realistic solution available to meet the need for the economical production of a bodyshell for such a highly individual specialist vehicle.

Work on the design of the new Bond began at the start of 1962, with early thoughts of using BMC A-series or Ford's Anglia engines as the basis for the new vehicle. These options were soon abandoned on commercial grounds and it emerged that there was only one serious contender to provide the basis for the new Bond - in the form of the contemporary Triumph Herald. There were a number of factors that led to this choice. Firstly, the Herald was almost unique at this time in that it retained 'traditional' separate chassis construction. This method had originally been forced on Standard-Triumph during the planning of their small-car project in the late 1950s because of difficulties in obtaining a supplier to produce a complete bodyshell for their new vehicle. The full story of the development of the Triumph Herald is covered by Graham Robson's excellent book, *Triumph Herald and Vitesse*, published by Osprey. Basically Standard-Triumph resolved the situation by effectively taking a step backwards to the days of separate chassis construction and designing a bodyshell that could be produced as separate sections which bolted together and mounted on it. This allowed the various sections to be sub-contracted to a number of different suppliers and had the additional advantage that a whole range of models could easily be derived from the same basic chassis and mechanical components.

By early 1961 Standard-Triumph had been taken over by Leyland Motors Limited, and this had been followed almost immediately by a restructuring of the Company and a review of the vehicles produced, including the Herald range. As part of this review, the slow-selling

Side view of the original Bond Equipe GT mock-up. Note the grafted-in sections of steel Herald panels in the hand-beaten aluminium bodyshell.

Herald Coupé, which had effectively been put in the shade by the introduction of the new Triumph Spitfire in 1962, was to be gradually phased out, finally disappearing in 1964. This would leave a gap in the Triumph range, which Bond's management saw as an ideal opportunity for them to approach Standard-Triumph with a view to securing the supply of the Herald's running gear as the basis of the new Bond Coupé. Obviously Standard-Triumph would have been reluctant to allow the use of their parts in any vehicle that was likely to compete with their

The original aluminium body buck for the Bond Equipe GT.

own existing models and they had, in fact, turned down a number of previous approaches by other companies on such grounds. This time, however, there were no such problems as Standard-Triumph had no plans to replace the Herald Coupé, and the new Bond was unlikely to compete with any of their other models. Links between the two companies were, in fact, already established through Sharp's parent company Loxhams Garages, who were major Triumph distributors in the North-West. Another factor that may also have helped to put this approach in a favourable light was the close geographical location of Lancashire-based Leyland Motors to that of Sharp's in nearby Preston. Standard-Triumph's Special Products Division Manager, Arthur Medlock, apparently took Sharp's proposition seriously and following discussion with Triumph management, the go-ahead was given for work on the project to commence.

Because of the lack of sheet-steel pressing facilities at the Bond Factory and of the fact that no other suppliers were available to carry out such work, it was decided from an early stage to incorporate as much of the Herald's bodywork as possible into the design. This led to the use of the Herald's steel floorpan, complete scuttle assembly and doors in the eventual bodyshell for the new Bond. The inclusion of the doors was especially important to Sharp's as these would otherwise have been prohibitively expensive and difficult to produce from scratch, although their use did restrict the styling of the new car considerably. Design work began immediately and Lawrie Bond was commissioned to draw up a number of alternative body styles for the proposed vehicle. Once the most suitable of these designs had been selected and approved, Lawrie worked in close association with Sharp's chief designer and development engineer Alan Pounder, and together they spent much time travelling back and forth along the M6 motorway to Standard-Triumph's Special Products Division at Coventry. Here the staff took a very close interest in every stage of the Bond project and Standard-Triumph were obviously keen to ensure that the finished car was of sufficient quality to enhance their own reputation through the best use of the components supplied to Sharp's Commercials.

Equipe GT

The prototype Bond Equipe GT (as the vehicle was to become known) was ready for inspection by early 1963 and it was dispatched to Coventry for approval along with a somewhat anxious group of

Britain's latest jet fighter, the Lightning, also built in the north-west, provides the ideal backdrop for this promotional photo shoot of the new Equipe GT in 1963.

Sharp's representatives. Apparently much now rested on all going well with the testing, as Tom Gratrix had also been negotiating with Standard-Triumph's home sales manager, Lyndon Mills, to see if an arrangement could be agreed for the new Bond Equipe to be sold and serviced through the Company's British dealership and service agent network. As it turned out, events on the day were to pre-empt these discussions as Stanley Markland, Standard-Triumph's recently-appointed Managing Director, appeared on the scene and requested a test drive of the prototype. On returning from this test, obviously suitably impressed, he stated that this new car should be sold only through Standard-Triumph dealerships, and therefore it would be eligible for a full warranty and servicing at any of the Company's service agents worldwide. Sharp's could not have hoped for any more and certainly had not expected to get such a deal so easily. This virtually guaranteed the success of the Equipe as no other limited-production specialist sportscar could boast such back-up facilities and access to such a worldwide dealership network. The agreement was put on a

TCK 301

Rear of pre-production Equipe GT shows the high standard of finish achieved by Bond Cars in 1963. Note the non-opening frameless rear-quarter light on this early vehicle – the seal-mounted glass being replaced by an opening aluminium-framed opening quarter light on the production vehicles.

more formal basis in late 1963 when Sharp's Commercials were given a three-year licensing agreement for the Equipe. The Bond Equipe GT was announced in May 1963 and immediately caused something of a minor sensation in the motoring press. The new car did indeed fill a gap in the market and was described as a smart, moderately-priced GT-style car that provided accommodation for two adults and two children in comfort. Although it was described as a four-seater by Sharp's, this was soon revised to a 2+2, due to the somewhat limited rear headroom due to the slope of the roof line that gave the car its 'fast-

Well-restored 1963 Bond Equipe GT, nicely set off with centre-lock wire wheels.

Early Bond Equipe GT interior with smart Microcell Contour 6 bucket seats and Les Leston wood-rimmed alloy steering wheel.

back' styling. Whilst anything more than a local journey was likely to lead to discomfort for an adult rear-seat passenger, this arrangement was quite suitable for two children and the appeal of the Equipe GT to the married man with a young family, but who still harboured sportscar inclinations, was promoted by Sharp's Managing Director, Tom Gratrix, and would feature in marketing material for the car.

The bodyshell of the new Equipe GT was cleverly constructed out of glassfibre around the Herald's steel floorpan and scuttle assemblies, with the bodyline moulding of the Triumph doors being continued in the design of the Bond as a neat finishing touch. The bonnet was also of glassfibre construction with steel inner-wheel arches and supporting frame taken straight from the Herald, despite it being quite different in appearance. It also retained the Herald's superb engine accessibility by tipping forward in a similar manner as a complete unit with the front wings and forming the whole front section of the car. This bodyshell was mounted on a modified Triumph Herald chassis, slightly shortened at the rear, but which retained the same wheelbase and front and rear suspension, with specially re-set springs to suit the lighter overall weight of the Bond. On the mechanical side, the Equipe GT was powered by the 63bhp Triumph Spitfire 1,147cc engine and was fitted with front disc brakes as standard, but otherwise the running gear was all pure Herald. The interior was also a mixture of parts from various Triumph models blended with specially-designed features unique to the Bond. The dashboard was basically that of the Triumph Vitesse, but with a slightly altered instrument layout incorporating a rev counter, separate temperature and fuel gauges, and a Spitfire 110mph speedometer. The use of the Herald's floorpan and scuttle assemblies

BTL 113B

Very rare gathering of five surviving Bond Equipe GT 2+2s, out of the only twenty-five or so believed to still exist, taken at the TSSC (see appendices) South of England Meet in 2013. (*Photo: G. Singleton.*)

meant that other fittings from this vehicle could also be used, including the main floor carpets, sun-visors, windscreen and wiper motor, rack and spindle mechanism. This saved considerable time and expense in the development and construction of the new Bond Equipe GT, allowing a very high standard of interior trim from the start. The seats were specially tailored to fit the Bond at the rear, with a folding-down rear seat-back that gave access to the luggage compartment, which also housed the spare wheel. As with the early Austin Healey Sprite, there was no external access to this space as no opening bootlid was fitted, but there was the advantage of a fully-carpeted platform with 25 cubic feet of luggage space with the rear seat folded down - ideal for continental touring! The front seats for the Equipe were Microcell Contour 6 bucket seats which, together with the Les Leston wood-rimmed alloy steering wheel, enhanced the sportscar feel of the Bond.

Amongst the many road tests of the Equipe GT published was that conducted by John Bolster for *Autosport* in 1964, a journal which featured tests of many of the sports cars of the time. The quality of both the exterior and interior finish was the subject of particularly favourable comment during this test. Although the limitation of the rear headroom was noted, it was not considered to be particularly disadvantageous considering that the most probable customers for the car were likely to be the predicted young family men. In this respect the Equipe GT was considered to be something of an ideal compromise, certainly more practical than an open two-seater and, although it could not really be described as a true sportscar, it was certainly lively enough to provide enjoyable 'sporting' motoring. Performance figures were said to be

The high standard of finish on the Bond Equipe GT was down to the skill and care of the Company's highly experienced (and mainly female) glassfibre workers. (*Photo: Peter G. Reed.*)

Full production of the Bond Equipe GT underway at the Firm's Ribbleton lane assembly line, circa 1963. (*Photo: Peter G. Reed.*)

LATHAM'S

A delivery of new Equipe GT 2+2s leaving Preston in 1964 for distribution to Triumph dealerships across the country. Why some of the cars are missing hubcaps, headlamps, windscreen wipers, etc. is a mystery.

quite respectable with a top speed of 83.3mph, a 0-60mph time of 17.6 seconds and a standing quarter mile time of 20.4 seconds. The favourable response of the motoring press was undoubtedly instrumental in the considerable interest from prospective purchasers for the car, which was priced at £822.4s.7d. including purchase tax. Because of the limited facilities at the Bond Factory, initial production was very slow with only about half-a-dozen Equipe GTs a week being built. This must have caused some frustration to many would-be customers, but by the time of the model's official début at Earls Court for the 1963 Motor Show in October, production had increased to some 15-20 cars per week. This figure may seem almost insignificant when compared to the production figures of Sharp's associate Standard-Triumph, who produced around 5,000 vehicles per week at this time, but before long the Equipe GT was appearing in many of their dealers' showrooms both at home and abroad.

The SAH Bond Equipe GT

From the introduction of the Equipe GT, Sharp's Commercials Limited were particularly keen to promote the 'sportscar' image for their new vehicle. The first steps towards enhancing this image began in late 1963 with the announcement in November of a specially-uprated version of the Equipe GT, modified by the Leighton Buzzard-based tuning specialists SAH (for Sid A. Hurrell) Accessories Limited, who specialised in uprating the performance of Triumph vehicles. The modifications to the car were almost entirely confined to the engine and suspension - the only change to the interior being a slightly smaller, flatter steering wheel to accommodate a 'straight-arm' driving position, as popularized by racing drivers of the time. Modifications to the engine included considerable work to the cylinder head, with enlarged and polished inlet and exhaust ports, a higher compression ratio of 10:1 and larger inlet valves. A high-lift camshaft was specified, with a choice of three different profiles available, and the bottom end was balanced and fitted with special competition bearings. Other features included a competition clutch to handle the extra power, an oil cooler and a twin-choke compound down-draught Solex carburettor with a special four-branch exhaust manifold. To improve the handling of the car and no doubt for appearance purposes, centre-lock wire wheels were fitted, shod with Dunlop SP tyres, and with a modified spring at the rear and competition-rated springs at the front. A set of chrome streamlined wing mirrors completed this conversion, which was road tested by *Motoring News* in late 1963. Performance figures given in this test were quite impressive, although the cost of the work on top of the relatively high price of the basic car was noted as likely to limit the popularity of this conversion. Acceleration figures for the SAH Equipe GT recorded a 0-60mph time of 14 seconds, somewhat better than the 18 seconds recorded for the contemporary six-cylinder Triumph Vitesse. The modified engine was rated at 85bhp at 6,000rpm and gave the car a top speed of 96mph in top gear or 99mph with the optional overdrive engaged. The SAH conversion work added some £236.10s to the price of the basic Equipe GT, but customers could specify that only certain parts of the conversion were to be carried out as required.

Monte Carlo Bond

The SAH-tuned Equipe GT may not have attracted many paying customers, but it certainly attracted the attention of the motoring press, and Sharp's, who were keen to capitalise on the car's image, began to consider the possibility of entering a works vehicle in competition. The first decision to be made was at which event the Equipe GT would make its competition début and Sharp's, perhaps a little over-ambitiously, decided to go for the next major international event on the motor sport calendar, the Monte Carlo Rally, which was to be held in January 1964! There was no time to lose and as early as November 1963 preparations began in earnest with an application to the RAC to gain the official form of recognition required for the Equipe GT to enter a vehicle in international competition. With this formality successfully completed, an approach was made to the motoring correspondent of the local *Lancashire Evening Post*, John Lambert, to help with the planning of Sharp's entry in the Monte Carlo Rally. The *Post* kindly agreed to provide sponsorship and press coverage for the event, and

Interior shot of the 1964 Monte Carlo Rally Bond Equipe GT. Note the leather-faced Restall Masterfit reclining competition seats, metal dash-mounted map case and map-reading lamp, radiator blind operating chain, steering column-mounted overdrive switch and, tucked behind the gear lever, a Halda Speedpilot.

John Lambert was asked to recommend a suitable driver for the car. As a result, a local international rally driver of some repute - John Cuff - was invited to drive the Monte Carlo Equipe GT.

One of the early demonstration Equipes, registered TCK 300, was now selected to undergo the transformation into a rally car that would be up to the rigors of the arduous Monte Carlo course. Whilst the car was being prepared, John Cuff and John Lambert - who was to be the navigator and co-driver for the event - set off in another works Equipe to spend several days reconnoitring the rally route in preparation for the event. Much of the modification work on the rally Equipe was carried out by SAH and resulted in a 35 per cent increase in power, up to 85bhp. This engine differed slightly from the previous SAH specification with a 9.7:1 compression ratio and a twin-choke horizontal-type Weber 40 DCOE carburettor on a special separate cast-aluminium inlet manifold. Other modifications included fitting a SU electric fuel pump, Laycock de Normanville Type C overdrive, a 4.55:1 ratio differential, a sump skid shield and adjustable Armstrong shock-absorbers all round. Testing of the rally Equipe began as soon as it was returned to Sharp's and a number of further modifications were carried out at the Bond Factory. Precautions were taken against the freezing conditions that were expected during the event, by fitting a radiator blind and a special duct on the bonnet to direct warm air from the engine compartment towards the windscreen, in order to keep it free from ice. Also special fully-adjustable rally seats were fitted, as well as the necessary map pockets, map-reading lights and other specialised equipment required

The Equipe GT 2+2 begins the next stage of the 1964 Monte Carlo outside the Excel Hotel, Garstang (*later the 'Chequered Flag' and recently re-opened after refurbishment as the 'Bellflower'*).

to aid navigation and timekeeping. During the testing of the car it was found that the wind noise (which had been commented on in some of the published road tests of the Equipe), now reached an unacceptable level at the high speeds required for the rally. To overcome this problem, the rain channels at either side of the windscreen were extended with specially-made strips which would interrupt the airflow slightly around the door windows.

Disaster struck the Bond team shortly before the start of the rally when the SAH-tuned engine apparently seized during testing. Because the spare engine was already on its way to France with the service van, a new engine had to be rushed to the factory from SAH in Leighton Buzzard. Unfortunately this also seized after only a few miles! So, with less than a day and a half before the Equipe was due to set off for the Glasgow starting point for the rally, it left Sharp's with a serious setback to their plans. The factory staff now worked through the night on the car, fitting an engine taken from one of the other 'works' Equipes that were used for demonstration purposes. Although these works car engines were tuned to some extent, they were basically as standard and this must have necessitated the salvage of many parts from the seized SAH engine. Certainly the Weber carburettor and the special manifolds were used, and probably the modified cylinder head as well, but it is not known exactly what the final specification for the rally car was when it departed on the following morning. Fortunately the official RAC recognition documents allowed for some flexibility in the specification and the car must have been within these limits for the scrutineering at Glasgow the following day. In the meantime further problems were encountered on the run to Glasgow when a faulty manifold gasket was diagnosed - but this was easily overcome by refitting the manifolds on their arrival at the city.

After scrutineering was complete, the various vehicles entered in the Monte Carlo Rally were waved off at one-minute intervals from a dramatically floodlit starting ramp in Blytheswood Square at dusk the following evening. Three and a half hours later the Equipe, numbered 253, arrived outside the Excel Hotel, Garstang, to be greeted by Tom Gratrix, Colonel Gray and other well wishers. Following a brief rest and refreshments for the crew, the car was under way once more, resuming its journey to the next check point at Llandrindod Wells in Powys, Wales. The first 650-mile leg of the rally to Dover was completed with time to spare and the Equipe reached Reims in France on the third morning without incident or incurring any penalty points. By the fourth day weather conditions were deteriorating and problems began to be encountered: the windscreen wipers jammed because of icing and the engine overheated when a sheet of ice formed over the front of the radiator. For the next section, from Reims to Gerardmer in the Vosges Department in north-eastern France, the Bond team, like many of the other competitors, switched to spiked tyres to help their car cope with the icy conditions. Despite this precaution, progress was slow, and the team's 'time in hand' was gradually lost. A headlamp 'shot-out' by a stone thrown up by the tyres of another competitor caused further delays because of the need to find a replacement. This was followed by a series of mishaps with further broken lights requiring repair and then to add insult to injury, a wrong turn put the Bond three miles off course. A puncture sustained whilst retracing their route further aggravated the Bond crew's problems and by the time the Uriage-les-Bains control point was reached they were 14 minutes down. Aware that they were behind time, John Cuff and John Lambert frantically tried to make up the lost minutes, resulting in a minor collision with a banking after the car skidded on an ice-covered corner. Fortunately, the damage was only minor, but yet another headlamp was lost, and, unable to effect repairs, they were forced to carry on as best they could. Monte Carlo was finally reached, following a second puncture, just 24 minutes too late for the Equipe to be given a classified position, but the car had made it. It seems unfortunate that the Equipe did not gain a classified place considering the effort that went into this, the Equipe's competition début. It was certainly commendable that the car made it to the finish without further serious mechanical problems, and, had it not been for a series of minor mishaps, the Equipe would undoubtedly have earned a respectable placing in the results of the rally.

253

TCK 300, the works rally Equipe GT 2+2 looking somewhat the worse for wear, with missing foglamps and minor scrapes, after completing the 1964 Monte Carlo Rally. It is shown on display at Bradshaw's Motor Showroom, Marsh Lane, Preston.

On returning to Preston the Monte Carlo Rally Equipe was used for promotional purposes, including a tour of various dealerships where it was displayed in their showrooms. The car is also understood to have competed in the 1964 Tulip Rally and it was used in May of that year for a 24-hour endurance run at the Oulton Park circuit. Modifications carried out to the car in preparation for this run included the fitting of a Pye radio telephone to enable it to keep in contact with the pits, and Dunlop C41 tyres were fitted to the knock-on wire wheels. The engine was said to be in 'perfectly standard tune', but it is believed that Knutsford-based Triumph tuning specialists Mangoletsi Limited had done some work on it. TCK 300 was to be driven at this attempt on the circuit's 24-hour endurance record by three well-known women drivers of the time: Pat Coundley, Liz Jones and Anita Taylor. Each was to drive the car for a three-hour shift during daylight, reduced to two hours after dark. The event received considerable press coverage, but all did not go according to plan on the day and a gearbox fault developed during practice, shortly before the proposed midday start. This was quickly replaced with a gearbox from another car and, following a sudden downpour, the run finally got underway at 3.20 pm. The run was fairly uneventful, with only a clogged radiator grill causing problems and the pit crew apparently singing over the radio telephone to keep the drivers awake through the night! The endurance run record

Anita Taylor trying out the Pye radio telephone fitted to the Equipe especially for the endurance challenge at Oulton Park.

Left to right, Pat Coundley, Liz Jones and Anita Taylor, with the 24-hour endurance Equipe GT 2+2 (*TCK 300*) at Oulton Park, May 1964.

was successfully broken by the Equipe which covered 1,435.72 miles during the 24 hours.

Equipe GT4S

EQUIPE
G.T.

The success of the original Equipe GT model was short-lived, however, and as the initial enthusiasm began to wear off, the motoring press became less forgiving with regard to the restricted rear headroom and the lack of an opening bootlid. Customer feedback to the newly re-named Bond Cars Limited in Preston also confirmed that such things did indeed matter to their customers and it was realised that an improved version of the Equipe was required. Discussion on this project began as early as April 1964 and it was established from the start that in order to maintain the level of interest in the Equipe, and maximise the impact of the new model, it needed to be ready for the Motor Show in October of that year. The specifications for the design of the new Equipe's bodyshell included the provision of adequate headroom over the rear seats to accommodate adult passengers and a lockable opening bootlid. Other

Original body buck for the Equipe GT4S in 1964.

new features were to be incorporated into the bonnet section of the new car, including a fresh-air intake duct for the heater, a four-headlamp system and provision to potentially accommodate the six-cylinder Triumph Vitesse engine when it became available. This design was to be based on the same basic Triumph Herald components as the existing Equipe model in order to simplify the changeover and allow production to commence as soon as possible. A number of drawings were considered, including a proposal submitted by Lawrie Bond, but the eventual winner was that drawn up in-house by Bond's own chief designer Alan Pounder.

Work on the Mk II version of the Equipe began immediately and by August 1964 the first prototype was nearing completion, with the target date for submission of the vehicle to Standard-Triumph for their approval set for September. Progress was certainly rapid - especially considering that Bond's workforce stood at little more than 300 and the Company had three major development projects under way at this time. All was not quite going smoothly for the Company, however, as although the new Equipe model and the last of the Minicars in the form of the Mk G Tourer were ready on time, the 875 project was by now getting into serious difficulties. The new Equipe, designated the GT4S (the 4S indicating four-seater), was unveiled at a ceremony laid on for the motoring press at the Dorchester Hotel in London in early October. Later that month it joined its predecessor, now retrospectively designated the Equipe GT 2+2, on the Company's stand at the Earls Court Motor Show. Initially the two models were intended to run side by side and there was even talk of making the lighter GT 2+2 the

The GT4S was initially unveiled to the motoring press at London's Dorchester Hotel in early October 1964. The car to the left is believed to be the fourth GT4S built, registered ARN 176B, which the author rescued from a Warrington scrapyard many years ago!

EQUIPE

sports model with an interim stage-tuned 70bhp version of the Spitfire engine as standard. In fact, three of the late GT 2+2 models were fitted with pre-production units of the new 67bhp Spitfire Mk II engine in September 1964, probably for demonstration purposes, with this plan in mind. One of these specially-modified cars, Reg. No CJX 856 C in fact survived and was for a number of years the everyday transport of this author's long-suffering wife! But sadly it was written off by a hit and run driver, fortunately whilst parked and unoccupied, and later had to be sold as salvage. (However it is believed to have survived and if anyone knows of its current whereabouts - please get in touch!) It soon became obvious to the Company from the response to the new GT4S, from both the public and the motoring press, that there was now little demand for the GT 2+2, even in a modified form, and the idea was dropped. The final GT 2+2 was completed at the end of October 1964 and the model was discontinued after only some 444 had been built.

The first GT4S cars off the production line were still fitted with the same 63bhp Mk I Triumph Spitfire engine used in the previous model, but customers were also demanding more power from the Equipe, especially now it could carry more passengers. Following the delayed introduction of the new Mk II Triumph Spitfire in December 1964, the new 67bhp engine was officially made available to Bond Cars Limited and from March 1965 was fitted to the GT4S. The new Bond featured major changes in its redesigned bodyshell which gave the GT4S a substantially altered appearance from the somewhat cleaner lines of its predecessor. The most obvious change at first sight was the completely

ACK 888B

Factory publicity photo showing the completely redesigned bonnet of the GT4S, which incorporated a new four-headlamp lighting system. The car featured is another early GT4S, ACK 888B, actually the first production vehicle, which has also survived and now awaits restoration alongside ARN 176B, with current owner and Bond enthusiast Claire Conway-Crapp.

ACK 888B

Factory publicity photo showing the rear view of the first production GT4S, showing the distinctive 'sawn-off' back end incorporating a neat rear spoiler and the new opening bootlid.

redesigned bonnet which incorporated a new four-headlamp system, borrowed from the Triumph 2000, and a chrome-trimmed air duct on top to improve the airflow to the car's heater and de-misting system. The rear of the car retained the distinctive 'fast-back' styling of the earlier Equipe, but this was subtly altered to increase the headroom over the rear seats by some three inches. This was a particularly successful compromise: the car retained its sporting character as well as boasting rear headroom only three inches shorter than that over the front seats. The redesigned rear panel also added to the distinctive appearance of the new Equipe with a 'sawn-off' rear end that incorporated a neat

ARN 176B

Bond Cars' plan to grab a 1965 publicity coup, with two GT4Ss to be used as press cars, and therefore the first vehicles to use a newly-opened section of the M6 motorway from Preston to Lancaster, which would have been big news at the time, were frustrated by the death of Sir Winston Churchill which, of course, completely dominated the news the following day.

HYUNDAI
ARN 176 B
D269 HMT
CJX 866C

ARN 176B at a recent Bond Rally – a far cry from its immaculate appearance at the 1964 Dorchester Hotel ceremony. This GT4S was the fourth off the production line, was one of the cars used for the model's launch ceremony, the first car on the new M6 Motorway, and was used in several magazine road tests. (*Photo: G. Singleton.*)

GT 4S 65
BOND
EQUIPE
GT 4S
Built by Bond in association with Standard Triumph and available from Standard Triumph dealers
12 MONTHS GUARANTEE AND STANDARD TRIUMPH SERVICE THROUGHOUT THE U.K.

Bond Cars Ltd, as the Company was by now known, began to use tongue-in-cheek references to the fictional James Bond character in their advertising.

Les Leston Grand Prix Steering Wheels

Period sales brochure for Les Leston accessories, featuring the 'Grand Prix' model steering wheel that was specified for the Equipe GT4S.

rear spoiler and the new opening bootlid, giving access to a generously proportioned luggage space and the spare wheel beneath the floor panel.

The GT4S was offered at only £817 including purchase tax at its launch in 1964, less than the original price of the GT 2+2 in 1963 and only £30 more than the discounted price of the final 2+2 models offered in late 1964 at £787.19s including purchase tax. There was certainly considerable interest from potential customers for the new model, but limited production facilities at Bond's Preston factories remained a problem. There were also issues with the early bodyshells produced at Bond's India Mill Premises which proved to be slightly out of line, but this was soon overcome and production settled down to around ten cars per week. Bond's two-site operation could not have helped things, with the bare bodyshells having to be transported from the New Hall Lane site to nearby Ribbleton Lane where final assembly and painting were carried out on the production line, and even at the height of GT4S production only around thirty cars a week were being built. Minor changes were made to the specification of the GT4S over the next few years, mainly to update the mechanical specification in accordance with changes made by Standard-Triumph. An early Bond-originated change was the fitting of a new Les Leston wood-rimmed alloy steering wheel - swapping the tapered slot spoke version found on the GT 2+2 and some early GT4S cars for the famous accessory manufacturer's most popular steering wheel, the Grand Prix model, with four graduated circular cut-outs in each spoke. Coincidentally, the bosses for Les Leston steering wheels were actually made under contract at Lawrie Bond's Loxwood premises. Other cosmetic improvements were offered by Bond Cars Limited in the form of a whole range of optional extras. These included centre-lock wire wheels, a heated rear window with ultra-fine elements bonded into the laminated glass, a fold-back Webasto sun roof and the option of finishing a new vehicle in any colour at all specified by the customer for an extra £26.

SAH Equipe GT4S

Ever keen to demonstrate the sporting potential of the Equipe, in the summer of 1965, Bond Cars Limited again looked to Triumph tuning specialists SAH Accessories of Leighton Buzzard to transform a GT4S into a 'True 100mph Grand Tourer'. This involved taking a standard GT4S fitted with the 67bhp Mk 2 Triumph Spitfire engine and carrying out a full 'Stage 2' conversion, to take the power output up to 90bhp and the top speed up to 106mph. Engine work for the conversion included: a new four inlet port gas-flowed cylinder head and matched manifolds, competition valves and valve springs, twin 40 DCOE twin-choke Weber carburettors, new stronger crankshaft, stronger connecting rods, new special pistons, new special 'racing' camshaft and new special distributor. Modifications were also made to the gearbox, including a diaphragm spring choke and new special close-ratio gear set. Other work included a twin tail pipe exhaust system, oil cooler, Lucas sports coil, Pirelli Cinturato tyres and full engine balancing.

Driving tests of the SAH GT4S noted that the standard quality of build of the car was high enough, that there was no additional engine or wind noise and that the front disc brakes were well able to cope

Engine of the SAH-tuned Bond Equipe GT4S, dominated by the twin 40 DCOE twin-choke Weber carburettors.

with the increased power. Impressions of the car's performance were favourable and the car was said to give the driver a feeling of 'driving something rather special'. There was plenty of power available and even at 100mph it was noted you could still hold a conversation without any difficulty. Yet it was also noted that the car had none of the other problems associated with high-performance cars, as it would still run smoothly in heavy traffic, and the exhaust note, though sounding

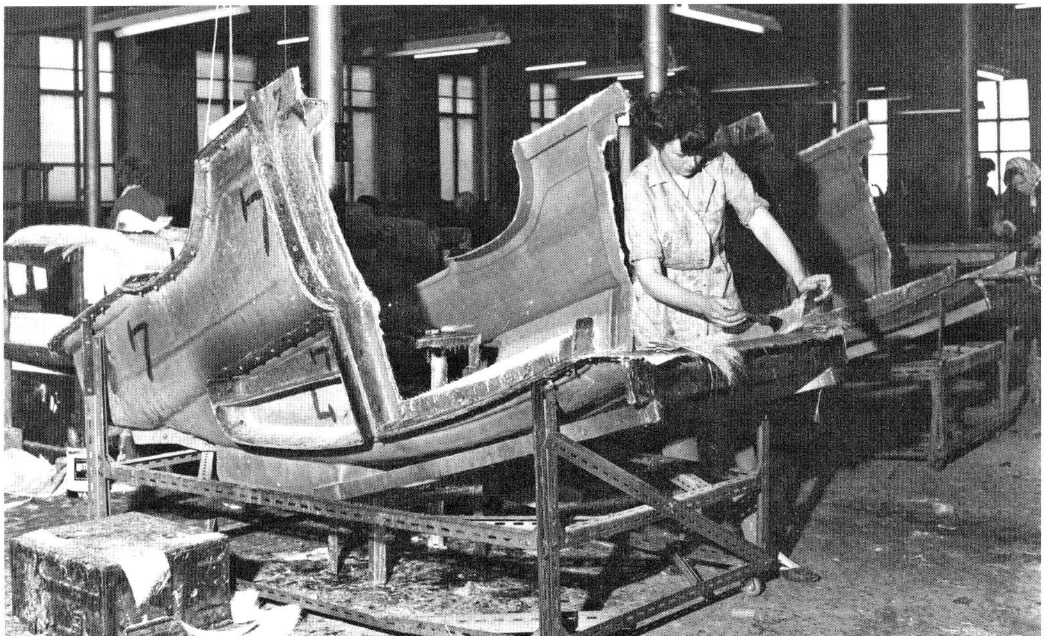

Laying glassfibre matting in Equipe GT4S bodyshell moulds at India Mill circa 1964. (*Photo: Peter G. Reed.*)

Chassis mounted and painted, Equipe GT4S bodyshells at India Mill, awaiting transport to the firm's Ribbleton Lane assembly line for completion. (*Photo: Peter G. Reed.*)

sporting, did not have the usual 'explosions' on over run that might attract the police! Bond Cars Ltd did not offer the SAH GT4S as an official model, though they did point out that the conversion was developed in association with Standard-Triumph and therefore did not invalidate the warranty on a new car in any way. SAH conversions were said to start from £99.1s.8d, with the model tested having cost £272.10s + £5.10s for labour to remove and then refit the engine and gearbox.

Equipe GT4S 1300

The next major change came in February 1967 with the introduction of GT4S 1300, powered by the new 75bhp 1,296cc Mk III Triumph Spitfire engine. Other than the new engine and minor modifications to the rear suspension, the Equipe GT4S 1300 was identical to the previous model and the car remained in production in this form until August 1970, when Bond's Preston factories were closed by their new owners, Reliant Motors Limited. In all, some 2,505 GT4S and GT4S 1300 Equipes were built, which - although a small figure by many manufacturers'

OOR 331G

OOR 331G

1968 Bond Equipe GT4S 1300. (*Photo: C. & A. Steggel.*)

Rear view of 1968 Bond Equipe GT4S 1300. Opening bootlid and increased rear-seat headroom made the GT4S models a more practical proposition. (*Photo: C. & A. Steggel.*)

standards - was a significant achievement for such a small firm, and the model proved to be the most successful of the four-wheel Bonds.

A new 2-Litre Bond Equipe

From the start of the GT4S project, Bond Cars Limited had been anticipating the availability of the Triumph Vitesse six-cylinder 1,998cc engine as a possible powerplant for their cars. Early plans for a six-cylinder version of the GT4S never got off the ground because ideas for a totally new and more ambitious Equipe began to take shape. As the initial development work for the new model began in mid-1965, Tom Gratrix was approached by a certain Trevor Fiore who announced himself as a professional car stylist and was said to have connections with the well-known Italian stylists and coachbuilders, Carrozzeria Fissore, located in Savigliano, near Turin. Fiore or Frost (as he was known before he changed his name in order to help his career), did indeed have such highly-placed connections and he had already done some work for another well-known Lancashire-based specialist sportscar manufacturer - TVR in Blackpool. He had been largely responsible for the striking but ill-fated TVR Trident in the early 1960s, which had never really progressed beyond the prototype stage. One of the four prototype Tridents built by Fissore had caused something of a sensation among the motoring press earlier in 1965 when it made its début at the Geneva Motor Show, but this success was short-lived. The Trident had been an ambitious step for TVR and was intended to be a top-quality sportscar designed to compete with the best, and that does not come cheap! TVR's sales at this time were not really up to supporting such a project and due to this and other financial problems, the makers of TVR cars, Grantura Engineering, went into liquidation for the second time in August 1965. Whilst a rescue deal for TVR was being put together, it seems a third party managed to acquire the Trident rights from Fissore - who were no doubt owed a lot of money by the now-bankrupt TVR Company. So when TVR re-emerged in 1966, all they had left was the four prototypes, with no way to put the vehicle into production.

With TVR's future so uncertain in 1965, Trevor Fiore was very keen to see his design concept take to the road, and Bond Cars Limited, with their close geographical location and similar, if less ambitious, product in the form of the Equipe, must have seemed an obvious place to start. A meeting was arranged at Bond's Preston factory and Trevor Fiore produced some impressive design sketches of his proposal. It was quickly obvious, however, that in order to make this design a viable proposition on the proposed Triumph Vitesse basis for the new Bond, considerable changes would be required, and Fiore, who was apparently unwilling to compromise, took his ideas elsewhere. The Trident design did eventually go into production in 1967 as the Trident Clipper V8,

Scale model proposal for the 2-Litre Equipe gets the approval of (*right to left*) Alan Pounder, Tom Gratrix and John Woods at Specialised Mouldings in 1966.

built by Trident Cars Ltd in Suffolk and based on Austin Healey 3000 running gear, fitted with a Ford 4.7 litre V8 engine and with a glassfibre bodyshell, but only some 130 vehicles were built before its demise in

Factory publicity photo of the Bond 2-Litre Equipe prototype, 1967.

ERN 656E

1975. The full story of the Trident saga and TVR cars is related in Peter Filby's book, *TVR: Success Against the Odds.*

Meanwhile, back at Bond's drawing office, Alan Pounder took up the challenge of translating the design sketches that Fiore had produced for Bond Cars Limited into a practical bodyshell design, utilising the specified Triumph components which were to form the basis of the new Equipe. The result, while still bearing some resemblance to the Fiore proposal, particularly in the treatment of the 'fastback' rear end, emerged as a substantially new design. Because of the limited facilities at the Bond Factory and the limited time scale for the development of the new Equipe, it was realised that some outside help would be needed to turn this ambitious new project into reality. At the Motor Show in October 1965, a meeting was arranged with Peter Jackson of Specialised Mouldings Limited to discuss the possibility that this Company carry out the necessary development work required to produce the initial body pattern. Soon afterwards Specialised Mouldings were commissioned to undertake the production of a prototype bodyshell, pattern master and a first working mould for the new shell. Throughout 1966 there were frequent visits to the Company's Crystal Palace works by representatives of Bond Cars Limited to check on each stage of the work as it progressed. Back at the Bond Factory in Preston, preparations for the production of the new model were also gaining momentum. The new design, although still based on the Triumph Herald / Vitesse chassis, now featured a completely Bond-designed bodyshell. Some Triumph parts, for example the steel floorpan and lower scuttle assembly, were still to be used, but would now require considerable modification as the outward appearance of the new Bond would give little indication of its Triumph origins. The scuttle assembly was remodelled by Bond with

Profile view of the 2-Litre Equipe prototype, 1967. The fuel filler was moved further back on the production model when the fuel tank was changed from that from the Triumph 2000 to the one from the Triumph Herald Estate.

Interior of the new 2-Litre Equipe, with newly-designed bucket seats, leather-bound alloy steering wheel, centre console, and polished wood door cappings and dashboard.

new, specially-made, windscreen pillars to accommodate the larger, more swept-back, windscreen that would be used. New specially-made pressed-steel door skins were also used, as were some other existing body parts (as on the earlier Equipes) such as the front and rear inner wheel arches, but unlike on the previous models these also required modification to fit the new bodyshell.

By January 1967 the first prototype bodyshell for the new Equipe had been received from Specialised Mouldings and work began on assembling the first prototype car. Progress was, however, slow, because of the large number of bought-in components and contracted-out work on special items required for the new car. Considerable time was spent in chasing up these suppliers and although the prototype was virtually complete by March, there were delays with small items like the windscreen wipers and some interior trim parts. The first prototype was finally ready to take to the road in May 1967 and work began immediately on the second car, intended to provide the standard for the production model. The new Bond Equipe 2-Litre GT (as the car was to be known) was announced to the motoring press in August 1967 with a launch ceremony held at London's Kensington Palace Hotel. The new car was powered by a 1,998cc Triumph inline six-cylinder engine that produced 95bhp at 5,000rpm giving the car a genuine 100mph capability and a 0-60mph time of 11.5 seconds, according to *Autocar* soon after the launch. Mechanically the Equipe 2-Litre was pure Triumph Vitesse, mounted on a slightly-modified chassis and using the Triumph all-synchromesh four-forward-speed gearbox, with Laycock de Normanville overdrive available as an optional extra. Substantial changes were made to the interior, in particular the use

Sorry–
no ejector seat!
ERN 656E

Early advertising brochure for the 2-Litre Equipe featured the prototype car and made even stronger references to the fictional James Bond character – which led to some confusion with one royal customer!

Leider keinen
Katapult-Schleudersitz!
ERN 656E

The Equipes were also marketed abroad, with exports claimed to twenty-six different countries.

of new specially-designed bucket seats with slightly less prominent side supports, to overcome the criticism over the difficulty which some owners had apparently experienced getting in and out of the old Microcell Contour 6 seats. Other improvements to the interior included extra rear-seat headroom, a centre console below the dashboard for fitting the optional radio and an integral radio aerial built into the glassfibre shell as standard. The overall appearance of the new Equipe was generally highly regarded and many reports at the time commented favourably on its sleek looks, professional standard of finish and highly individual lines. The Equipe 2-Litre GT did not come cheap, however, and at £1,095.13s, including purchase tax, plus an additional £58.7s for the preferable optional overdrive, it could hardly be called competitive,

A well-restored 1968 2-Litre Equipe Coupé – note the location of the fuel filler cap on the production model and the optional extra Webasto sunroof.

though, didn't compare too badly with the MGB GT, which could be had from £1,064,19s.

Equipe 2-Litre Mk II

Although the Equipe 2-Litre was intended to expand the Bond range as a complimentary model to the existing GT4S, it soon became clear that the new model somewhat over-shadowed its predecessor from the start. This led to a drop in demand for the GT4S and production was cut back accordingly, allowing the Factory to concentrate on the new model. As sales steadily grew the Equipe 2-Litre began to suffer from criticism directed at its high-speed handling abilities, especially on hard cornering. This was hardly surprising when considering the car's basis on Triumph Herald suspension components - and Triumph were also experiencing similar problems with their Vitesse and GT6 models, which although now considerably more powerful than the Herald, still used the same basic rear suspension layout. Consequently Triumph completely redesigned this layout for their Herald chassis-based six-cylinder models, replacing the old swing-axle arrangement (which had been satisfactory for the lower-powered Herald) with an improved system able to cope with the demands of the more powerful, faster, Vitesse and GT6 models. This was done by incorporating a newly-designed vertical link assembly, now secured at its bottom end by an independent lower wishbone system. This made the whole system far more rigid and necessitated alterations to the rear half-shafts, now incorporating rubber Rotoflex couplings and universal joints to allow the whole assembly to move freely. The result of these improvements was the introduction of the Vitesse Mk II 2-Litre, launched in October 1968. Bond had been kept informed of these developments and the new chassis was simultaneously incorporated into their Equipe 2-Litre model in September 1968, and the new Mk II version was also launched

ALFA ROMEO
CITROEN
AUSTIN
EQUIPE
EQUIPE
G.T.
BOND

Bond Cars Ltd stand at the 1968 Motor Show with the new 2-Litre Mk II Convertible stealing the show.

The Gold Medal for Coachwork was won by the 2-Litre Convertible Equipe Mk II at the 1968 Motor Show, and in recognition these gold windscreen stickers were produced to be placed on the cars on the Bond stand.

COACHWORK
COMPETITION
ORGANISED IN CONJUNCTION WITH
THE 1968
MOTOR EXHIBITION
BY PERMISSION OF THE SOCIETY OF MOTOR
MANUFACTURERS AND TRADERS
SECTION Nº 14
STANDARD CONVERTIBLE COACHWORK
FIRST PRIZE
INCORPORATED

at the Motor Show in October that year. As with the new Mk II Vitesse model, the Bond also featured a new uprated version of the Triumph six-cylinder engine, which now produced some 104bhp, giving a top speed of 103-104mph. Interior changes to the Bond Equipe 2-Litre Mk II were minimal, the main change was the use of textured-black Ambla PVC trim material to replace the wood-veneered finish on the facia and door cappings, as well as a black leather-bound version of the Les Leston steering wheel, both enhancing the all black 'sporting' trim.

A Convertible Bond

The real eye-catcher on the Bond stand at the 1968 Motor Show was, however, the striking new Bond 2-Litre Mk II Convertible. From the start of the Equipe 2-Litre project, plans for a convertible version of the car had always been in the background. It was not until mid-1968 that these plans were turned into reality when the prototype convertible took shape at the Bond Factory in July of that year. The process of producing a convertible version of the Equipe 2-Litre had in fact been surprisingly straightforward, although the large swept-back windscreen had caused some problems and required major modification of what was basically a Herald / Vitesse convertible hood frame. Apart from the first prototype convertible, all the Equipe 2-Litre convertibles were built to the new Mk II specification, for it was decided to leave the launch of the new model to coincide with the introduction of the Mk II model once the specification was finalised. It is not known exactly how many of these convertible Equipes were built, but from the Mk II model's introduction approximately 50 per cent of Equipe 2-Litre production was made up by the convertible model - indicating a total figure of around 400 convertibles.

The new Bond Convertible was once again considered something of a 'gap filler' as no new British four-seat convertible had appeared at the Motor Show for some six years. This factor must undoubtedly have

The 2-Litre Equipe Mk II range for 1968. The Rostyle stainless-steel wheel trims and black-painted sills enhance the low, sleek look.

been significant in the amount of interest that the new model attracted at the show. But at £1,277.6s, including purchase tax, it also attracted comments from the motoring press with regards to the relatively high price of Bond's advertised 'low cost individuality'. By the time the first road tests of the new convertible began to appear in early 1969 this price had in fact risen further to £1,305, some £284 more than the equivalent Vitesse Mk II convertible and £433 more than the Vitesse Mk II saloon model. Bond's advertising made much of the four-seater accommodation offered by their convertible and this apparently led to an embarrassing incident for the Company at the Motor Show launch, when four rather large press reporters were invited to try out this feature for themselves. Unfortunately the Bond's glassfibre bodyshell proved to be somewhat less rigid than its Vitesse cousin and allowed a slight flexing of the chassis because of the weight, resulting in the doors jamming shut and refusing to budge. Following a rather undignified exit, when the offending reporters climbed out of the car, the doors once again opened freely, and a number of blocks were discreetly placed under the car to support the chassis and prevent a repeat performance! Fortunately for Bond, little was made of this incident by the motoring press and the production model was immediately modified with extra strengthening in order to overcome the problem. The new Bond Convertible soon redeemed itself at the Motor Show, however, winning a gold medal for coachwork, and, despite the price,

Bond Cars Ltd's marketing for the new Mk II 2-Litre Equipes seems to have become far less restrained! Though as well as the car's 100mph performance and 'knock-out looks', the copy also emphasised the hand-built quality of the vehicle, and for the more level-headed, the access to Standard Triumph's servicing network too.

Bond Bombshell
Bond Equipe 2 Litre GT.
This is the Bond Equipe GT. A fleet, four-seater fastback with a smooth 95 b.h.p. 2-litre engine. A car that can soar to 70 m.p.h. in seconds, reach 100 in top – and a knock-out to look at!
In design (and by design) the Equipe's a great deal like the most expensive car in the world. It's largely and quite distinctively hand-built. Its rustproof moulded glass fibre body displays a seven times hand-sprayed coach finish.
And servicing? No problem. The Equipe GT can be taken for a check-up or spares or servicing to any Standard Triumph servicing centre sited in the U.K.
A fast hand-built car with country-wide servicing facilities. That's the pride and practicality of owning an Equipe GT. And with the one you buy, you receive a 12,000 mile/12 month warranty on its performance and reliability. £1,223 - purchase tax included.
… and the convertible Equipe GT. Fast. Fantastic suspension. Hand-built. £1,305 including purchase tax.
NAME
ADDRESS
Saloon
Convertible
Many Standard Triumph dealers have the Bond Equipe GT in their showrooms now. The coupon brings you their names and full Equipe GT details.
To: Bond Cars Ltd., Preston, Lancs. Please send full information on the Equipe GT and tell me where I can see it.
Built by Bond in association with Standard Triumph.

Montage of features from the new Mk II 2-Litre Equipes, showing black-textured Ambla covering on the dashboard, engine accessibility and generous boot space, etc.

initial orders proved that there was indeed considerable demand for such a car. A *Motor* brief test on the Equipe Convertible appeared in March 1969, again commenting on the high price of the vehicle and also noting the limited rear-seat accommodation which resulted from the intrusion of the hood well into the passenger space (though no more so than on the Herald and Vitesse before it). This led *Motor* to revise the four-seater description of the car made by Bond to their own 2+2 version, but there were favourable comments with regard to the high overall standard of finish, the improved handling characteristics and the car's 'lively' performance.

These improvements in handling and performance of the Mk II Equipe 2-Litre also prompted *Motor* to reassess the Coupé version of the car which had been the subject of a full road test in the journal the previous November. Performance figures for the new Mk II model recorded a top speed of 103.5mph with a rather disappointing 0-60mph time of 13.2 seconds, although weather conditions for the test were described as 'poor - wet and windy'. A road test of the mechanically-identical Triumph Vitesse recorded a more respectable 0-60mph time of 11.3 seconds in more favourable conditions. Bond's own sales literature for the Equipe gives a 0-60mph figure of 10.6 seconds. Also it was stated in *Motor*'s re-test of the Equipe that the overdrive unit fitted to the test car had unfortunately developed a fault and this was given as the reason why the car failed to record a 100mph lap at the MIRA circuit.

A Bright Future for the Equipe?

With the introduction of the Equipe 2-Litre Mk II range, the outlook certainly seemed promising for Bond Cars Limited, with a secure future assured. The new Equipes were proving popular, and orders were coming in from dealerships at home and abroad - in fact, the Equipe now boasted exports to some twenty-six different countries. France, Belgium, Holland and Portugal were all regular destinations for new Equipes. Bond's advertising no longer contained references to predicted mass production, but played on the 'hand-built exclusivity' of the Bond Equipe. Clearly the production of such an exclusive high-quality vehicle required such care and attention that only a limited number could be produced each year, or so Bond Cars Limited would have had their customers believe. Certainly this image received something of a boost

Bond's stand at the 1969 Motor Show – no longer tucked away at the edges, the Company opted for a large premium main-floor space alongside mainstream manufacturers.

BOND
ASTON MART
LAGONDA

BOND
1300 GT

Bond also splashed out with added glamour at the 1969 Motor Show!

late in 1968 with the placing of an order for an Equipe 2-Litre Coupé by the King of Nepal. The King required the car to be finished to his own specifications and even enquired about the fitting of an ejector seat! Apparently he had seen some of Bond's promotional literature which included a humorous reference to such an option, playing on the link between the brand name of the vehicle and the fictional James Bond character. The 'Royal' Bond Equipe was the first such car to be finished by the factory in black and was trimmed in red leather with matching seatbelts supplied free of charge by Britax. The car was shipped from Birkenhead Docks for the first leg of its journey by sea to Calcutta and then 600 miles by train to Nepal, finally to be delivered to the Royal Palace at Kathmandu - where it possibly still resides to this day.

As sales of the Equipe range remained steady, further development work and discussion of proposed new models took place behind the scenes at the Bond Factory. This included a proposal for an S/E Special Equipment model of the 2-Litre Equipe, to include a whole range of luxury features as standard. It was to be fitted with a radio, tape player, wire wheels, heated rear window, sunroof, burglar alarm, overdrive, hazard warning lights and other gadgetry. In other words, every optional extra available on the existing 2-Litre model plus almost every conceivable gadget on the market as well. The projected price for the S/E model was never finalised and it was perhaps fortunate for the Company that the model never went into production as the cost of all these features, on top of the already high price of the Equipe, would have certainly made it a very expensive proposition indeed. Attempts to revive the flagging sales of the Equipe GT4S were also under discussion at this time. Perhaps the most promising of all these ideas

A striking 1968 Mk II 2-Litre Equipe Convertible – in 20 years Bond cars had come a long way from the first Minicar! (*Photo: C. & A. Steggel.*)

Engine bay of a restored 1968 Mk II 2-Litre Equipe, showing Triumph's 1998cc straight-six cylinder engine. The alternator conversion would be a recent modification.

was a proposal for a convertible version of the vehicle. Certainly such a model would have been straightforward enough to develop in view of the GT4S model's standard Herald scuttle and floorpan assemblies, but events were rapidly coming to a head that were to have disastrous consequences for Bond Cars Limited.

Although the Equipe range continued in production after the takeover of Bond Cars Limited by Reliant in early 1969, all development work on the cars was immediately stopped at the Preston factories. The final Equipe 2-Litre and GT4S models produced in August 1970 were virtually unchanged from their 1968 specification, other than minor modifications to simplify production or overcome parts shortages. There were, however, drastic differences apparent in the build quality of these later cars, resulting in a stream of complaints from dissatisfied customers and dealerships alike. Various attempts were made to overcome this situation and to placate the dealerships - who were rapidly running out of patience with the Reliant-owned-and-run Bond Factory. By August 1970, however, Reliant had given up on the Equipe and the last few, hastily-built, vehicles were sold off at a Midlands motor auctioneers to ensure that there would be no further comeback to the Firm. Production figures for the three years that the Equipe 2-Litre models were produced indicate that only 1,431 such vehicles were built. Around 600 of these were Mk I models, and the remainder

This 2-Litre Equipe is the very last car built (V10 – 5431), and is now abroad and undergoing a full restoration (*Photo: G. Singleton.*)

BOND
FMK 980J

NATIONAL
'DRIVE IT' DAY
9

One of the last 2-Litre Equipe Mk II Convertibles, which formed part of the batch sold off at auction by Reliant – all have consecutive 'CBF' (Staffordshire) registration numbers. Note the lack of chrome body strips and badging, also a feature of these cars. This vehicle was, in fact, at one time owned and driven by the author, but before it looked this good! (*Photo: C. & A. Steggel.*)

were divided fairly equally between the Mk II Coupé and Convertible models. Certainly the Equipe 2-Litre had remained 'exclusive', but considering the expenditure on the development of the model, profits were undoubtedly minimal, despite the vehicle's relatively high price.

Chapter Seven

The Final Phase

The factors behind Reliant's takeover of Bond Cars Limited in February 1969 have often in the past been somewhat over-simplified. Many people saw the move as a means of removing Reliant's main competition in the three-wheeler market, but with the total production of Bond's 875 model at 3,400 vehicles, compared to Reliant's own 15,000 three-wheeler sales per year at this time, Bond hardly posed a serious threat. It seems that the main reason for Reliant's interest in fact lay in Bond's successful association with Standard-Triumph, which was by now well established, with access to Triumph's dealership and servicing facilities worldwide.

This was not some modern-day aggressive takeover bid by a rival company, but rather a series of unfortunate circumstances which left the way open for Reliant to move in. The reasons for the sale of Bond Cars Limited, in fact, went back to the death of Ewart Bradshaw some years before in 1959. This event had led to the reorganisation of the Bradshaw Group of companies, including Colonel Gray becoming the Chairman of Loxhams Garages Ltd, and leaving Tom Gratrix in charge of Sharp's Commercials (known as Bond Cars Ltd from 1964) as Managing Director. By 1968 the decision had been taken to sell off Loxhams Garages following an approach by the Dutton Forshaw group who were looking to expand their dealership organisation in the north-west. Dutton Forshaw were mainly interested in the sales and service activities of Loxhams, and prior to their takeover of the Company, Colonel Gray was instructed to sell Loxhams' shareholding in Bond Cars Ltd, though ownership of the buildings occupied by the Company was to be retained. Because of difficulties in finding a buyer for Loxhams' stake, and also because other shareholders were reluctant to remain as minority shareholders to an outside majority, there was apparently little alternative, but to sell Bond Cars Limited outright. For Bond Cars itself, a management buyout seemed the preferable option, but although the Company was by no means in financial difficulties at this time, it could hardly be described as thriving either. Bond's management realised that outside backing for such a takeover of the Company would not be easy to secure. Initially they attempted to raise the financial backing required themselves and an approach was made to Standard-Triumph, with whom Bond had enjoyed a close association for several years during the production of the various Equipe models, but this proved unsuccessful. Another company approached was the Wales-based Gwent and West of England Enterprises Limited, a subsidiary of Julian Hodge (Finance) Ltd. This Company already had

TRIUMPH

What Reliant coveted! Bond Cars Ltd's arrangement with Standard Triumph's dealership and servicing network.

extensive motor industry and engineering interests, including a certain Reliant Motor Company, which they had taken over control of in 1962.

Reliant take over Bond Cars

As Dr Dan Lockton outlines in the first volume of his outstanding and comprehensive work on the Reliant story - *Rebel without Applause: Vol.1*, Reliant, who were now alerted to Bond's predicament, took the opportunity to suggest that Gwent and West of England Enterprises make a bid to purchase Bond Cars Limited. Negotiations began with Loxhams late in 1968, and public assurances were made that the Preston Factory would continue to operate and be run as a separate complementary entity to Reliant's Midlands-based concern. However, local concerns that production would be soon be transferred to the Midlands continued and in January 1969, Preston North MP Ron Atkins became involved and suggested that the merger should be referred to the Board of Trade. The situation was not helped by Col. Gray's refusal to disclose the duration of the leases on the Preston factories to be taken up by Reliant. But both Loxhams and Reliant stuck to their story, repeatedly stating that it was intended that production at Preston would continue, and Bond became a subsidiary of the Reliant Motor Company in February 1969. To begin with there was little change for the 300-strong work force at Preston, although Reliant soon rearranged Bond's management structure, with Ray Wiggin replacing Tom Gratrix as Managing Director, who left to become managing director of the Watson Motor Group chain of garages.

Reassurances of Reliant's intention to keep the Bond factories running as a going concern also continued, and there was some

Scooter Ski production gets underway at Bond's India Mill Premises.

evidence of this in July 1969 with the introduction of a new product for the Preston factories: the Scooter Ski. This glassfibre single-hulled water-borne 'motor-scooter' was basically an up-to-date, more practical, interpretation of a previous Bond product, the twin-hulled Power Ski. It was powered by a 185cc single-cylinder Rotax two-stroke engine with a recoil rope pull-start, accessed by lifting the hinged scooter-style seat. Steering was via motorcycle-style handlebars,

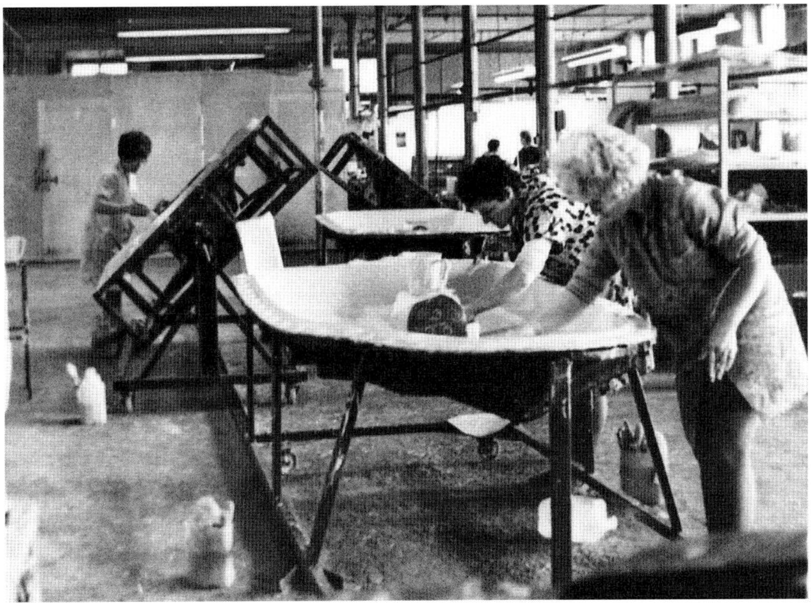

Bond employees laying glassfibre in the new Scooter Ski hull moulds that seem to have replaced the Bond 875 moulds at India Mill, circa 1970. (*Photo: Peter G. Reed.*)

Alan Pounder testing one of the first Bond-built Scooter Skis in the Lake District in 1969.

which also incorporated s twist-grip accelerator - a centrifugal clutch allowed the engine to idle whilst the craft remained stationary. Despite its modern looks, it was a far cry from today's sophisticated jet-skis! The engine drove a rear-mounted propeller beneath the hull, giving a claimed top speed of 25mph, whilst the steering was connected to a small front-mounted rudder, assisted by the rider banking the machine over, as on a motorcycle. Reliant had, in fact, first announced that they were to produce the Scooter Ski in 1967, following negotiations with the UK sales agent, Scooter Ski Sales Limited of Draycott, Derbyshire. This was followed by a well-publicised demonstration in St Katherine's Dock, London, filmed by Pathé News. But it seems that initially, as with Bond's Power Ski previously, domestic orders were slow to materialise, though this did allow time for Reliant to develop and improve the Scooter Ski. By 1969, Scooter Ski Sales Ltd's marketing was reaching an international audience and sales were picking up, and it was reported that Bond's production capacity would be required to fulfil a recent order for 500 Scooter Skis. Following the Earls Court International Boat Show in January 1970, further export orders for 3,500 Scooter Skis were announced, seemingly securing the Preston Factory's immediate future.

Whilst production of the GT4S and Equipe 2-Litre models continued, it was not long before Reliant's attention turned towards the 875 three-wheeler. To many it came as no surprise that Bond's new owners wanted to discontinue 875 production, since the model appeared to compete directly with their own products, and with the 875's troubled production history they would hardly have needed to look far for an excuse to do so. But the 875 had by now developed into a much more practical proposition. With its issues overcome it began to carve its own niche in the market and certainly in performance terms it easily outstripped Reliant's own three-wheel offerings. But although Bond had only recently secured a new three-year contract with Rootes to continue to supply the Imp engine and running gear for the 875, Reliant now reported that there had been a significant price increase for these parts. The result was that the 875 would have either been uneconomic to produce or would have to be priced above what Reliant felt the market could support, and winding down of production was announced, with the blame being laid, perhaps rather conveniently, at Rootes' door. Early in 1969, production of the 875, which stood at around forty-five vehicles per week, was drastically cut back and only two to six vehicles a week were produced until existing orders had been fulfilled and stocks of major components used up early in 1970, when it was finally discontinued.

Bond's by-now highly-organised product development committee was another early casualty of the takeover: it was virtually disbanded, and the existing projects in the pipeline abandoned. These included the S/E version of the Equipe 2-Litre, and a totally new Equipe which was to have been based on the Triumph 2000 floorpan and mechanical components. Also abandoned was Bond's own Apex project (named after the Rootes project name that resulted in the Imp prototype), which had reached a fairly advanced stage with the first of two proposed prototypes already under construction. The Bond Apex or Competition 875 was to be a glassfibre monocoque construction sports-style two-seater coupé based, like the 875 three-wheeler, on Hillman Imp mechanical components. Unfortunately the prototype was never completed and only the initial design sketches have survived to give an indication of what could have been a very interesting sportscar.

Reliant were very keen at this stage to develop their access to Bond's arrangement with Triumph, and realising that any new vehicle that

COMPETITION
'875'

Alan Pounder's initial concept sketch for the Bond 875 Apex project in 1968 – although work was apparently started on a prototype vehicle, the project was scrapped shortly after Reliant's takeover.

Front view of Reliant's proposed face-lift for the Equipe, which featured glassfibre door shells and scuttle assembly.

Side profile of Reliant's proposed updated Equipe, which although featuring some of the styling cues of the original car, seems to have lost the character and clean sleek lines of the Bond version.

would be sold through these dealerships would have to be largely based on Triumph components, they set to work designing their own version of the Equipe at Tamworth. The new vehicle, code named FW8, was apparently intended to fill a gap in Reliant's range between their three-wheeler models and the prestigious Scimitar. The styling was done in-house, with no input from Ogle, who did much of Reliant's design work by this time, and resulted in a rather uninspiring fixed-

Rear view of Reliant's proposed update of the Equipe.

head coupe based on a loose interpretation of the basic Equipe shape, but which had lost many of the characteristic Fiore design features. The new Reliant Equipe, which never progressed beyond the prototype stage, was still based on the separate chassis and running gear from the Triumph Vitesse. This choice seems at first to be a little surprising, as by that time the separate chassis Triumph design, which had been conceived out of necessity in the late 1950s, was now looking somewhat dated. Triumph were in fact already considering abandoning the Herald and Vitesse range in favour of the more modern monocoque construction Triumph 1300 and 2000 models. Bond apparently were also aware of this and hence their proposed design for a new Equipe had been based around the Triumph 2000's steel floorpan, giving a semi-monocoque bodyshell in place of the old separate chassis configuration. It should be remembered, however, that Reliant's production facilities at Tamworth were considerably more advanced than Bond's Preston operation, so the production of their own chassis frame would have presented few problems. Also, the separate chassis method of construction would undoubtedly have been a lot more straightforward and therefore cheaper to produce.

As in the past, it was events beyond Bond's control that were to deal the final blow, initially to the Equipe and ultimately the Company, with the merging in 1968 of the Leyland Group (which included Standard-Triumph) with the rival BMC Group. This led to a major reorganisation of both groups, with the result that Triumph, Rover and Jaguar found themselves grouped together as manufacturers of 'specialist' vehicles. The new British Leyland Motor Corporation also began to rationalise the various manufacturers' model ranges and dealership networks.

This left the three 'specialist' car manufacturers sharing a combined dealership network, meaning that the showrooms could now offer a much wider range of models. As part of this rationalisation process it was decided to finally replace the Herald/Vitesse range with the new Toledo and 1500 models launched in 1970, though as already outlined, this would not have been a major issue for Bond, and it may be noted that other companies that also used Triumph engines and parts continued to be supplied. But these developments did mean that there was no longer room for the Equipe models within the new Triumph range and therefore Reliant effectively lost the hoped-for access to this international dealership network. This was undoubtedly a major blow to Reliant because it was this access to Triumph dealerships that had clearly been a major factor behind the acquisition of Bond Cars Limited. Apparently Reliant had little idea of the problems that lay ahead and they certainly appear to have failed to realise the likely implications of the Leyland/BMC merger, despite the fact that it was already well advanced at the time of their takeover.

Chapter Eight

The Bond Bug

Whilst the events surrounding the creation of the British Leyland Motor Corporation were unfolding, Reliant had already set into motion plans for the production of a completely new vehicle that would bear the Bond name. Code named TW11, this was a revolutionary new three-wheeler created by the talented designer, Tom Karen, then managing director at Ogle Design Ltd, a company that had developed a close relationship with Reliant since 1963, one that had resulted in a number of distinctive vehicle designs. His fascination with three-wheelers had begun in 1954 when he produced a tiny one-off, all-aluminium-bodied, two-seat, three-wheeler called the Vimp - interestingly it had featured a windscreen frame mounted on part of the bonnet section, which hinged forwards for passenger/driver access. It seems the idea planted a seed, and later, at Ogle, he began to develop a concept for a sporty, two-seat three-wheeler, which he presented to an initially, decidedly unenthusiastic, Reliant. Certainly Reliant's three-wheelers up to now had developed an image more inspired by economy and some might say even austerity, making it difficult for the Company's management to see how such a 'fun car' concept could fit in with the range. But Tom Karen persisted with his idea, even having some 1/8th scale models made, and eventually, in 1967, Ogle got the go ahead to develop a full-scale mock-up. This allowed a number of design features to be seen in a 'real' context and tried out, leading to some being rejected, such as the original idea to have a fixed canopy with large side openings that driver and passenger had to scramble in and out of, and other features to be developed further, like getting the fixed seating position just right for a range of heights of driver.

By now Reliant seemed to be warming to the concept, and were looking to it as a means of attracting younger drivers/owners and even termed it 'The Youth Car of the Seventies' at its eventual launch. Though at this stage there was still no firm plans to put the vehicle into production, Ogle were now commissioned to continue development in 1968 and produce a full prototype. The basis for the new vehicle was to be inspired by the separate steel chassis that had been a feature

One of a series of original concept sketches for what became the Bond Bug. (*Photo: T. Karen.*)

of the Company's Regal 3/25 model introduced in 1962. This model's successful combination of steel chassis coupled with a moulded all-glassfibre shell was a concept that at the time was being re-styled by Ogle, working in association with Reliant's chief engineer John Crosthwaite, who was responsible for redesigning a lighter-weight chassis and updating the running gear for project TW8, that would become the new Reliant Robin in 1973. John Crosthwaite had joined Reliant in 1966, as a chassis specialist, having considerable experience in the field, having worked with the likes of Cooper, Lotus and BRM, as well as being responsible for a number of pioneering racing-car designs in the USA. His first task at Reliant was to carry out improvements to the SE4 Scimitar's chassis, which led to his first association with Tom Karen the following year, when he designed a completely new chassis for the newly-styled SE5 Scimitar. The new chassis for the TW11

Another original concept sketch for what became the Bond Bug. (*Photo: T. Karen.*)

bond
BUG
750ES

Tom Karen attending a recent Bug Club event. (*Photo: J. Scratch Platts.*)

prototype was developed by John Crosthwaite from the new frame being prepared for the TW8 project, which was shortened and fitted with a revised rear suspension set-up. The intention was to improve the car's cornering ability, which had become something of an issue on the Regal, and obviously as the new car was to be promoted for its sporty image, this needed sorting out! The new rear set-up utilised a live axle mounted on double trailing arms each side, with combined coil spring and telescopic shock absorber units, and a Panhard rod to help compensate for when only one occupant was carried, with an antiroll bar to help control body roll. Stability was also helped by the choice of 10in wheels, as popularised by the Mini, and the low seating position and low centre of gravity of the design.

It was clear from the outset that mechanically, at least, Tom Karen's

First prototype from early 1969. Still named the Reliant Rogue at this stage, it featured flip-up headlamps, a more rounded frontal appearance and convertible style roof section. (*Photo: T. Karen.*)

new design should use as many off-the-shelf Reliant components as possible, including the all-alloy 701cc engine from the Regal, producing 29bhp at 5,000rpm, as well as its front suspension and steering. But the new bodyshell bore no resemblance to any previous Reliant product - or anything else on the market for that matter! To overcome the access issues noted on the mock-up, Tom Karen seems to have partly revisited his earlier Vimp creation and also been inspired by his aeronautical engineering background. The result was a one-piece moulded glassfibre aircraft-style canopy, incorporating the windscreen and hinged to the front, to allow it to open upwards. Opening was assisted by a pneumatic gas strut that held the canopy open, and detachable flexible side-screens covered the 'door apertures' when it was closed. The resulting prototype TW11 was completed in early 1969 and provisionally named the Reliant Rogue, and featured retractable headlamps and a more rounded frontal appearance than the sharp angular lines shown in the initial concept sketches, though this would have greatly simplified production, as all of the glassfibre parts that made up the shell could be lifted straight from their moulds, with no undercuts or bolted sections to contend with. However, it seemed the concept remained a step too far for Reliant's management, who were reluctant to take the risk of going ahead with the vehicle under the Reliant name. But the recent acquisition of Bond Cars Ltd in early 1969 gave fresh momentum to the project, as it was felt that under the Bond brand name such a bold totally new vehicle might just work from a marketing point of view. Initially, work on a second prototype was given the green light

Rear view of the first Rogue prototype, with open luggage compartment and roof cover, and side-screens fitted. (*Photo: T. Karen.*)

and several largely cosmetic features of the first prototype that were regarded by Reliant as impractical or in need of improvement were attended to. The vehicle was widened slightly and the roofline raised to increase headroom, the adjustable steering wheel proved unnecessary and the front end was restyled more in keeping with the original

Looking somewhat well worn from testing – the second prototype now featured a closable locking luggage compartment, full-length canopy section with rigid roof, and fixed protruding pod-style headlamps. It also had a more angular front end closer to the original design sketches that would be carried forward on to the production model. (*Photo: T. Karen.*)

Photo of a very early production model Bug, which was supplied as part of the original press pack for the model's launch at Woburn Abbey.

concept sketch, emphasising the 'wedge'-like appearance. Also gone were the unnecessarily complex retractable headlamps, replaced by fixed rectangular units mounted in angular pods that complimented the new frontal appearance, which now incorporated one of the more iconic features of the eventual production vehicle - the aircraft-inspired low-drag NACA duct to improve airflow to the engine's cooling system. Other detail changes included moving the window back to create a rear parcel shelf, better side-screen weather sealing and a practical enclosed boot space to the rear in place of the previous open luggage shelf.

Though the completed second prototype would still see some further minor development before the details of the actual production model were finalised, work was now halted, whilst final decisions were made on the specifications and range of models that would be offered. Also under consideration was the final finish of the car and, of course, the name, which Reliant management selected, after apparently considering 'dozens' of options! Tom Karen had come up with the bold idea of standardising the colour for the new vehicle, partly to simplify production, but also because such a vehicle couldn't be just any old colour - it had to be conspicuous and stand out in traffic! The choice

LBF 367D

Preston built
Bond Bugs being delivered to Reliant's factories at Tamworth in preparation for the Bug's launch in 1970.

was narrowed down to a bright lime green or even brighter tangerine orange, though as usual there was sound design thinking behind this choice, as both were noted to keep their bright appearance even when the car became dirty. Tangerine was noted to be slightly more effective in this respect, so the choice was made. To enhance the aviation/racing car image that would be reflected in the marketing of the 'Bond Bug', Tom Karen set to work designing a series of bold graphics to take the place of conventional badges on the new car. This 'high-tech' look was further emphasised by aircraft-style instruction decals applied to appropriate parts of the bodywork to indicate the correct tyre pressures, fuel octane rating and cockpit-opening instructions.

The eventual production version of the new Bond Bug featured relatively few modifications, mostly to the rear end appearance, including a neater, but larger boot that could now also accommodate the side-screens when not in use. Minor changes were also made to the rear 'skirt' to bring it into line with the new boot and accommodate better quality built, in rear light clusters. The finished Bug would certainly still attract attention, as even after all the development work, it remained true to Tom Karen's idea and continued to look more like some futuristic motor show concept car than an actual road-going vehicle. Reliant now looked towards the Bug's public debut, with all publicity put in the hands of Adrian Ball and Associates Ltd, and an ambitious launch event was planned at Woburn Abbey in Bedfordshire for June 1970. The car was claimed to be the first vehicle designed exclusively for the 17 to 25 age group, and in the press pack put together for the event, it was stated that they were confident of it becoming 'as

SOMETHING NEW
UNDER THE SUN

From the start, Reliant's marketing campaign for the Bug was certainly not restrained and clearly focused on their intended young driver customer base.

big a trend-setter in the 1970s as the Mini was' followed by a cutting 'in the last decade'!

To help their young customers, Reliant put together a special finance package that included hire purchase, two-years' insurance, two years' road tax and a two year warranty (or 24,000 miles, whichever came first). The insurance element was particularly notable and was arranged by Hodge Insurance at a premium of £25, irrespective of the driver's age and vehicle's location, which seems remarkable by today's standards! Additionally, although it covered named drivers only, any number could be nominated at no extra cost. Although Reliant certainly appeared to be serious in their intention to attract younger buyers, the Bug was not cheap, with three models

Dolly
bug
the bird puller
CBF 819H
bond
BUG
Get the facts, man! Send for our poster and leaflet to Rodney Hackett, Bond Cars, Dept. 220, Tamworth, Staffs.

By today's standards some of Reliant's marketing for the Bug might be seen as questionable, as apart from the cringe-worthy attempts to be 'cool' and 'trendy', much of their marketing was quite obviously aimed solely at male customers.

ETO 209L

A restored 1972 Bug. Today the Bug is very highly sought after, and most survivors have already been acquired and restored by enthusiasts.

offered, starting at £548 including purchase tax, compared to the rather better-appointed new Mk III Mini 850 at £596. This was for the basic '700' model version, with the standard 7.35:1 compression ratio engine, rated at 29bhp at 5,000rpm. It came without sidescreens, sunvisors, heater or spare wheel and the canopy fixed in place for normal use, as no pull handle, catch or external lock was supplied - certainly a car for fresh-air lovers (as Reliant's sales literature put it!). But such frugality, to save just a few pounds, clearly wasn't what Bug customers wanted and it failed to attract any interest, with only one believed to have ever been built. Next in the range was the mid-specification 700E model, priced at £579.7s with the same standard specification engine, fully operational and lockable canopy, sidescreens, heater, driver's sun visor, interior light, chrome hubcaps and chrome trims for the gutters and rear lamps, as well as chrome strips inset in the windscreen and rear window seals. But it was the top of the range 700ES Bug that was to prove the most popular version, priced at £628.19s including purchase tax. This model featured a higher 8.4:1 compression ratio engine, rated at 31bhp at 5,000rpm and, in addition to the features of the 700E, it came with Goodyear Decathlon tyres, alloy rear wheels, two wing mirrors, twin horns, rear-wheel mud flaps, rubber front bumper and chrome exhaust trim. The interior of the 700ES was also upgraded with head rests, two sun visors, seat side and centre supports, headlining, ash tray, two map pockets, engine cowl cover and 'Formula One steering wheel' - seat belts were still optional though!

As production got underway in preparation for the Bug's official launch, everything behind the scenes at Bond's Preston Factory was not quite so bright and cheerful, with the production of the Bug being beset with problems from the start. Not least of these was the poor quality of the bodyshells and canopies, which were manufactured at

FRE 517K

Period sales brochure photo of the Bug and intended 'young professional' driver, showing excellent detail of the opening canopy and car's interior.

Reliant's recently-acquired Kettlebrook Works at Tamworth, where all the Company's specialist glassfibre moulding was carried out, and were then transported to Preston for assembly. With any new product it is inevitable that problems will arise, but this arrangement must surely have exacerbated any issues that arose by leading to delays in identifying where things were going wrong and solutions being implemented. The relatively complex two-piece mouldings that made up the shell of the Bug required a high degree of accuracy in manufacture and those arriving in Preston were soon found to be a poor fit, plus many supposedly pre-cut holes for cables and mounting components were not present, and certain bonded-in sections, such as the rear wheel arch extensions, were already coming adrift. Most of these problems were soon overcome by Bond's experienced staff, but led to production delays and missed targets, which Reliant were quick to pick up on, though they did eventually acknowledge where some of the problems lay. As considerable demand for the Bond Bug was anticipated, Reliant wanted to be prepared to cope with initial orders on the model's launch, so early production of the Bug had been conducted at Preston under a certain degree of secrecy since March, and despite the problems outlined, some 350 Bugs had been built prior to June 1970. However, it was whilst Bond staff were checking on the security of these stored vehicles that another problem emerged - it was noticed that many of the cars had developed a distinct bulge in their canopies immediately over the gas strut mounting point. All the vehicles' canopies were quickly released to relieve the strain on the glassfibre panel and each car had then to be modified by the fitting of a steel strengthening plate over the area.

The Bug's launch certainly turned out to be a huge success, as it was accompanied by a well-planned and organised publicity drive that not only encompassed the motoring press, whose representatives were invited to Woburn Abbey to try out the vehicle, but also the popular press - newspapers, magazines and even TV coverage. At least partly responsible for this positive reaction, apart from the appearance of the car itself that is, was the innovative and upbeat approach Reliant's publicity agents took to promoting the Bug. At the launch, motoring journalists were each presented with a pack of press releases and photographs, describing the evolution of the Bug from Tom Karen's initial concept drawings right through to the vehicle they were about to see, together with a specially orange highlighted (blue being the usual colour) issue of *Reliant News*, the Firm's in-house news sheet, specifications and prices of the Bug models that would be available, and details of the intended market and the special finance/insurance package being offered. All this came in a predictably bright orange folder titled *'For those too young to be square'* - referring to the conventional wheel alignment of the Bug's perceived rival, the Mini! Amongst the claims made for the Bug was an impressive potential fuel consumption of 60mpg, but the figure that caught most people's attention was a top speed in excess of 75mph! It is perhaps with this in

Although the Bond Bug conformed to all the basic safety regulations of the time, it became caught up in an ongoing media campaign against three-wheelers due to claims of instability – despite statistically being some of the safest vehicles on the road at the time! The Bug's striking appearance, young drivers and sports performance were probably not factors in its favour in this respect.

K6

PADGETTS
RELIANT
700E

Reliant's show stand in the early 1970s, with predictable added glamour and sectioned Bond Bug. Presumably the apparent colour sample swatches across the front of the desk do not apply to the Bug!

mind that Reliant chose the Woburn venue for the Bug's launch with its private, traffic-free roads for the invited journalists to try out the new car - each accompanied by a Reliant representative, to help those new to three-wheel motoring accustom themselves to the experience! But, perhaps inevitably, there was always going to be one driver who just pushed his luck a little too far.

At Woburn it was Stuart Marshall, editor of *TAB*, the British tyre industry's business magazine, and later *Financial Times* motoring correspondent. Accompanied by a works employee, he put the Bug into a rather tight right-hand bend at around 25mph, resulting in the rear end sliding sharply to the left. In trying to regain control he, by his own admission, over-corrected and the car then skidded to the right, left the road and did a full 360-degree roll across the Duke of Bedford's manicured front lawn. Apart from losing a wing mirror the car and its occupants were unharmed, probably in part due to the safety features built into the Bug's shell, and on trying the ignition, the engine started immediately and Marshall continued with his test drive. Something of an expert on tyres and their grip characteristics, he, perhaps a little unfairly, received a fair amount of criticism for the incident, though it did not stop Reliant from, 'rather sportingly' as he put it, lending him a Bug for a week, and although not altogether convinced of the car's merits, he suffered no further mishaps. Later in life Stuart Marshall

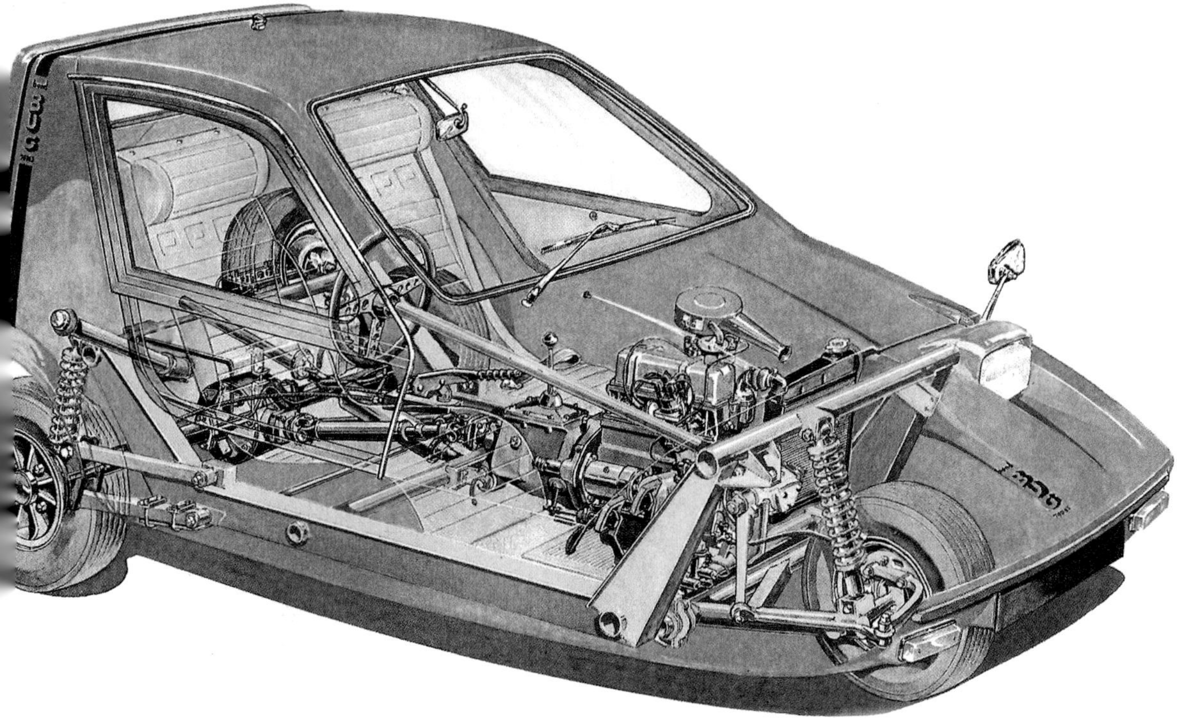

Cutaway drawing of the Bond Bug revealing the separate steel chassis and mechanical layout of the vehicle.

was to describe his experience with the Bond Bug as being 'shaken, not stirred!'

Despite all the preparations and carefully-orchestrated publicity, Reliant still seem to have been taken by surprise by the scale of the reaction to the Bond Bug, and the 350 or so Bugs prepared to fulfil anticipated early orders proved woefully inadequate. Considering the production figures of Reliant's existing three-wheelers by this time, such low-volume output seems at best rather short-sighted. and probably also an indication of the troubled relationship between Bond Cars Ltd and Reliant. The Bug continued to turn heads wherever it went, generating considerable attention from other motorists and passers-by, just as previous Bond products had in years past. It wasn't just idle interest either and orders continued to come in, despite the sharp intakes of breath from much of the motoring press over the price. But by now there were supply problems, and despite promises to increase production, delays were inevitable and the waiting list for the Bug began to grow. Another problem was that clearly the Bond Bug 'Funabout' concept, with its less than perfect weatherproofing and heating, was undoubtedly best enjoyed in summer. But due to developments now taking place behind the scenes, it would be some time before the supply situation improved and as autumn approached, the Company was in serious danger of losing the product's initial market momentum. It is perhaps ironic that, whilst Reliant were now heralding the success of the new car as a 'Bond Bug Bonanza', likening the demand to something of a gold rush, they were also setting in motion events that would seal the fate of Bond Cars Ltd in Preston.

Closure of Bond's Preston Factories

Under the guise of rationalising production, Ray Wiggin, Reliant's Managing Director, announced in July 1970 that both Preston factories were to be closed by the end of the year, citing their failure to operate economically, even suggesting that Bond had been making consistent losses for some years before being acquired by Reliant. Clearly there was more to the story, however, as by this time some 500 Bugs had been assembled at Preston, and Reliant themselves were celebrating the healthy order book for the new vehicle. True, there had been earlier friction between Bond and Reliant over the problems encountered with the early production of the Bond Bug, but even Reliant admitted that many of these were in fact beyond the control of Bond Cars Limited. To those working in the Preston Bond factories, it would perhaps have appeared logical to retain their production capacity for the Bug and that their future was actually more secure. But Reliant had invested heavily in organising their considerably more prolific vehicle production

BOND CARS
NEC 964
257 ETJ

Bond Cars Ltd's Ribbleton Lane Factory circa 1964. The entrance to the main assembly lines, housed in an old rope works, was via the large doors straight ahead. To the right are the stores and parts departments. The four cars parked in the foreground are situated on the site of a short row of terraced houses, named Gosford Street, which were used as office and storage space for a time by the Company, but eventually demolished.

LANCIA
Lookers Grosvenor Motors
MORE SELECTED
USED CARS
INSIDE
BRAVO DELTA

By the 1990s the car park in front of the old Bond Factory on Ribbleton Lane had been built over with a car show room, at that time occupied by Lookers Grosvenor Motors Ltd, and the stores buildings had been demolished to make way for a new petrol filling station and car wash. Today the fuel station is still there, but the showroom is now a specialist food supermarket, with numerous large signs obscuring the old factory features.

around a number of specialised sites in and around Tamworth, and they certainly had such capacity nearer to home. Unfortunately for Bond Cars Ltd, the success of the Bug was likely to have actually had a detrimental effect, as continuing to transport components for assembly in another part of the country really didn't make sense from an economic or practical point of view. But, whilst these may have been contributory factors, it would appear that the decision had in fact already been taken some time before this point, probably as the implications of the BMC/Leyland merger finally became clear to the Reliant Motor Company, denying them one of the key perceived advantages of their acquisition of Bond.

As early as August 1970 the Bond production lines were being wound down and the Scooter Ski that had appeared to hold so much promise for continued production at Preston was relocated elsewhere. But it would have probably made little difference, as the first signs were appearing that its recent, much-heralded, popularity was already waning. Cheaper, similar, products had already started to take a significant share of the market away, leading to the cancellation of some of the much-publicised orders. But more importantly the first 'Jet Ski' type Personal Water Craft (PWC) had begun to appear in Australia in the late 1960s, and in 1973 Kawasaki introduced the first mass-produced Jet-Ski (Kawasaki actually registering the name as their trademark). These new PWCs featured a fully-enclosed impeller pump that produced a high-powered water jet to provide the thrust to propel and steer the vehicle, dramatically improving manoeuvrability and safety over previous propeller-driven designs like the Scooter Ski,

Inside the old Bond production line on Ribbleton Lane during the 1990s when part of it served as a service and repair workshop for Lookers Grosvenor Motors Ltd. Today no such comparisons are possible as the whole factory has been split up into small light industrial and storage units.

effectively rendering them obsolete. Also in August 1970, the last of the Bond Equipes rolled off the production line in Preston, though some of the last 2-Litre Equipes have been noted to have vehicle number date codes indicating September and possibly even October production. It would seem that Reliant staff realised that sufficient major components were present to assemble a final ten 2-Litre Equipe cars, which were then sold off via a Midlands-based motor auctioneer - apparently all to the same buyer. Around 200 employees were left by this time and a few found alternative positions within Reliant, with the remainder being offered assistance to find new jobs locally - some ending up working for TVR in nearby Blackpool. The Bond spare parts business and all remaining stock of Bond Equipe, Bond 875 and Bond Minicar parts was sold to Bob Joyner & Son of Oldbury in Worcestershire. Bob Joyner had begun his motorcycle parts and repair business just before the war, going on to manufacture complete motorcycles, and becoming the largest manufacturer and supplier of spares for British motorcycles in the world. Following the decline of the British motorcycle industry in the 1960s and '70s he bought up the spares stock, rights and patterns of many companies, including Norton Villiers Triumph (NVT) in 1974. Without his business sense and foresight, there is little doubt that far fewer British motorcycles would have survived to today.

By the end of 1970 the two Bond factories in Preston were empty and any remaining equipment either removed by Reliant or sold off locally,

BOND 875

Comparison shot of the Bond production line on Ribbleton Lane, taken circa mid-1965, with the first Bond 875 and Equipe GT4S vehicles being completed alongside the last of the Minicars – Mk G Tourers. (*Photo: Peter G. Reed.*)

and both premises had reverted back to the new owners of Loxhams - Dutton Forshaw. On Ribbleton Lane, the open parking area to the front of the old Bond Works and part of the Factory itself was sold off and soon occupied by a newly-built car showroom for Grosvenor Motors (Preston) Ltd, and operated as a Fiat and Lancia dealership, using part of the old factory as their paint shop and for storage. In 1973 they leased another part of the road frontage to Total Oil (Great Britain) Ltd and a new petrol filling station was built. The site expanded beyond the old factory frontage and in 1983 became part of the Lookers Group. More recently the site has been split up again, with the old Bond assembly line building now being divided into small light industrial units for rent. India Mill's fate was less drawn out, with the former cotton mill, built circa 1864, being partially demolished circa 1973 and eventually completely demolished, leaving an empty 2.8 acre site used for various purposes up until 2014 when construction of fifty-one affordable, energy-efficient homes got underway, which were due to be completed by October 2015.

The Bug carries on

The Bond name was to continue, at least for now, as the production of the Bug was transferred to Reliant's factories at Tamworth, where around forty a week were coming off the production line by late 1970. Although Reliant had a backlog of orders for the Bug, they realised that with summer now just a memory they needed to rekindle interest in the Bug to keep the orders coming in. The Company already had a stand booked at the prestigious London Motor Show, held at Earls Court in October, but of course three-wheel vehicles were not eligible and were supposed to be shown at the later Motorcycle Show in November. Clearly Reliant were by now coming around to the idea that the market for the Bug was somewhat different to the traditional buyers of their austerity-inspired three-wheelers of the recent past, and were determined it should take its place at the main Motor Show. To achieve this, they came up with a remarkable if unorthodox plan, to

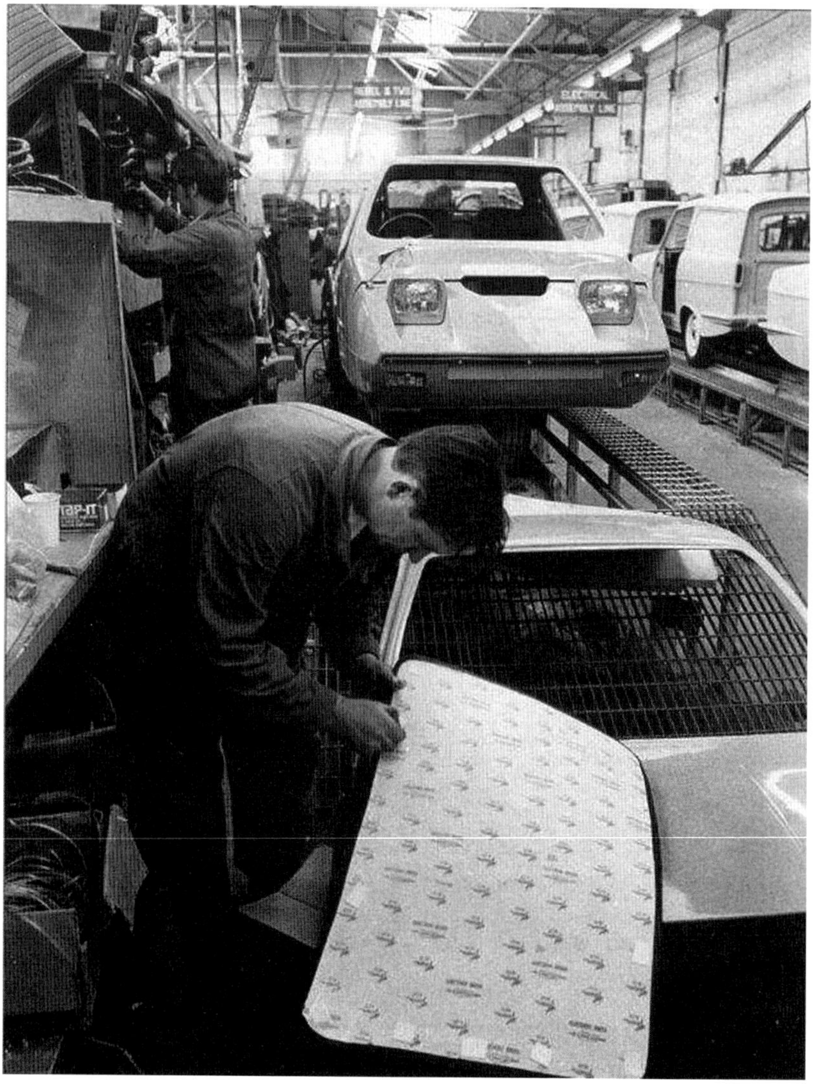

Bond Bug production transferred to Reliant's factories at Tamworth.

FRE 51 8K

Factory publicity shot of a 1971 Bond Bug 700ES.

create a four-wheel Bug that would be eligible for the show - by joining two three-wheel Bugs back to back on a common rear axle! The ruse worked and the 'Push-Me-Pull-You' Double Bug duly appeared on the stand, with potential customers being told that they could only buy half the car on show. Reliant even pushed the boat out, hiring two young female models dressed as 'Bug Bunnies' to pose with the car.

Certainly young ladies, often with little on, draped over the show cars, was considered *de rigueur* at the time, though at the 1970 show one company, TVR, took it perhaps a step too far even for the '70s, by having their models completely naked. At the time, however, they simply stole the show! Despite such competition, the Bug still attracted plenty of the attention at the show from both the public and the press, but it seems Reliant still couldn't let go of the concept of the three-wheeler as an economy vehicle. Whilst the Bug grabbed attention wherever it went and accolades for its bold design, it was still being largely sold at three-wheeler dealerships alongside Reliant's less-glamorous products, and the Company's in-house magazine regularly reported on such routine fare as 'challenging' long-distance journeys in Bugs that demonstrated their reliability and economy. Even today, Tom Karen maintains that it

BUG

Reliant's unorthodox scheme to get the Bond Bug featured on their stand at the main Earls Court Motor Show in November 1970 – where three-wheelers were considered to be motorcycles and therefore excluded – was to build this four-wheel 'Double Bug'. It did indeed form the centrepiece of the Firm's stand, alongside a sign to prospective customers warning that they could, in fact, only buy half the car shown! (*Photo: C. Stanley.*)

was this mindset that held the Bug back, as the dealerships selling the Bug did not really get the concept or market. In his eyes it would have been better to have been sold by sportscar or even supercar dealerships, where a father could buy his Ferrari and also a Bug for his sixteen-year-old son or daughter. But the nearest the Bug got to this was a handful of Scimitar dealerships, who perhaps understood the concept a little better and also offered the Bond Bug alongside Reliant's flagship product.

The Bug continued to attract perhaps more than its fair share of attention, when considering the car's actual sales figures, which were certainly falling well below the levels Reliant anticipated. Sales did, however, remain steady and production soon settled down to around twenty per week, which is perhaps surprising, as the Company were still claiming that demand was outstripping supply. It is also interesting to note that Reliant commented in December 1970, that whilst initial sales had shown that some 60 per cent of buyers were aged over twenty-five, the Bug now appeared to be reaching its intended target audience, with 59 per cent of sales now being to buyers aged twenty-five or under. In London a Bug featured for three weeks in September 1970 as the main display in the Council of Industrial Design's 'shop window' for British design at the Design Centre, near Piccadilly Circus - the first vehicle to do so and where it was seen by an estimated 70,000 visitors! The press also maintained their coverage of the Bug, especially as a number of firms saw the potential of the vehicle for advertising purposes,

The Bond Bug featured for three weeks in September 1970 as the main display in the Council of Industrial Design's 'shop window' for British design at the Design Centre, near Piccadilly Circus – the first vehicle to do so and where it was seen by an estimated 70,000 visitors!

including Rothmans International Ltd, who ordered six Bugs in late 1970 to be used to promote their brand of cigarettes. Earlier in that year Rothmans had begun to sponsor an aerobatic team flying Stampe SV4 biplanes finished in the Company's colours, and appearing at airshows and events throughout the country. Their marketing department clearly thought a complimentary fleet of Bond Bugs would make a good marketing tool and specified that the cars should be finished in white with black roofs, the first departure from the Bug's standard tangerine colour scheme. After purchase, the Rothman's Bugs would also feature the Rothman's blue pack label emblem, and toured UK seaside resorts with young female drivers distributing prizes and Green Shield stamps. The cars had consecutive registration numbers believed to run from AME 191H to AME 196H, and amazingly, two have survived and have been restored by the same owner, though one white-finished car in this sequence also appeared in a TV commercial advertising Cape fruit. Bugs began popping up all over the place, including the Isle of Man TT races, Biggin Hill Airshow, and major motor racing meetings at Silverstone and Brands Hatch, but then they did standout somewhat. Toy firms also got in on the act, with Airfix announcing a 1:32 scale plastic kit of the Bug to be released in 1971, and Corgi Toys released their 'Whizzwheels' 1:43 scale diecast 700ES Bug in April of the same

AME 194H

Not all Bugs were tangerine! This 700ES was one of six specially ordered in White by Rothmans International Ltd. (*Photo: J. Scratch Platts.*)

year, as Model No. 389, available in orange, and much scarcer, in lime green.

Bug Production comes to an End

There were relatively few changes made to the Bug during its production. August 1971 saw an improved gearbox with synchromesh on all gears and, in September 1972, minor changes to the steering

BUG
700ES

Profile view of the white Rothmans Bond Bug 700ES. This is one of two of the specially-ordered white Bugs known to survive – both have been restored and looked after by the same owner. (*Photo: J. Scratch Platts.*)

wheel and column to meet new safety regulations. Through 1972 and 1973 production was largely confined to 700 ES models, and gradually fell to around fifteen vehicles per week. A more significant change came later in 1973, when in October the Bug received the larger capacity 748cc engine that was also being fitted to Reliant's new three-wheeler, the Ogle-designed Robin, which was to be officially launched in November of that year. The new Bug models were designated the 750E and 750ES respectively, and immediately superseded the older 700E and 700ES models, with the basic 700 model having been finally dropped as an option back in April 1973. The new engine produced 32bhp at 5,500rpm, giving the new Bug models slightly better acceleration and potential top speed of up to 105mph, which a 750ES reputedly achieved during a test run at Brands Hatch. Other than the engine change and updated decals featuring the new model names, the specifications of the new models remained the same as their respective predecessors and there was little fanfare to welcome the new Bugs, as Reliant concentrated their efforts on the new Robin. By May 1974 it was all over and the Bond name finally faded into history when Reliant announced that Bug production would cease, in order to concentrate all the Firm's available facilities on the Robin. Production of the Bug ceased almost immediately, although there was apparently still at least a limited demand and Reliant did consider, albeit very briefly, the possibility of a more practical four-wheel Bug in response to some of the criticisms the car was by this

In the end it needed more than a trendy, possibly rebellious, image to sell cars, and Reliant dropped the Bond Bug to concentrate on its traditional market with the new Reliant Robin.

time attracting. But the idea was dismissed (at least for the time being) as Reliant, perhaps unsurprisingly, considered the more conventional, from their point of view, Robin to be a far more commercially viable proposition in the long term.

The Mighty Metronome

In all 2,268 Bugs are believed to have been built between 1970 and 1974, and it seems remarkable the impact this little car made for such a relatively short and limited production run. It is therefore hardly surprising that interest in what had become something of a design icon continued long after it had gone. However, the first of a number of variations on the Bond Bug theme actually came whilst the Bug was still in production. This was the mighty Metronome, a Methanol Fuel, Altered Wheelbase Experimental Class, Drag Racing Car built in 1971 after its creator, Mark Stratton from Hustler Racing, succeeded in persuading Reliant to build him a specially-made, super-thin, Bond Bug shell weighing only 35lbs, approximately one tenth of the normal shell weight, and with an average thickness of only 1/8th of an inch. This shell was fitted around a specially-constructed tubular-steel, four-wheel frame with the front axle mounted ahead of the Bug shell. In its first incarnation, power came from a supercharged and fuel-injected 6.5 litre Chrysler Fire Power V-8 engine (the famous 392 cubic inch 'Hemi').

The mighty Metronome at speed. Built by Mark Stratton of Hustler Racing, the Metronome was powered by a supercharged and fuel-injected 6.5 litre Chrysler Fire Power V-8 engine, and achieved 154mph! *(Photo: Roger Phillips collection via the Acceleration Archive.)*

HUSTLER
RACING
WYNN'S
Metronome

The car was commissioned and driven by Steve Cryer, and achieved 10.8 seconds at 136.7mph (though he was also noted to have achieved a 154mph run). Later on it was driven by Ed Shaver and then later still by James Leech in 1975, by that time re-engined with a slightly more sensible and less top-heavy Daimler 2.5 litre V-8, as the car had proved somewhat difficult to handle in its original form. The Metronome does not seem to have raced after 1975, which was the same year another somewhat unorthodox version of the Bug theme appeared, this time in the US.

The Spi-Tri

The new vehicle in the USA was a prototype three-wheeler called the Spi-Tri and built by Structural Plastics Inc. in Oklahoma, and designed by Larry Barker, a partner in the Company. The prototype vehicle was obviously very heavily influenced by the Bond Bug, though contrary to a number of sources, it was not based on an actual Bug shell. It seems that Barker's business partner had owned a vehicle repair workshop, where a Bond Bug that had been imported in to the USA had arrived for repair. Whilst working on the vehicle he became interested in its design and began to think about how it could be improved. The prototype Spi-Tri featured an all-glassfibre shell with an elongated rear section when compared to the Bug; it had a fixed 'canopy' roof and glassfibre forward-hinged doors, with a pronounced wrap-around moulded bumper/join line that ran around most of the vehicle. It was powered by an Elecxtro electric motor that gave the vehicle a top speed of around 50mph and

The 1984 production version of the Spi-Tri built by Structural Plastics Inc. in Oklahoma and designed by Larry Barker. (*Photo: H. Kraemer.*)

WARNING
Maryland
471 2L9
Historic

Interior view of the 1984 production version of the Spi-Tri. (*Photo: H. Kraemer.*)

a range of 40 miles between charges. After considerable development and testing, a production version was finalised in 1984, which differed from the prototype as it included larger-diameter wheels and had large impact bumpers at the front and rear of the vehicle. Also, it was now powered by a compact three-cylinder 993cc Daihatsu CB series engine with Daihatsu transmission, after an earlier plan to use a Reliant 848c engine was dropped. The engine choice resulted from an intention for the Spi-Tri to be a world car, that is, it could be built anywhere in the world and use a readily-available engine. However, Daihatsu would not begin importing their cars to the US until 1987, so in 1984 Barker and his partner had to convince the Company to send them an engine along with a supply of spare parts. In total, three Spi-Tri vehicles were built with the last one undergoing vehicle stability testing at Edwards Air Force Base in Southern California, and it saw a return to electric power, being fitted with a custom-made Baldor electric motor that utilized an infinite ratio transmission.

Doodle Bug

The next extreme Bug appeared in the UK in 1979 in the form of another Methanol Fuel Altered Dragster named the Doodle Bug. For some time

DOODLE BUG

The Doodle Bug built and driven by Roy Jaggar, and powered by a Daimler 2.5 Litre supercharged V-8 engine that could take it to over 120mph. (*Photo: R. Jaggar.*)

mistakenly believed to have been a later reincarnation of the celebrated Metronome, this was in fact a totally new creation, which was built around a standard Bond Bug body from a scrapped car, lengthened by 18 inches and mounted on a specially-made, four-wheel, box-section ladder frame chassis. Like the last seen configuration of the Metronome, the Doodle Bug was powered by the widely-used Daimler 2.5 litre supercharged V-8 engine, which has perhaps led to past confusion. It

DOODLE BUG
FCA 43
Transmatic
Auto Specialist
Middleton
061 653 4023
Snap-on
RACEMASTER

Last-minute adjustments being carried out on Roy Jaggar's Doodle Bug. Note the complex and substantial chassis frame that forms the basis of the car. (*Photo: R. Jaggar.*)

was built and driven by Roy Jaggar, and its best recorded time was 10.96 seconds at 123mph. It underwent various modifications and a change of colour scheme, until sold in the late 1980s, after which it seems to have been dismantled and eventually lost.

Webster Motor Company Ltd

In 1977 a change of ownership for Reliant saw not only a major overhaul of the Company's management, but also a shift in direction away from their staple three-wheeler fare, which had begun to suffer from falling sales and increasing public safety concerns. Both Reliant's three-wheelers and their up-market four-wheel Scimitar products were losing ground to increased competition in their respective markets. Reliant understandably began to look for a gap in the market that they could exploit and obviously thought they had found it with their new Michelotti-designed small two-seat sportscar, the Scimitar SS1, launched in 1984. Though they had other work, the Company had clearly pinned their hopes in the SS1, but despite investing heavily in the car, everything did not go to plan and it was beset with production difficulties coupled with poor sales. By the late 1980s Reliant was even selling off assets to help raise much-needed cash flow and one of the projects sold off around this time was the Bond Bug, as much of the tooling for this vehicle had been retained at the factory. This was bought by Mike and Gary Webster, confirmed Bug enthusiasts, who set up the Webster Motor Company Ltd (WMC), based in Hampshire, UK, in 1990.

Gary Webster had already built a four-wheel prototype based on a damaged original Bug shell and now, with a set of original factory

KDT 22K

Four-wheel 'standard' WMC Bug from Mike and Gary Webster's Webster Motor Company Ltd.

WMC's open sport model dispensed with the canopy altogether, replacing it with a moulded apron surmounted with twin aero screens.

moulds and the production rights to build new Bugs, he saw an opportunity to cash in on the now re-emerging popularity of the Bug design. Apparently the deal even included the rights to the Bond name, but early enquiries with insurance companies soon persuaded him to use his own company's name to differentiate the new vehicles from the original Bond Bug, which had by now gained something of a poor reputation, risk-wise. Initially offered in the-then popular, kit-car format, the new WMC Bug featured a brand-new strengthened chassis, modified to take a standard Mini front sub-frame to provide the front suspension and steering rack, with suitably revised rear-suspension, incorporating a new full-width Panhard rod, to improve the ride and cornering of the new four-wheel car. Another feature adopted to improve the car's handling was the use of standard 10in wheels to the front of the vehicle, but 12in to the rear, with other wheel size options and combinations also offered. The mid-engined layout was retained, and the engine and transmission were also to come from a donor vehicle, with the 850cc, 41bhp unit from the Standard Reliant Robin being recommended, with a suitably shortened prop-shaft. The bodyshell was all-new, produced from the now-refurbished original Reliant moulds and available in various options; one with rigid, folding, front-hinged doors, to eliminate the need to keep opening the canopy, another with a sunroof built into the canopy and finally one which dispensed with the canopy altogether, replacing it with a moulded apron surmounted with twin aero screens to give a completely

WMC BUG

WMC also offered their vehicles in the-then very popular kit form and although, as with many kit cars, this initially looked to be a good way to save money, buyers soon found that desirable features, such as alloy wheels, sunroof and upgraded interior trim were all optional extras that soon bumped up the cost.

open 'sport' model. Additionally WMC offered a new standard three-wheel chassis for would-be restorers of original Bugs and proposed to produce similarly-configured new bodyshells to allow 'new' original specification Bugs to be built as well.

The WMC Bug was launched in March 1990 and was certainly well received, with reviews commenting favourably on its handling, performance and economy, though its spartan interior, whilst true to the original Bug fun-car concept, was noted as still somewhat lacking in creature comforts. It seemed there was undoubtedly a demand for a four-wheel version of the Bug, but the WMC models were not cheap, with the basic open 'Sport' model in kit form starting at £1,758, a Standard model at £2,475 and the Super (with hinged folding doors) at £2,775 - all subject to VAT, of course! Desirable goodies, such as alloy wheels, sunroof and a Deluxe padded seat trim set were all optional extras at additional cost.

By the 1980s the British kit car scene was well established and was undergoing something of a boom, with manufacturers mainly concentrating on either traditional-looking roadsters or lookalikes of well-known but expensive sports cars, such as the Lotus Seven, AC Cobra and Lamborghini Countach. Though some could be built on a fairly low budget, many were relatively expensive to build, especially for those wanting to achieve the high standard of finish they had seen on the shiny demonstration models they had originally viewed. In this market, the price of the WMC Bug was probably not seen as especially excessive, but then few other kits had the option for the buyer of buying and restoring a fairly recent original of the car it was based on! Additionally, by the early 1990s, the formerly buoyant kit car market was showing definite signs of sinking as the economic climate changed dramatically. As sales began to tail off and a number of manufacturers went under, a further blow was dealt in the mid- 1990s, when rumours began to circulate of impending legislation to regulate the building of such vehicles. Sales of the WMC Bug were certainly limited and some sources quote as few as five kits sold, though photographs of more than this number appear to exist. Another quotes a total of ten vehicles, comprising five four-wheeled Bugs, four three-wheeled and one open Sports. This still seems low, as other sources quote twenty-plus four-wheel Bugs, but it is more likely to be correct. As with the original Bug, the impact of the WMC version seems to far outweigh the numbers actually produced and is still regularly discussed today, despite WMC having folded in February 1998.

'Official' attempts to revive the Bug

This was not quite the end of the Bond Bug's story, however, as in the meantime events at Reliant seemed to have gone from bad to worse, the Company having gone into receivership in 1990 and being acquired by Bean Industries Limited. Bean had bought the engine and gearbox manufacturing operation of Reliant in 1988, but continued production as a major sub-contractor to Reliant, so had more to lose than most when Reliant got into trouble, so they ended up buying the Company. Bean Industries themselves then got into financial difficulties of their own and went into receivership in late 1994, meaning that Reliant was again under threat. This time the Company was acquired by the Avonex

Reliant's in-house attempt to give the Bug a facelift, with new metallic paint, revised headlamp housings and indicator/sidelight units, and updated wing mirrors, failed to achieve the desired results. (*Photo: T. Touw.*)

Tom Karen's proposed 1990s facelift resulted in the Reliant Sprint with a more rounded profile, reminiscent of the original Reliant Rogue prototype. (*Photo: T. Touw.*)

Group Ltd in January 1995 and one of the projects they initiated, in the hope of reviving Reliant's fortunes, was a revamp of the Bond Bug, now to be called the Reliant Sprint. After an in-house attempt to restyle the Bug failed to achieve the desired results, Tom Karen was commissioned to create an updated Bug for the 1990s. He came up with a more rounded form with cleaner, uncluttered lines, somewhat reminiscent of the original Rogue prototype of 1969, but still unmistakably a Bug. The Sprint was to remain a three-wheeler, as the new management clearly felt this was where Reliant's customer base lay, and a prototype Sprint was exhibited along with other new proposed Reliant three-wheelers at a dealer event held at the National Motorcycle Museum in 1995. But the Sprint went no further, as the Avonex Group proved to have troubles of its own and they too went into receivership in December 1995.

This time salvation came in April 1996, in the form of a group of business investors headed by Jonathan Heynes, who had twenty-five years' experience with Jaguar. They made a successful bid for the ailing Reliant Company, and amongst the various stalled projects they inherited at the Factory was the Sprint, which had been almost ready for launch. Heynes was keen to restart some form of production as

Sprint

Rear view of Tom Karen's proposed 1990s facelift continued the more rounded profile, with neat updated lighting, and extended re-shaped wheel arches and rear skirt. (*Photo: T. Touw.*)

Believing there was likely to be more demand for a four-wheel Bug-style vehicle, Reliant's new owners set about modifying a prototype Sprint as the basis to create a mould for a new four-wheel shell, both seen seemingly abandoned in this shot of the factory yard. (*Photo: T. Touw.*)

soon as possible, starting with the Robin, but he also wanted to look at potential new products, and with a little persuasion saw the potential of the Sprint as a new four-wheel sports model. The new four-wheel Bug project was designated RFW9 and work started on designing and fabricating a completely new chassis for the car. Design work also began on modifying an existing Sprint shell to produce a new four-wheeler bodyshell mould. Power for the prototype was to be provided

RFW 9
22

Two prototypes of the new four-wheel Bug project, designated RFW9, are believed to have been completed, and one survives and can be seen at the Bubblecar Museum (*see appendices*).

by a standard Reliant 850cc engine, though various other options were discussed for the production vehicle. One option was the often-discussed Reliant/BRM single-overhead cam engine developed in the 1970s, but the test engines were reputedly ordered to be scrapped when the agreement with BRM ended. At least one of these engines seems to have escaped this fate and was acquired by Jonathan Heynes, who intended to re-manufacture it as an 850cc OHC unit for the Four-wheel Kitten and Bug models. However, just as the new Bug was announced in 1998, the European Commission and industry associations of the major motor vehicle manufacturers agreed to reduce the average CO2 emissions of new cars, and although the agreement was to be voluntary at first, it became obvious that the 850cc Reliant engine in its current form was going to have problems meeting any such new targets. One solution looked at was to convert the Reliant engine to fuel injection, with some success, but other options considered for the Bug included the possibility of electric power or a small diesel engine.

In the end, the departure of one of the key investors led to a change in priorities, and precedence was given to production of the new Mk 2 Robin and to development of what would be the new Mk 3 model, announced in 1999. All work on the various sporting model projects virtually ceased, including the Bug. However, the prototype was tested by representatives of the motoring press and was well received, with favourable comments regarding its performance and handling. The Company's direction also began to change at this time, as Reliant became involved in importing Piaggio and Ligier 'light cars', as well as the Renault-powered San coupes and convertibles, designed in France, but built in India. Initially these were to be sold alongside the Reliant three-wheelers, which at this point were subject to a two-month waiting list. Soon after, it was announced that by 2001 even this limited Reliant production would cease and the Firm would concentrate on its new role as an importer. Jonathan Heynes sold his stake in the Company and left Reliant.

Rear view of the surviving RFW9 prototype reveals the car's apparently unfinished state.

Appendices

1. Owners Clubs - Keeping the Cars Running.

For some time Bond vehicles have had a dedicated and enthusiastic following, and for those who are looking for rarity and individuality from a classic car, there can be few marques that can compete with the variety of vehicles under the Bond name. There are a number of specialist clubs catering for Bond vehicles, offering events, advice from other owners, and information on spares availability and restoration. Brief details of the main clubs are included here.

Bond Owners' Club

The first Bond Minicar Owners' Club was formed circa 1951, just a couple of years after the earliest Bond Minicars, the Mk As, began to leave the Factory in Preston. It was felt that as the Minicar represented a new mode of motoring, it would be beneficial to have means by which owners could talk to each other and share their experiences. By the 1960s there was a network of over forty individual Bond clubs all over the country, whose activities were covered in the *Bond Minicar Magazine* produced by Sharp's Commercials, a journal that provided an invaluable source of all sorts of information for Bond owners, as well as keeping these clubs in touch with each other. These individual organisations varied in size considerably and organised their own events, such as rallies, camping weekends, picnics, social evenings, dances and film shows, etc. Such events were advertised in the magazine and owners from one club would often attend those in other areas for joint activities. Additionally there were annual National Bond Rallies, organised by Sharp's, held at Morecambe and Clacton, attracting owners from all over the country.

At the time of the closure of the Bond Factory in 1970, a group of Bond three-

Minicar
BOND
Scooter
OWNERS CLUB

20

The Bond Owners' Clubs organised all sorts of activities and driving skills competitions etc. at their meetings and weekend get-togethers, with the more competitive members often taking home a trophy or two. This display at the Bubblecar Museum includes several such trophies, as well as literature and photographs all connected with one such owner.

The model Minicar was apparently given by Sharp's Commercials Ltd to owners whose Minicars completed their first 10,000 miles without any form of breakdown – but as they are only made of plastic and were no doubt usually passed on to children, very few seem to have survived.

wheeler enthusiasts formed *Bond Info*, an information service to keep all the various Bond clubs in touch with one another and to provide a central source of information on all aspects of Bond ownership, now that the *Bond Magazine* was no more than an afterthought incorporated into Reliant's own in-house journal. Over the years these individual owners clubs have combined into the present single national organisation known as the Bond Owners' Club (BOC), making it one of the longest running one-make car clubs in the country. Membership of the club is open to owners and enthusiasts of Bond Minicars (Marks A to G), Bond 875s, Equipes, Bond Bugs or any other product bearing the Bond name. The Club welcomes members from all around the world and current membership stands at around 300, though unusually the Bond Owners Club requests that, 'Overseas enthusiasts applying to join must currently own a Bond, as the future of our Club depends on us keeping the few remaining Bonds in the UK.'

Services offered to Club members include: a monthly magazine still titled *Bond Info*, but now in full-colour, technical advice, a spare parts department and information on spares availability, details of club rallies and other events, club publications (reprints of owners handbooks and so on), club regalia, and a free small ads service for cars and spares through *Bond Info* (though car sales are restricted to the UK edition only). The Club's main event of the year is the National Rally held at the National Watersports Centre, Holme Pierrepont, Nottingham, over the Spring Bank Holiday, which usually attracts a selection of all types of Bond two-, three- and four-wheel vehicles, and is well worth attending.

Full details of the Bond Owners Club, including membership application and contact details, can be found online at: http://www.bondownersclub.co.uk/

KENNETH GARDNER
PHONE
4468
PHONE
4468

The main event of the Bond owner's calendar was the Club's National Rally, held at Morecambe from 1955 through to 1967 and later revived from 1986 through to 2003, when local council sponsorship ended and a new venue had to found. Here a 1951 Mk A Minicar warms up for one of the driving tests on the promenade at Morecambe during an early rally held there.

Berkeley Enthusiasts Club

The Berkeley Enthusiasts Club was founded in 1964, initially called the International Berkeley Enthusiasts Club, but the name was changed in 1967 to the Berkeley Enthusiasts Club (BEC). This was due to the RAC Competitions Committee, who would not officially recognise a one-car make club as 'International', and with many Berkeleys still participating in competition events, clearly this was a problem. From the outset, the Club's main aim was to assist owners to keep their

A line-up of superbly restored Bond Minicars at the 2011 Bond Owners' Club National Rally. (*Photo: C. & A. Steggel.*)

166 ERA
RFH 512
946

Berkeley Enthusiasts Club annual AGM and Rally weekend in 2016. (*Photo: L. Smyth.*)

Berkeleys on the road, and initially this took the form of providing a means for owners to stay in contact with each other, provide a source of spares and technical literature and even help to develop modifications to update the various models.

However, in recent years, all three- and four-wheel Berkeley car models have become recognised as historic cars in their own right, and the emphasis of the Club has now shifted towards helping members to restore cars to their original specification. Membership of the BEC currently stands at around 200, most being in the United Kingdom, but also with representation covering many parts of the world. Services offered to Club members include: a monthly *Bulletin* featuring; club news, technical articles, event reviews, diary of forthcoming events, news on spares sources, and members 'for sale and wanted adverts' for vehicles and parts. BEC also provides an online forum and a popular Facebook Berkeley Car Owners group with around 200 members.

To help their members maintain and restore the vehicles, the Berkeley Enthusiasts Club provides a technical service, giving members access to a wide range of service sheets, parts books and archive material. It also has a spares service, which can supply selected parts or help members locate difficult to obtain items, and when it is found that a part is no longer available anywhere, the Club will endeavour to see they are re-manufactured. A stock of second-hand and re-conditioned parts are also available. A Berkeley register is held by the Club, listing all known cars, past and present, and the BEC can assist members with claiming lost registration numbers on vehicles returning to the road after long intervals.

The BEC holds an annual AGM, and a rally weekend for members, as well as supporting other rallies and special or local events where microcars are welcome. Classic car and motorcycle shows are also attended, and regular monthly meetings are held in some areas of the UK.

Full details of the Berkeley Enthusiasts Club, including membership application and contact details, can be found online at: http://www.berkeleycarclub.com/

The Bug Club

The Bond Bug - produced between 1970 and 1974 - has over the years inspired several groups of enthusiasts to attempt to set up a club exclusively for this revolutionary and highly-individual vehicle. All these previous clubs have unfortunately, for one reason or another, fallen by the wayside - though usually not through a lack of enthusiasm! Therefore, for many years, the Bond Bug was represented by the Bond Owners' Club. However, with changing circumstances, not least being the recent massive growth in popularity of the Bug, it became apparent that it was in the best interests of both the BOC and Bug owners to once again attempt to set up a separate club exclusively for the Bond Bug. Although the Bug bears the Bond name, it was totally a Reliant design and built by them, and although some early ones were assembled at

Impressive line-up of Bond Bugs at the Wickenby Wings And Wheels Bug Club Rally. (*Photo: R. Biggin.*)

bond
700ES

Tom Karen discuses the finer points of the Bug design with Bug Club members at a Club event. (*Photo J. Scratch Platts.*)

the Bond Factory in Preston, most were built at the Reliant Factory at Tamworth. In many Bond purists' eyes the Bug was not seen as a 'proper' Bond and this was often pointed out at events, albeit amiably. In late 1990 it was decided to set up a separate club for the Bug and by January 1991 The Bug Club had been formed, and although the Bond Owners Club will still accept Bug owners as members, it is pointed out to prospective members that there is a dedicated club for Bond Bugs.

Such is the following for the Bond Bug that membership soon climbed to over 240 members, including owners as well as enthusiasts, though at present it has settled down to around 170 members. The Bug Club's first major event coincided with 1991 being the Bug's 21st birthday, which provided an ideal opportunity to organise a major celebration of the successful establishment of the Bug Club and the Bug's coming of age. The Club holds its own annual rally in June and also attends several other major events a year. The Club maintains a register of details of known Bond Bugs, which covers around 1,500 of the 2,250 or so built, though this includes historic information and not all survive to this day. This is, however, especially useful as no production records from the factory survive, and the register can help owners identify newly-found Bugs or fill in gaps in the history of their vehicles. It is believed around 700 to 750 Bugs actually survive to this day, including a number of derelict and yet to be restored vehicles though not all of these are ever likely to appear fully restored, as they may have been converted to trikes or cannibalised for spares etc. Newly-found Bugs still turn up regularly and seven previously unknown Bugs turned up in 2015 alone. Club records also show that Bugs have appeared in some twenty different countries, and surviving Bugs are known in Ireland, the Netherlands, Germany, France, Belgium, Norway, Switzerland, Spain, Japan, US, Australia and New Zealand. Recently a Bond Bug has been exported to Thailand to be exhibited in a museum there.

No doubt the healthy survival rate for Bond Bugs has been helped in recent years by the recognition of the vehicle's status as a design icon - leading to a massive rise in demand for Bugs and in turn an increase in values. This has led to more potential owners actively seeking out Bond Bugs and being prepared to spend more on restoring them, thus making previously uneconomic projects now viable.

The Bug Club is now firmly established as 'the' club for Bug owners and potential owners. The Club provides a colour bi-monthly magazine, website and members' forum, active social media presence (with two Club pages on Facebook), advice and encouragement, details of spares availability, etc.

Full details of the Bug Club, including membership application and contact details, can be found online at: http://www.bondbugs.co.uk/

Triumph Sports Six Club - Bond Equipe Register

The Triumph Sports Six Club (TSSC) was formed in 1977 by a group of enthusiasts with the aim of 'promoting and preserving all cars based on the Herald chassis'. This definition included the Herald, Vitesse,

RLG 45OH

Line-up of Bond Equipes at the 2013 TSSC South of England Meet. (*Photo: G. Singleton.*)

REGALIA & BOOKS
TSSC CLOTHING
INSURANCE
VALUATIONS
CONCOURS
TRIUMPH
CLUB
BOND

The 50th anniversary of the first Bond Equipe being celebrated at the TSSC International Weekend in 2013. The blue Equipe GT is 516 FYL (O5/101), the first production vehicle, which usually resides in the TSSC Museum. (*Photo: G. Singleton.*)

Spitfire and GT6 models, along with their derivatives - including the Bond Equipes. Today they have expanded their scope further to include Triumph TRs 1 to 8, Triumph 2000, Dolomite, 1300/1500, Acclaim, and the Triumph Stag. The Club is very business-like, with office premises, professional staff and online shop for Club-branded clothing and regalia, as well as books, vehicle accessories and parts. The Club HQ is located on Main St, Lubenham, Market Harborough, Leicestershire, and houses the archive, a small museum with several historically significant vehicles and a Club shop. On a regional level it operates on a more informal basis through a network of area organisers who hold friendly monthly meetings and often organise their own local events.

Membership of the world's largest Triumph club does have many advantages, including a 130-page monthly magazine *The Courier*, an agreed value insurance scheme, special offers, Club regalia sales, and separate registers for each model. The Club also organises a number of national meetings, of which the premier event is TriumphFest in July, now in association with the Santa Pod Raceway near Wellingborough as part of their annual Retro Show. Other benefits of membership include discounted insurance with agreed valuation, certified by the Club's Insurance Panel, a members' self-help scheme and an additional bi-annual magazine, *The Turning Circle*, each edition of which focuses on a particular model.

The Bond Equipes have their own Register, and, like the other registers, it has a secretary to assist members with technical queries, spares information, and to maintain a comprehensive listing of all known surviving Equipes. This covers some 300 cars, including a pre-production 2+2, the first production 2+2 and several of the examples used in contemporary road tests. A considerable number of Equipes were exported, and contact has also been established with owners in Greece, South Africa, Australia, Canada and in Europe. The Register, through present secretary Guy Singleton, has arranged for a number of parts to be re-manufactured, including all the badges for the various models, commission plates and door window glass. Many second-hand spares can also be located - information is collected from fellow owners and held by the Register Secretary, who can also help would-be purchasers locate an Equipe by supplying a 'cars for sale' listing. Copies of a number of factory records and other documents can be consulted to help owners with questions on production dates and paint colours, and also to confirm correct original specifications and equipment. The premier event in the Equipe Register calendar is the Bond Equipe Weekend, which was conceived in 1986 as 'a friendly get-together for Equipe owners', though this is now often held in conjunction with other club events.

Full details of the Triumph Sports Six Club, including membership application and contact details, can be found online at: http://www.tssc.org.uk/

Vintage Motor Cycle Club

The Vintage Motor Cycle Club (VMCC) has been around since 1946 and operates a system of over 180 'marque specialists' who look after the interests of the owners of machines built by a specific manufacturer. Owners of early Bond/BAC machines are particularly fortunate in having the services of Nick Kelly to call on as their official VMCC marque specialist. Nick can advise owners on all aspects of the maintenance and the restoration of these machines through his own wide practical experience of the marque. He is also an authority on the historical aspects of the marque, and holds comprehensive records of all known surviving Minibykes, Lilliputs and Gazelle scooters, as well as catering for these machines (and the later Bond P1-4 scooters) for the Bond Owners' Club. Another important service offered by the VMCC through the various marque specialists is the issuing of certificates, acceptable to the DVLA, to allow the retention of original registration marks.

The VMCC organises a number of rallies, which makes for a busy annual events calendar for enthusiasts, a number of which are attended by many of the marque specialists. Such events provide an ideal opportunity to exchange information, examine surviving machines (particularly useful if you are currently undertaking a restoration project) and obtain spare parts.

Should any readers of this book own or know the whereabouts of any Bond/BAC machine, irrespective of its condition, or even incomplete machines or spare parts, Nick Kelly would always be extremely interested to hear from you, for it is important that the few surviving machines are recorded (Nick's phone no. is: 01273 703489 - please leave a message and he will get back to you).

Full details of The Vintage Motor Cycle Club, including joining information, details of services to members, contact details, etc. can be found online at: http://www.vmcc.net/

Register of Unusual Microcars (RUMcars)

The Register of Unusual Microcars was set up in 1981 and covers any three- or four-wheeled road vehicle with an engine size of 700cc or under, or any small electric-powered road vehicle, manufactured after 1945. In particular, it caters for those makes not at present covered by any other club or register, although no marque is excluded. The Register is not a commercial enterprise. It exists purely to maintain records of the existence of these rare little vehicles, and to encourage their preservation and restoration. Its aim is to obtain as much information as possible on surviving microcars, regardless of a vehicle's condition or its country of origin. In order to keep track of such surviving cars, a vehicle registration certificate is issued by the Register and is intended to remain with the car. Whilst ideally, owners will notify the Register of any changes in a vehicle's circumstances, it is hope this certificate will encourage new owners to contact the Register if the car is sold. RUMcars is recognised by the DVLA and can also help with re-registering microcars that have been off the road for a long time or have lost their paperwork.

There is a small administration fee to register a vehicle, which covers the cost of the certificate and postage, but owners may also subscribe to the register magazine, *Rum Car News*, which comprises approximately thirty-six pages in full colour and is published quarterly. Innovatively, subscribers have the option of either hard copy or an eMagazine version at a significantly reduced cost, especially for those overseas. Through the medium of this magazine, RUMcars endeavour to keep all microcar enthusiasts (even those without cars) informed on all matters relating to such vehicles, including news and events, cars and parts for sale or wanted and information on available spare parts. There is also an active online forum for microcar enthusiasts to keep up to date with the latest news and announcements, as well as various discussion categories, and it has nearly 600 registered members.

RUMcars has also built up a comprehensive archive of material related to microcars, including original sales literature, owner's manuals, photographs, magazine articles and so on. All this material provides an invaluable resource, not only for microcar owners, but for writers, journalists, historians and anyone requiring related information. It is refreshing to see such material being preserved and organised in a way that it may directly benefit anyone with an interest in microcars.

When the Register of Unusual Microcars was first started in 1981, it became actively involved in the setting up of the National Microcar Rally, now an established annual event. The rally, held in September, is organised in turn by various groups of enthusiasts and is attended by many members of the various microcar clubs, as well as many of those whose vehicles are on the RUMcars Register.

Finally, RUMcars do hold their own informal get-together, usually in July each year, when the Hammond Collection of Microcars (see Museums section for full details) holds its open day. The collection is located near Staplehurst in Kent and camping facilities are available on site. A selection of owners usually attend with their own vehicles, and the 2015 event saw visitors from The Netherlands, Germany and France as well as all parts of the UK - though attendance was somewhat limited due to poor weather and travel concerns due to the disruption caused by 'Operation Stack' on the M20.

Full details of The Register of Unusual Microcars, including magazine subscription (with Paypal accepted), contact details and link to the forum, can be found online at: http://www.rumcars.org/

Vintage Motor Scooter Club

The Vintage Motor Scooter Club (VMSC) was formed in 1985 to cater for scooter owners not covered by the existing one-make clubs and provides a more informal alternative to the VMCC for Bond Scooter owners, etc. It is dedicated to the care, preservation and restoration

VINTAGE MOTOR SCO
CLUB
www.vmsc.co.uk
243
249

A selection of vintage scooters on display at a Vintage Motor Scooter Club event. (*Photo: I. Harrop.*)

(where necessary) of all motor scooters, and offers a service of expert advice and support to anyone with an interest in these machines. The VMSC has an international membership of around 650 individuals, including a handful of Bond Scooter owners and even an Oscar Scooter owner, and as a result can often obtain information on the most obscure machines. Membership is by annual subscription, which six magazines and entry to three camping weekend-type rallies organised by the Club each year. The Club's main annual event is the 'VMSC Vintage and Custom Scooter Extravaganza' held at Coventry in April and usually attracting around 80 to 100 scooters.

The Club is also authorised by the DVLA to provide a dating service for appropriate vehicles for which a registration number is required, and can help in either providing a Certificate of Recommendation for applications to retain an original number, or a Dating Certificate, which accurately dates the machine for which an age-related registration mark is being applied for.

Full details of The Vintage Motor Scooter Club, including joining information, details of services to members, contact details, etc. can be found online at: http://www.vmsc.co.uk

2. *Museums and Collections where Bond Vehicles may be seen*

Today, vintage transport, and especially microcars, seem to arouse considerable interest for a number of reasons: nostalgia for times past, whether actually experienced personally or vicariously through reminiscences of parents or grandparents, etc; curiosity to see how people lived in the past and how they used what was available to overcome adversity due to the economic conditions they lived through; and also the technology that developed through necessity as these diminutive vehicles evolved. Whilst it is possible to gain some insight into this past era of motoring through books, photographs and even occasionally film, the actual small size of many microcars still surprises many people when they see the real thing.

Sadly, in recent years we have seen many small privately-run museums closing, but one that took many people by surprise was the largest microcar museum of all - The Bruce Weiner Microcar Museum, in Madison, Georgia, United States. The collection of over 200 vehicles (at one time it had reached 350!) was put together by Bruce Weiner, whose collecting does appear to have got out of control! Finally he decided that maintaining and preserving the collection, in its own climate-controlled museum opened in 1997, was taking up too much of his time for what was basically supposed to be a hobby and the fun had gone out of it. With neither of his two offspring showing any inclination towards the Museum either, he decided to close the doors in 2013 and auction off the entire collection - apart from keeping some ten 'favourite' microcars! The auction set new heights in microcar prices, with the top bid going to a 1958 F.M.R (Fahrzeug und Maschinenbau GmbH) Tg 500 'Tiger', an 80mph four-wheeler based on the Messerschmitt Kabinenroller design, at $322,000. Bond-related cars sold at the same auction included: 1958 Berkeley Sports SE328 at $23,000, 1951 Bond Minicar Mk B at $19,550, 1972 Bond Bug 700E at $17,250, 1960 Berkeley T60 at $13,800, 1953 Bond Minicar Mk C at $13,800, 1959 Bond Minicar Mk F at $11,500, 1957 Bond Minicar Mk D at $11,500, 1950 Bond Minicar Mk A at $10,350 (unfinished restoration), 1959 Opperman Unicar at $9,200 and a 1953 Bond Minicar Mk C at $4,025 (unfinished restoration).

Lancashire County Museum Service, Preston

In the United Kingdom, two Mk A Bond Minicars have found their way into publicly-funded museums. The first, registration number NYA 538

Lancashire County Museums Service's Mk A Bond Minicar, 'as found'.

Lancashire County Museums Service's Mk A Bond Minicar, now fully restored, but in store.

(Chassis code BC/6/1492) was donated in a dilapidated condition and was restored to full working order. It is fitted with a 197cc engine and has undergone a rack and pinion conversion to update its steering (though the original parts have all been kept for reference). Though it has been used for a few special events and exhibitions, there is no room to permanently display the vehicle, so it is presently in store at the Lancashire Museum's store, Preston, and may be viewed by serious researchers only, by prior appointment.

The Science Museum

The other car is registration number BKS 448 (Chassis code (B/2/634) and is in the collection of the Science Museum, and located at the Museum's large object storage facility at Wroughton Airfield, Wiltshire, and is again only accessible by appointment. This vehicle is fitted with a 122cc engine and modified with the later Triplex-toughened glass windscreen. It was donated by Dr R.J.B. Marsden in 1955 having covered only 20,000 miles and was completely refurbished by Sharp's Commercials Ltd to 'as new' condition. Apart from one or two scratches the Science Museum's Minicar remains in excellent condition, but unfortunately there are no plans to display it.

The Bubblecar Museum

The Bubblecar Museum first opened in 2004 and moved to its present location at Clover Farm, Main Road, Langrick, near Boston, Lincolnshire, circa 2012, where it is now housed in larger premises with additional facilities including: a Camping and Caravanning Club-certificated camp site, tearoom, shop and rally field available for events. It is owned and run by Mike and Paula Cooper, both very knowledgeable microcar enthusiasts, and the new site has become the venue for a number of club events, camping weekends, etc.

BUBBLE
CAR
MUSEUM

The Museum itself houses over fifty microcars as well as several period scooters, vintage mopeds and a small selection of more recent French 'Sans Permis' microcars. Though space is obviously at a premium with having so many vehicles to accommodate, significant effort has still been made to display several of the microcars in imaginative diorama settings, and a variety of 1950 and 1960 period memorabilia is also incorporated into several excellent shop window-style displays,

WELCOME
RELIANT
NTX 362
WJN 896

Ground floor of the Bubblecar Museum, with three Bond Minicars (*Mk B, Mk C and Mk F*) to the left and Berkeleys to the right. Despite the crowded appearance, there is still room for a number of vehicles to be imaginatively displayed as well as additional fascinating displays of period memorabilia.

period rooms, a garage forecourt and even a microcar scrap yard! Apparently further cars are still in store or awaiting restoration.

Though displays are subject to change from time to time, the current collection includes: Bond Mk B, Mk C, Mk D and Mk F Minicars, Bond P3 Scooter, Berkeley T60 (two vehicles, one a hard top and the other a soft top), SE328, B105 models, Bond Bug 700E and 700ES, and the Reliant RFW9 Bug four-wheel prototype. Other makes represented include: Isetta, Messerschmitt, Goggomobil, Nobel, Scootacar, Heinkel, Trojan, Meadows, Suzuki, Zundapp, Vespa, Reliant, Piaggio, Fiat, New Map, Peugeot, Tomcar, Seab, Comtesse, Lawil, Cursor, Ligier, Bamby, and Maico.

Further details of the Bubblecar Museum, admission times and prices (you can even book a ride in a bubblecar!), location details, and information on camping and rally facilities, can all be found online at: http://www.bubblecarmuseum.co.uk/

The Hammond Microcar Collection

The Hammond Microcar Collection began in 1975 with the purchase of a 1958 Heinkel Kabine Model 153 by Edwin and Jean Hammond for their teenage son, in the hope of diverting his motorcycle aspirations. Apparently it worked, and father and son rebuilt the Heinkel together, but it also led to Edwin Hammond becoming hooked on microcars. By 1980 he was running out of room, with microcars even stored in neighbours' garages, and had formed the Register of Unusual Microcars

134 KKM
JDY 95

Jean Hammond showing the author around the new purpose-built museum that houses most of the Hammond Collection.

(RUMcars) to record the surviving vehicles that were not covered by other clubs and help bring like-minded enthusiasts together. In 1985 the Hammonds moved to a former farm in Kent, with plenty of outbuildings to house the still-growing collection, and Edwin began making plans for a museum building, but sadly had only just started this when he passed away in 1999. His wife Jean and three children, along with a group of enthusiasts, carried on his work to see his dream fulfilled. The result is a purpose-built single-storey museum housing some forty-five microcars, with attached workshop where visitors can see those project vehicles currently under restoration. Nearby are still the numerous outbuildings containing further project vehicles, and numerous new and used parts that Edwin collected, knowing that they would come in useful one day!

The Collection includes three vehicles related to Lawrie Bond: a 1957 Berkeley SA322, unusually still fitted with its 322cc British Anzani engine and currently awaiting restoration; a 1959 Opperman Unicar built from a kit; and the sole surviving 1958 Opperman Stirling prototype. Other notable microcars include: a 1965 Peel Trident; 1954 Allard Clipper; 1959 Lloyd LS600; 1958 Tourett; AC Petite; 1958 Heinkel 153 (the one that started it all); New Map Solyto; 1985 Replicar Cursor; 1963 Peel P50; 1959 Goggomobil TS300; 1956 Gordon; 1960 Scootercar; 1961 Meadows Frisky; 1960 Messerschmitt KR 200; BMW 600; 1967 Velorex 16/350; 1955 Champion Kombi; 1953 Champion 400; 1975 Casalini Sulky; 1962 Nobel 200; 1954 SNCAN Inter Torpedo; and 1967 Autobianchi.

The best time to see the Hammond Collection is during their annual open day, each July, when RUMcars members and other microcar owners are likely to be visiting, often in their own vintage vehicles, but you may visit at other times by prior appointment. Located near Staplehurst in Kent, it is an ideal destination for a car club visit or stopping-off point, as it is not far from the Channel ports and Tunnel, and there is a Camping and Caravan Club certified campsite on the farm.

Contact details for the Hammond collection can be found on the RUMcars website at: http://www.rumcars.org under 'Links and Contact Details'.

Location information and tariffs / booking details for the camp site can be found online at: http://www.schoolhousefarmcamping.co.uk

PS.SPEICHER, Einbeck

One of the very first dedicated microcar museums was Automuseum Störy, near the town of Bockenem in Lower Saxony, Germany. For many years this collection of some 260 vehicles (half being motorcycles and scooters) was the scene of annual gatherings of microcar enthusiasts from across Europe. The Museum was the result of a lifetime's collecting by its owner, Otto Künnecke, but after facing long-running issues trying to make the old building meet modern safety regulations and other obstacles placed by the local authorities, it closed for good in 2005. However, despite substantial offers for his collection from as far away as the United States, Otto Künnecke wanted the vehicles to remain in Germany and preferably to be placed on public display again.

This is where PS.SPEICHER comes in - a relatively new museum housed in a fully-restored listed building which was once used as a grain store in Einbeck, a town in the district of Northeim, in southern Lower Saxony, Germany. Opened in 2014, this organisation is not a traditional museum, but a sophisticated exhibition design, blending

HEINKEL TOURI

Part of the microcar exhibition area in the imaginatively-restored former grain store building at PS.SPEICHER, Einbeck. (*Photo: PS.SPEICHER.*)

BOND MINICAR MARK C 1952-56

1959 Mk F Bond Minicar Tourer on display at PS.SPEICHER, Einbeck. (*Photo: PS.SPEICHER.*)

genuine historic exhibits with new technology to provide better interpretation and a learning experience - a concept that has met mixed reviews in the UK, usually due to the paucity of actual exhibits, but a number of German museums seem to be getting the balance right. PS.SPEICHER comprises eight exhibition rooms over some 4,000m on six floors taking visitors on a chronological journey through all ages and development phases of private motor transport.

In 2012 the Künnecke family entered into a partnership with the non-profit Kulturstiftung Kornhaus charitable foundation that is behind the PS.SPEICHER project. The result being that when planning the new automotive collection, they had the pick of the world's largest collection of microcars, still stored at the old Automuseum Störy. Initially twenty-six exhibits were selected, focusing on the age of Germany's economic miracle in the 1950s. During this period, microcars, which were designed to cater for customer demands for greater comfort at an affordable price, eventually ousted two-wheel motorcycles as the main everyday transport of working Germans. Initially the exhibition at Einbeck only featured one Bond car, a 1959 Mk F Minicar Tourer, but plans are underway to increase the microcar presence at PS.SPEICHER and they have a number of Bond vehicles available, including: 1955 Mk C Tourer; 1965 250G Twin Estate; 1967 Bond 875 Ranger Van; 1970 Bond Bug 700ES; and a 1959 Opperman Unicar.

Further details of PS.SPEICHER, including location details, admission times and prices, special exhibitions, news and local information for visitors, can be found online at: https://ps-speicher.de (for English language option, select 'EN' on homepage).

Haynes International Motor Museum

Following the successful Scootermania exhibition at the Coventry Transport Museum in 2012, which featured the British Scooter collection of Robin Spalding (see *British Motor Scooters 1946-1970* by

Robin Spalding, published by Bavarov Ltd, 2012, ISBN 095731440X), the collection was sold to the British Motorcycle Charitable Trust (BMCT). This allowed Robin to concentrate on new projects, and ensured that the collection would be kept together and remain in the UK. This collection includes a 1951 Bond Minibyke, built by Ellis Ltd, a 1953 BAC Gazelle scooter (believed to be the only survivor) and a 1961 Bond P3 Scooter built by Sharp's Commercial's Ltd.

The BMCT has been in negotiations with the Haynes Museum, which recently reopened following a £6 million extension, renovation and refurbishment project, to provide a new home for the Collection. This has resulted in the development of a new British Scooter Collection Hall at the Museum, which opened at the end of May 2016. This will allow for a permanent exhibition to display the over forty machines in the collection and a few additional machines in a purpose-built gallery. Though it might be advisable to contact Haynes before visiting to see a particular model.

The Haynes Motor Museum is located at Sparkford near Yeovil in Somerset, and details of their over 400 exhibits, contact and visitor information, and much more, can be found online at: http://www.haynesmotormuseum.com/

3. Sharp's Commercials/Bond Cars Ltd Chassis Numbers

As with many other motor vehicle manufacturers, Sharp's Commercials developed their own unique numbering system for the various models that were produced over the years. This chassis number was marked on the maker's plate, which was attached to the bulkhead in the case of the Minicars and to the left-hand side of the scuttle assembly on the Equipe models. On the Bond Bug the plate is found at the top of the passenger-side footwell, although Bugs which were not built in Preston are marked Reliant Motor Co. rather than Bond Cars Limited.

This chassis number is made up of an alpha-numeric code that can be interpreted to give the year and month in which the vehicle was completed, the vehicle's individual production number, and in some cases the specification to which the vehicle was built when new. In the case of the Minicars, Bond 875s and the Equipes, the year comes first and is indicated by a single-letter code. This is followed by the numerical month code, which is logically indicated by '1' for January, '2' for February and so on up to '12' for December. It should be remembered that the date indicated refers to when the vehicle was built and it is unlikely that this will coincide with the date when the vehicle was first registered. Finally, many Minicar chassis numbers additionally have a one or two letter suffix which indicates the specification that the vehicle was originally built to.

Year Letters

A = 1949, B = 1950, C = 1951, D = 1952, E = 1953, F = 1954, G = 1955, H = 1956, I = 1957, J = 1958, K = 1959, L = 1960, M = 1961, N = 1962, O = 1963, P = 1964, Q = 1965, R = 1966, S = 1967, T = 1968, U = 1969, V = 1970.

Minicar Specification Suffixes:

C = Convertible (or Saloon Coupe), D = Deluxe, E = Estate, F = Family, R = Reverse, S = Standard, T = Twin engine, V = Van.

Chassis Numbers for the Various Models

Model	From	To
Minicar Mk A	A/1/1	C/4/1973
Minicar Mk B	C/6/1974	D/10/3391
Minicar Mk C *	E/1/5000	H/5/11796
Minicar Mk D	H/5/11797	J/11/15542
Minicar Mk E *	I/12/20000	J/11/21180
Minicar Mk F	J/11/21181	O/1/27679V
Minicar Mk G *	M/8/40000	R/11/43246E
Bond 875 Mk I	Q/8/50000	T/3/52037
Bond 875 Mk II	T/3/52039	V/2/53441V
Bond Bug **	BB/60000	BB/62569
Equipe GT 2+2 ***	0/5/101	P/10/544
Equipe GT4S	P/9/1001	S/1/2934
Equipe GT4S 1300	S/2/2935	V/8/3505
Equipe 2L Mk I *	S/8/4000	T/9/4590
Equipe 2L Mk II	T/9/4591	V/8/5431

(Compiled from information provided by the Bond Owners' Club)

Notes

* Not all chassis numbers ran consecutively from model to model - some new models were given fresh starting points when production commenced, namely the Mk C, Mk E and Mk G Minicars, Bond 875 Mk I, Bond Bug, Equipe GT and 2-Litre Equipe, and therefore these invariably do not account for pre-production prototypes and development vehicles, etc. in the sequence.

** All Bond Bugs have the prefix BB indicating Bond Bug, followed by the production number and then the relevant suffix depending on which version of Bug the vehicle is, ie: 700, 700E or 700ES. eg: BB/625051ES = Bond Bug No. 2,051 700ES version.

*** The maker's chassis numbers referred to here for the Equipe models are in fact marked on the maker's plates as the vehicle's 'Serial No.' The chassis number or 'Comm. No.' marked on the Equipe's maker's plate is in fact derived from the vehicle's engine number and therefore provides a simple means of checking if an Equipe's engine is the original one or not. eg. Comm. No. - BFC 53232HE. Engine number - FC 53232HE.

SHARPS COMMERCIALS
LTD.
PRESTON ENGLAND
BOND MINICAR
CHASSIS No.
LUBRICATION
PRICE'S
SHELL
VACUUM
WAKEFIELD
ENGINE
ENERGOL SAE 40
DOUBLE SHELL
MOBILOIL A
ENERGOL SAE 140
SHELL SPIRAX C
MOBILUBE C

Bond Minicar maker's plate. Chassis No. BC-6-1492 for June 1951. No explanation has been found for some 1951 cars having the 'BC' prefix instead of just 'C'.

Examples

I/ 4/13469RC	=	1957, April, Mk D No. 1672, Reverse Convertible.
K/ 8/23156F	=	1959, August, Mk F No. 1975, Family Model.
T/ 1/51888	=	1968, January, Bond 875, No. 1888
P/ 9/492	=	1964, September, Equipe GT 2+2, No. 392

Index